The Oxford School Spelling Dictionary

Robert Allen

Education consultant Michele Chapman

OXFORD
UNIVERSITY PRESS

OXFORD
UNIVERSITY PRESS

Great Clarendon Street, Oxford OX2 6DP

Oxford University Press is a department of the University of Oxford.
It furthers the University's objective of excellence in research, scholarship,
and education by publishing worldwide in

Oxford New York

Athens Auckland Bangkok Bogatá Buenos Aires
Cape Town Chennai Dar es Salaam Delhi Florence Hong Kong Istanbul
Karachi Kolkata Kuala Lumpur Madrid Melbourne Mexico City Mumbai
Nairobi Paris São Paulo Shanghai Singapore Taipei Tokyo Toronto Warsaw

with associated companies in Berlin Ibadan

Oxford is a registered trade mark of Oxford University Press
in the UK and in certain other countries

British Library cataloguing in Publication Data available

Hardback ISBN 0-19-910713-0
Paperback ISBN 0-19-910714-9

1 3 5 7 9 10 8 6 4 2

Typeset in Gill Sans
Printed in Italy

Introduction

The Oxford School Spelling Dictionary is a special dictionary designed to help students with their spelling. Generally speaking there are three main areas of spelling difficulty for users of English whatever their age.

- Some words are difficult because they have unusual or unpredictable features. **Eighth**, **guard**, and **niece** are often spelt wrongly because they have awkward letter sequences. **Disappear** and **embarrass** are confusing because some letters are doubled while others are not. Words such as **desperate** and **separate** seem inconsistent because one has an **e** in the middle where the other has an **a** for no apparent reason.

- Then there are words that are easily confused. **Vain**, **vein**, and **vane** sound the same but have different meanings. Some words change their spelling according to how they are used. For example, **dependant** as a *noun* is spelt with an **a**, but as an *adjective*, it is spelt with an **e**.

- The third type of difficulty arises when suffixes and endings are added to words. It is not easy to remember to keep an **e** in **changeable**, to replace **y** with **i** in **happily**, and not to double the **p** in **galloping**.

With increased interest in spelling, reading, and writing in schools today we hope that *The Oxford School Spelling Dictionary* will provide a valuable tool offering useful strategies for dealing with spelling difficulties. We also hope that it will support teachers and parents whose task is to enable young writers to become confident, accurate spellers and to express themselves with a voice of their own.

How to use
The Oxford School Spelling Dictionary

Entries

Words are listed alphabetically in **blue** and the part of speech (e.g. *noun, verb, adjective*) follows in black. If the word has endings (called inflections), these are also listed in black below the headword.

Decide on the first sound of the word you are looking for. Some first sounds can be confusing. If you cannot find the word you are looking for, use the **Try also** tips which will guide you to other possible spellings.

Footnotes

Some words have footnotes attached to them. These identify words when you need to check that you have the right one. For example, at **bite** you will find a footnote to tell you that there is another word that sounds like it but is spelt a different way, **! byte**. Words that sound the same but are spelt differently are called homophones. Some footnotes also give extra information on usage and grammar.

Panels

There are about 250 panels which highlight particular problems. For example, you may want to know which words are spelt **-able** like **bendable**, and which are spelt **-ible** like **accessible**. Or you may want to know how you form plurals of nouns ending in **-f** such as **calf** or **roof**. Use these information panels to build your knowledge of spelling rules and practices.

It may be useful to keep a spelling jotter for new words. When using a new word, say it aloud several times before you write it down. When you go on to use it in your writing, try not to copy it but to write the word from memory.

Try also

Entry word

Panel

selfishness
selfless *adjective*
 selflessly
self-service
★ sell *verb*
 sells
 selling
 sold
semaphore
semen

> **semi-**
> *semi-* makes words
> meaning 'half', e.g.
> *semi-automatic,*
> *semi-skimmed.*
> A few words are spelt
> joined up, e.g.
> *semicircle,*
> *semicolon,* but most
> of them have hyphens.

semibreve *noun*
 semibreves
semicircle *noun*
 semicircles
semicircular
semicolon *noun*
 semicolons
semi-detached
semi-final *noun*
 semi-finals
semi-finalist *noun*
 semi-finalists
semitone *noun*
 semitones
semolina
senate
senator *noun*
 senators

send *verb*
 sends
 sending
 sent
senior *adjective* and
 noun
 seniors
seniority
sensation *noun*
 sensations
sensational *adjective*
 sensationally
sense *noun*
 senses
sense *verb*
 senses
 sensing
 sensed
senseless *adjective*
 senselessly
sensible *adjective*
 sensibly
sensitive *adjective*
 sensitively
sensitivity *noun*
 sensitivities
sensitize *verb*
 sensitizes
 sensitizing
 sensitized
sensor *noun*
 sensors
☆ sent see send
sentence *noun*
 sentences
sentence *verb*
 sentences
 sentencing
 sentenced
sentiment *noun*
 sentiments

sentimental
 adjective
 sentimentally
sentimentality
sentinel *noun*
 sentinels
sentry *noun*
 sentries
separable
separate *adjective*
 separately
separate *verb*
 separates
 separating
 separated
separation *noun*
 separations
September *noun*
 Septembers
septic
sequel *noun*
 sequels
sequence *noun*
 sequences
sequin *noun*
 sequins
serene *adjective*
 serenely
serenity
sergeant *noun*
 sergeants
sergeant major
 noun
 sergeant majors
○ serial *noun*
 serials
series *noun*
 series
serious *adjective*
 seriously

Inflections

Part of speech

. . . .

★ To sell something means 'to exchange it for money'. **!** *cell.*
☆ You use sent in e.g. *he was sent home.* **!** *cent, scent.*
○ A serial is a story or programme in separate parts. **!** *cereal.*

Footnote

Do not confuse with

Aa

-a
Most nouns ending in
-*a*, e.g. *amoeba, gala,*
have plurals ending in
-*as*, e.g. *amoebas,*
galas. A few technical
words have plurals
ending in -*ae*, e.g.
antennae.

aback
abacus *noun*
  abacuses
abandon *verb*
  abandons
  abandoning
  abandoned
abbey *noun*
  abbeys
abbot *noun*
  abbots
abbreviate *verb*
  abbreviates
  abbreviating
  abbreviated
abbreviation *noun*
  abbreviations
abdomen *noun*
  abdomens
abdominal
abduct *verb*
  abducts
  abducting
  abducted
abide *verb*
  abides
  abiding
  abided

ability *noun*
  abilities
ablaze
able *adjective*
  abler
  ablest

-able and **-ible**
You add -*able* to a
verb to make an
adjective that means
'able to be done', e.g.
bendable means 'able
to be bent'. Some
adjectives that have
this meaning end in
-*ible*, e.g. **accessible,**
convertible and
incredible. You
cannot use -*ible* to
make new words as
you can with -*able*.

ably
abnormal
  abnormally
abnormality *noun*
  abnormalities
aboard
abode *noun*
  abodes
abolish *verb*
  abolishes
  abolishing
  abolished
abolition
abominable
aboriginal
Aborigines
abort *verb*
  aborts
  aborting
  aborted

abortion *noun*
  abortions
abound *verb*
  abounds
  abounding
  abounded
about
above
abrasive
abreast
abroad
abrupt
abscess *noun*
  abscesses
abseil *verb*
  abseils
  abseiling
  abseiled
absence *noun*
  absences
absent
absentee *noun*
  absentees
absent-minded
  absent-mindedly
absolute
  absolutely
absorb *verb*
  absorbs
  absorbing
  absorbed
absorbent
absorption
abstract *adjective*
  and *noun*
  abstracts
abstract *verb*
  abstracts
  abstracting
  abstracted

absurd
  absurdly
absurdity *noun*
  absurdities
abundance
abundant
abuse *verb*
  abuses
  abusing
  abused
abuse *noun*
  abuses
abusive
  abusively
abysmal
abyss *noun*
  abysses
academic
academy *noun*
  academies
accelerate *verb*
  accelerates
  accelerating
  accelerated
acceleration
accelerator *noun*
  accelerators
accent *noun*
  accents
accent *verb*
  accents
  accenting
  accented
★ **accept** *verb*
  accepts
  accepting
  accepted
acceptable
acceptance
access *noun*
  accesses

access *verb*
  accesses
  accessing
  accessed
accessibility
accessible
accession *noun*
  accessions
accessory *noun*
  accessories
accident *noun*
  accidents
accidental
  accidentally
acclaim *verb*
  acclaims
  acclaiming
  acclaimed
accommodate *verb*
  accommodates
  accommodating
  accommodated
accommodation
accompaniment
  noun
  accompaniments
accompanist *noun*
  accompanists
accompany *verb*
  accompanies
  accompanying
  accompanied
accomplish *verb*
  accomplishes
  accomplishing
  accomplished
accomplished
accomplishment
  noun
  accomplishments

accord *noun*
  accords
according
  accordingly
accordion *noun*
  accordions
account *noun*
  accounts
account *verb*
  accounts
  accounting
  accounted
accountancy
accountant *noun*
  accountants
accumulate *verb*
  accumulates
  accumulating
  accumulated
accumulation
accuracy
accurate
  accurately
accusation *noun*
  accusations
accuse *verb*
  accuses
  accusing
  accused
accustomed
ace *noun*
  aces
ache *noun*
  aches
ache *verb*
  aches
  aching
  ached
achieve *verb*
  achieves
  achieving
  achieved

· ·

★ To **accept** something is to take it. ! **except**

achievement
achievements
acid *noun*
acids
acidic
acidity *noun*
acknowledge *verb*
acknowledges
acknowledging
acknowledged
acknowledgement
noun
acknowledgements
acne
acorn *noun*
acorns
acoustic
acoustics
acquaint *verb*
acquaints
acquainting
acquainted
acquaintance *noun*
acquaintances
acquire *verb*
acquires
acquiring
acquired
acquisition *noun*
acquisitions
acquit *verb*
acquits
acquitting
acquitted
acquittal *noun*
acquittals
acre *noun*
acres

acrobat *noun*
acrobats
acrobatic *adjective*
acrobatically
acrobatics
acronym *noun*
acronyms
across *adverb* and
preposition
act *noun*
acts
act *verb*
acts
acting
acted
action *noun*
actions
activate *verb*
activates
activating
activated
active
activity *noun*
activities
actor *noun*
actors
actress *noun*
actresses
actual
actually
acupuncture
acute
Adam's apple *noun*
Adam's apples
adapt *verb*
adapts
adapting
adapted
adaptable
adaptation

adaptor *noun*
adaptors
add *verb*
adds
adding
added
adder *noun*
adders
addict *noun*
addicts
addicted
addiction *noun*
addictions
addictive
addition *noun*
additions
additional
additive *noun*
additives
address *noun*
addresses
address *verb*
addresses
addressing
addressed
adenoids
adequate
adhere *verb*
adheres
adhering
adhered
adhesive *noun*
adhesives
adhesion
adhesive
Adi Granth
adjacent
adjective *noun*
adjectives

adjourn *verb*
adjourns
adjourning
adjourned
adjournment
adjudicate *verb*
adjudicates
adjudicating
adjudicated
adjudication
adjudicator
adjust *verb*
adjusts
adjusting
adjusted
adjustment *noun*
adjustments
administer *verb*
administers
administering
administered
administration
noun
administrations
administrative
administrator
admirable
admirably
admiral *noun*
admirals
admiration
admire *verb*
admires
admiring
admired
admirer *noun*
admirers
admission *noun*
admissions
admit *verb*
admits

admitting
admitted
admittance
admittedly
ado
adolescence
adolescent *noun*
adolescents
adopt *verb*
adopts
adopting
adopted
adoption
adoptive
adorable
adorably
adoration
adore *verb*
adores
adoring
adored
adorn *verb*
adorns
adorning
adorned
adornment
adrenalin
adrift
adult *noun*
adults
adulterer
adultery
advance *noun*
advances
advance *verb*
advances
advancing
advanced
advanced
advantage *noun*

advantages
advantageous
★ **Advent**
adventure *noun*
adventures
adventurous
adjective
adventurously
adverb *noun*
adverbs
adversary *noun*
adversaries
adverse
adversity *noun*
adversities
advertise *verb*
advertises
advertising
advertised
advertisement
noun
advertisements
advice
advisable
advise *verb*
advises
advising
advised
adviser *noun*
advisers
advisory
advocate *noun*
advocates
advocate *verb*
advocates
advocating
advocated
aerial *adjective* and
noun
aerials

· ·

★ Use a capital A when you mean the period before Christmas.

aero-
You use *aero-* to make words to do with the air or aircraft, e.g. **aerobatics**. If the word is a long one you spell it with a hyphen, e.g. **aero-engineering**.

aerobatic
aerobatics
aerobics
aeronautical
aeronautics
aeroplane *noun*
  aeroplanes
aerosol *noun*
  aerosols
aesthetic
  aesthetically
affair *noun*
  affairs
★ affect *verb*
  affects
  affecting
  affected
affection *noun*
  affections
affectionate
  affectionately
afflict *verb*
  afflicts
  afflicting
  afflicted
affliction
  afflictions
affluence
affluent
afford *verb*
  affords

affording
  afforded
afforestation
afloat *adjective* and *adverb*
afraid
afresh
African *adjective* and *noun*
  Africans
aft
after
afternoon *noun*
  afternoons
afterwards
again
against
age *noun*
  ages
age *verb*
  ages
  ageing
  aged
aged
agency *noun*
  agencies
agenda *noun*
  agendas
agent *noun*
  agents
aggravate *verb*
  aggravates
  aggravating
  aggravated
aggravation
aggression
aggressive
  aggressively
aggressor
  aggressors

agile
agility
agitate *verb*
  agitates
  agitating
  agitated
agitation
agitator *noun*
  agitators
agnostic *noun*
  agnostics
ago
agonizing
agony *noun*
  agonies
agree *verb*
  agrees
  agreeing
  agreed
agreeable
agreement *noun*
  agreements
agriculture
agricultural
aground
ahead
ahoy
aid *noun*
  aids
aid *verb*
  aids
  aiding
  aided
☆ Aids
ailing
ailment *noun*
  ailments
aim *verb*
  aims
  aiming
  aimed

★ **Affect** means 'to make something change'. ! ~~effect~~.
☆ Use a capital A when you mean the disease.

aim *noun*
aims
aimless
aimlessly
★ **air** *noun*
airs
air *verb*
airs
airing
aired
airborne
air-conditioned
air-conditioning
aircraft *noun*
aircraft
Airedale *noun*
Airedales
airfield *noun*
airfields
air force *noun*
air forces
airgun *noun*
airguns
airline *noun*
airlines
airlock *noun*
airlocks
airmail
airman *noun*
airmen
airport *noun*
airports
airship *noun*
airships
airstream *noun*
airstreams
airtight
airy *adjective*
airier
airiest

airily
☆ **aisle** *noun*
aisles
ajar
✪ **akela** *noun*
akelas
alarm *verb*
alarms
alarming
alarmed
alarm *noun*
alarms
alas
albatross *noun*
albatrosses
album *noun*
albums
alcohol
alcoholic *adjective*
and *noun*
alcoholics
alcoholism
alcove *noun*
alcoves
✳ **ale** *noun*
ales
alert *verb*
alerts
alerting
alerted
alert *adjective* and
noun
alerts
algebra
algebraic
alias *noun*
aliases
alibi *noun*
alibis

alien *adjective* and
noun
aliens
alienate *verb*
alienates
alienating
alienated
alienation
alight
alike
alive
alkali *noun*
alkalis
alkaline
alkalinity
Allah
allegation *noun*
allegations
allege *verb*
alleges
alleging
alleged
allegedly
allegiance *noun*
allegiances
allegorical
allegory *noun*
allegories
allergic
allergy *noun*
allergies
alley *noun*
alleys
alliance *noun*
alliances
allied
alligator *noun*
alligators

- -

★ You can use a plural in the phrase *to put on airs*.
☆ An **aisle** is a passage in a church or cinema. ! **isle**.
✪ **Akela** is a Scout leader.
✳ You can use a plural when you mean 'different types of ale'.

allot verb
allots
allotting
allotted
allotment noun
allotments
allow verb
allows
allowing
allowed
allowance noun
allowances
alloy noun
alloys
all right
all-round
all-rounder
ally noun
allies
ally verb
allies
allying
allied
almighty
almond noun
almonds
almost
aloft
alone
along
alongside
★ **aloud**
alphabet noun
alphabets
alphabetical
alphabetically
alpine
already
Alsatian noun
Alsatians
also

☆ **altar** noun
altars
✿ **alter** verb
alters
altering
altered
alteration
alternate
alternately
alternate verb
alternates
alternating
alternated
alternation
alternating current
alternative noun
alternatives
alternative
alternator noun
alternators
although conjunction
altitude noun
altitudes
altogether
aluminium
always
amalgamate verb
amalgamates
amalgamating
amalgamated
amalgamation
amateur adjective
and noun
amateurs
amateurish
amaze verb
amazes
amazing
amazed

amazement
ambassador noun
ambassadors
amber
ambiguity
ambiguities
ambiguous
ambiguously
ambition noun
ambitions
ambitious
ambitiously
amble verb
ambles
ambling
ambled
ambulance noun
ambulances
ambush noun
ambushes
ambush verb
ambushes
ambushing
ambushed
amen
amend verb
amends
amending
amended
amendment
amenity noun
amenities
American adjective
and noun
Americans
amiable
amiably
amicable
amicably
✳ **amid**

. . . .

★ **Aloud** means 'in a voice that can be heard'. ! allowed.
☆ An **altar** is a raised surface in religious ceremonies. ! alter.
✿ **Alter** means to change something. ! altar.
✳ You can also spell this word *amidst*.

amidships
ammonia
ammunition
amnesty *noun*
  amnesties
amoeba *noun*
  amoebas
★ among
amount *noun*
  amounts
amount *verb*
  amounts
  amounting
  amounted
amphibian *adjective*
  and *noun*
  amphibians
amphibious
ample *adjective*
  ampler
  amplest
  amply
amplification
amplifier *noun*
  amplifiers
amplify *verb*
  amplifies
  amplifying
  amplified
amputate *verb*
  amputates
  amputating
  amputated
amputation
amuse *verb*
  amuses
  amusing
  amused
amusement *noun*
  amusements

amusing
☆ an
anaemia
anaemic
anaesthetic *noun*
  anaesthetics
anaesthetist
anaesthetize *verb*
  anaesthetizes
  anaesthetizing
  anaesthetized
anagram *noun*
  anagrams
analogous
❍ analogue
analogy *noun*
  analogies
analyse *verb*
  analyses
  analysing
  analysed
analysis *noun*
  analyses
analytical
anarchism
anarchist *noun*
  anarchists
anarchy
anatomical
anatomy

> **-ance and -ence**
> Most nouns ending in
> *-ance* come from
> verbs, e.g.
> disturbance,
> endurance. Some
> nouns end in *-ence*,
> e.g. dependence,
> obedience, and you
> need to be careful not
> to misspell these.

ancestor *noun*
  ancestors
ancestral
ancestry *noun*
  ancestries
anchor *noun*
  anchors
anchorage *noun*
  anchorages
ancient
anemone *noun*
  anemones
angel *noun*
  angels
angelic
anger
angle *noun*
  angles
angle *verb*
  angles
  angling
  angled
angler *noun*
  anglers
Anglican *adjective*
  and *noun*
  Anglicans
Anglo-Saxon
  adjective and *noun*
  Anglo-Saxons
angry *adjective*
  angrier
  angriest
  angrily
anguish
angular
animal *noun*
  animals
animated
animation

★ You can also spell this word *amongst*.

☆ You use *an* instead of *a* before a word beginning with a vowel, e.g. *an apple*, or before an abbreviation that sounds as though it begins with a vowel, e.g. *an MP*.

❍ You will sometimes see the spelling *analog*, especially when it is about computers.

animosity *noun*
  animosities
aniseed
ankle *noun*
  ankles
annex *verb*
  annexes
  annexing
  annexed
annexation
annexe *noun*
  annexes
annihilate *verb*
  annihilates
  annihilating
  annihilated
annihilation
anniversary *noun*
  anniversaries
announce *verb*
  announces
  announcing
  announced
announcer
announcement *noun*
  announcements
annoy *verb*
  annoys
  annoying
  annoyed
annoyance *noun*
  annoyances
annual *adjective*
  annually
annual *noun*
  annuals
★ anonymity
anonymous
  anonymously
anorak *noun*
  anoraks

anorexia
anorexic
another
answer *noun*
  answers
answer *verb*
  answers
  answering
  answered

-ant and -ent
Many adjectives end in *-ant*, e.g. abundant, important. Some adjectives end in *-ent*, e.g. dependent (dependant is a noun), permanent, and you need to be careful not to misspell these.

antagonism
antagonistic
antagonize *verb*
  antagonizes
  antagonizing
  antagonized
Antarctic *adjective* and *noun*
anteater *noun*
  anteaters
☆ antelope *noun*
  antelope *or* antelopes
antenna *noun*
  antelopes
anthem *noun*
  anthems
anthill *noun*
  anthills
anthology *noun*
  anthologies

anthracite
anthropologist
anthropology

anti-
anti- at the beginning of a word makes a word meaning 'against something' or 'stopping something', e.g. antifreeze means 'a liquid that stops water from freezing'. If the word you are adding *anti-* to begins with a vowel, you use a hyphen, e.g. anti-aircraft.

antibiotic *noun*
  antibiotics
anticipate *verb*
  anticipates
  anticipating
  anticipated
anticipation
anticlimax *noun*
  anticlimaxes
anticlockwise *adverb* and *adjective*
anticyclone *noun*
  anticyclones
antidote *noun*
  antidotes
antifreeze
○ antipodes
antiquated
antique *adjective* and *noun*
  antiques
antiseptic *noun*
  antiseptics

★ The noun from anonymous.
☆ You use antelope when you mean a lot of animals and antelopes when you mean several you are thinking about separately.
○ A word Europeans use for Australia and New Zealand.

antler noun
  antlers
anus noun
  anuses
anvil noun
  anvils
anxiety noun
  anxieties
anxious
  anxiously
anybody
anyhow
anyone
anything
anyway
anywhere
apart
apartment noun
  apartments
apathetic
apathy
ape noun
  apes
aphid noun
  aphids
apiece
apologetic
  apologetically
apologize verb
  apologizes
  apologizing
  apologized
apology noun
  apologies
apostle noun
  apostles
apostrophe noun
  apostrophes
appal verb
  appals

  appalling
  appalled
appalling
apparatus noun
  apparatuses
apparent
  apparently
appeal verb
  appeals
  appealing
  appealed
appeal noun
  appeals
appear verb
  appears
  appearing
  appeared
appearance noun
  appearances
appease verb
  appeases
  appeasing
  appeased
appeasement
appendicitis
★ **appendix**
  appendixes or
  appendices
appetite noun
  appetites
appetizing
applaud verb
  applauds
  applauding
  applauded
applause
apple noun
  apples
appliance noun
  appliances
applicable

applicant noun
  applicants
application noun
  applications
applied
apply verb
  applies
  applying
  applied
appoint verb
  appoints
  appointing
  appointed
appointment noun
  appointments
appraisal
  appraisals
appraise verb
  appraises
  appraising
  appraised
appreciate verb
  appreciates
  appreciating
  appreciated
appreciation
appreciative
apprehension noun
apprehensive
apprentice noun
  apprentices
apprenticeship
approach verb
  approaches
  approaching
  approached
approach noun
  approaches
approachable
appropriate

- -

★ You use **appendixes** when you mean organs of the body and **appendices** when
  you mean parts of a book.

approval
approve *verb*
  approves
  approving
  approved
approximate
  approximately
apricot *noun*
  apricots
April
apron *noun*
  aprons
aptitude *noun*
  aptitudes
aquarium *noun*
  aquariums
aquatic
aqueduct *noun*
  aqueducts
★ Arab *noun*
  Arabs
★ Arabian *adjective*
☆ Arabic
☆ arabic
arable
arbitrary
arbitrate *verb*
  arbitrates
  arbitrating
  arbitrated
arbitration
arbitrator
○ arc *noun*
  arcs
arcade *noun*
  arcades
arch *noun*
  arches
arch *verb*
  arches

arching
arched
archaeology
archaeological
archaeologist
archbishop *noun*
  archbishops
archer *noun*
  archers
archery
architect *noun*
  architects
architecture

-archy
-archy at the end of a
word means 'rule or
government', e.g.
anarchy (= a lack of
rule) and **monarchy**
(= rule by a king or
queen). The plural
forms is *-archies*, e.g.
monarchies.

Arctic
are
area *noun*
  areas
arena *noun*
  arenas
aren't *abbreviation*
argue *verb*
  argues
  arguing
  argued
argument *noun*
  arguments
arid
aridity
arise *verb*
  arises

arising
arose
arisen
aristocracy *noun*
  aristocracies
aristocrat *noun*
  aristocrats
aristocratic
arithmetic
arithmetical
* ark *noun*
  arks
arm *noun*
  arms
arm *verb*
  arms
  arming
  armed
armada *noun*
  armadas
armadillo *noun*
  armadillos
armaments
armchair *noun*
  armchairs
armful *noun*
  armfuls
armistice *noun*
  armistices
armour
armoured
armpit *noun*
  armpits
army *noun*
  armies
aroma *noun*
  aromas
aromatic
arose *see* arise
around

· ·

★ You use **Arab** when you mean a person or the people, and **Arabian** when you
  mean the place, e.g. *the Arabian desert.*
☆ You use **Arabic** when you mean the language, and **arabic** when you mean
  numbers, e.g. *arabic numerals.*
○ **Arc** means a curve. ! **ark.**
* **Ark** means a boat. ! **arc.**

arouse *verb*
  arouses
  arousing
  aroused
arrange *verb*
  arranges
  arranging
  arranged
arrangement
array *noun*
  arrays
arrears
arrest *verb*
  arrests
  arresting
  arrested
arrest *noun*
  arrests
arrival
arrive *verb*
  arrives
  arriving
  arrived
arrogance
arrogant
arrow *noun*
  arrows
arsenal *noun*
  arsenals
arsenic
arson
artefact *noun*
  artefacts
artery *noun*
  arteries
artful
  artfully
arthritic
arthritis
article *noun*
  articles

articulate *adjective*
articulate *verb*
  articulates
  articulating
  articulated
artificial
  artificially
artillery *noun*
  artilleries
artist *noun*
  artists
artiste *noun*
  artistes
artistic
artistry
asbestos
ascend *verb*
  ascends
  ascending
  ascended
ascent *noun*
  ascents
★ **ash** *noun*
  ashes
ashamed
ashen
ashore
ashtray *noun*
  ashtrays
Asian *adjective* and
  noun
  Asians
aside
ask *verb*
  asks
  asking
  asked
asleep
aspect *noun*
  aspects

☆ **asphalt**
aspirin *noun*
  aspirins
ass *noun*
  asses
assassin *noun*
  assassins
assassinate *verb*
  assassinates
  assassinating
  assassinated
assassination *noun*
  assassinations
assault *verb*
  assaults
  assaulting
  assaulted
assault *noun*
  assaults
assemble *verb*
  assembles
  assembling
  assembled
assembly *noun*
  assemblies
assent
assert *verb*
  asserts
  asserting
  asserted
assertion
assertive
assess *verb*
  assesses
  assessing
  assessed
assessment
assessor

- -

★ The tree and the burnt powder.
☆ Note that this word is not spelt *ash-*.

asset *noun*
  assets
assign *verb*
  assigns
  assigning
  assigned
assignment *noun*
  assignments
assist *verb*
  assists
  assisting
  assisted
assistance
assistant *noun*
  assistants
associate *verb*
  associates
  associating
  associated
associate *noun*
  associates
association *noun*
  associations
assorted
assortment
assume *verb*
  assumes
  assuming
  assumed
assumption *noun*
  assumptions
assurance *noun*
  assurances
assure *verb*
  assures
  assuring
  assured
asterisk *noun*
  asterisks
asteroid *noun*
  asteroids

asthma
asthmatic *adjective*
  and *noun*
  asthmatics
astonish *verb*
  astonishes
  astonishing
  astonished
astonishment
astound *verb*
  astounds
  astounding
  astounded
astride
astrologer
astrological
astrology
astronaut *noun*
  astronauts
astronomer
astronomical
astronomy

-asy
Not many words end in *-asy*. The most important are ecstasy, fantasy, idiosyncrasy. There are a lot of words ending in *-acy*, however, e.g. accuracy.

★ **ate** see eat
atheist *noun*
  atheists
atheism
athlete *noun*
  athletes
athletic

athletics
atlas *noun*
  atlases
atmosphere *noun*
  atmospheres
atmospheric
atoll *noun*
  atolls
atom *noun*
  atoms
atomic
atrocious
  atrociously
atrocity *noun*
  atrocities
attach *verb*
  attaches
  attaching
  attached
attached
attachment *noun*
  attachments
attack *verb*
  attacks
  attacking
  attacked
attack *noun*
  attacks
attain *verb*
  attains
  attaining
  attained
attainment
attempt *verb*
  attempts
  attempting
  attempted
attempt *noun*
  attempts

★ **Ate** is the past tense of eat e.g. *I ate an apple.* ! eight.

attend *verb*
attends
attending
attended
attendance *noun*
attendances
attendant *noun*
attendants
attention
attentive
attic *noun*
attics
attitude *noun*
attitudes
attract *verb*
attracts
attracting
attracted
attraction *noun*
attractions
attractive
auburn
auction *noun*
auctions
auctioneer
audibility
audible
audience *noun*
audiences

audio-
audio- makes words with 'sound' or 'hearing' in their meaning. Some of them have hyphens, e.g. **audio-visual** (= to do with hearing and seeing).

audiovisual
audition *noun*
auditions

auditorium *noun*
auditoriums
August
aunt *noun*
aunts
★ **auntie** *noun*
aunties
☆ **au pair** *noun*
au pairs
○ **aural**
austere
austerity
Australian *adjective*
and *noun*
Australians
authentic
authentically
authenticity
author *noun*
authors
authority *noun*
authorities
authorize *verb*
authorizes
authorizing
authorized
autistic

auto-
auto- at the beginning of a word means 'self', e.g. **autobiography** (= a biography of yourself), **automatic** (= done by itself). But some words beginning with *auto-* are to do with cars, e.g. **autocross** (= car racing across country).

autobiography *noun*
autobiographies
autograph *noun*
autographs
automate *verb*
automates
automating
automated
automatic
automatically
automation
automobile *noun*
automobiles
autumn *noun*
autumns
autumnal
auxiliary *adjective*
and *noun*
auxiliaries
availability
available
avalanche *noun*
avalanches
avenue *noun*
avenues
average *adjective*
and *noun*
averages
average *verb*
averages
averaging
averaged
avert *verb*
averts
averting
averted
aviary *noun*
aviaries
aviation
avid

★ You can also spell this word *aunty*.
☆ **Au pair** means a young person from another country who works in your house.
○ **Aural** means 'to do with hearing'. **! oral**.

avoid *verb*
avoids
avoiding
avoided
avoidance
await *verb*
awaits
awaiting
awaited
awake *adjective*
awake *verb*
awakes
awaking
awoke
awoken
awaken *verb*
awakens
awakening
awakened
award *noun*
awards
award *verb*
awards
awarding
awarded
aware
awareness
awash
away
awe
awed
awful
awfully
★ **awhile**
awkward
awoke see awake
awoken see awake
axe *noun*
axes

axe *verb*
axes
axing
axed
axis *noun*
axes
axle *noun*
axles
Aztec *noun*
Aztecs
azure *adjective*

Bb

babble *verb*
babbles
babbling
babbled
baboon *noun*
baboons
baby *noun*
babies
babyish
babysit *verb*
babysits
babysitting
babysat
babysitter *noun*
babysitters
bachelor *noun*
bachelors
back *noun*
backs
back *verb*
backs
backing
backed
backache *noun*
backaches

backbone *noun*
backbones
background *noun*
backgrounds
backing
backlash *noun*
backlashes
backlog *noun*
backlogs
backside *noun*
backsides
backstroke
backward *adjective*
and *adverb*
backwards *adverb*
backwater *noun*
backwaters
backyard *noun*
backyards
bacon
bacteria
bacterial
bad *adjective*
worse
worst
badly
baddy *noun*
baddies
badge *noun*
badges
badger *noun*
badgers
badger *verb*
badgers
badgering
badgered
badminton

★ **Awhile** means 'for a short time', e.g. *Wait here awhile.* You spell it as two words in e.g. *a short while.*

baffle *verb*
baffles
baffling
baffled
bag *noun*
bags
bag *verb*
bags
bagging
bagged
bagel *noun*
bagels
baggage
baggy *adjective*
baggier
baggiest
bagpipes
★ **bail** *noun*
bails
☆ **bail** *verb*
bails
bailing
bailed
Bairam *noun*
Bairams
Baisakhi
bait *noun*
bait *verb*
baits
baiting
baited
bake *verb*
bakes
baking
baked
baker *noun*
bakers
bakery *noun*
bakeries
baking powder

balance *noun*
balances
balance *verb*
balances
balancing
balanced
balcony *noun*
balconies
bald *adjective*
balder
baldest
✪ **bale** *noun*
bales
✲ **bale** *verb*
bales
baling
baled
ballad *noun*
ballads
ballerina *noun*
ballerinas
ballet *noun*
ballets
ballistic *adjective*
balloon *noun*
balloons
ballot *noun*
ballots
ballpoint *noun*
ballpoints
ballroom *noun*
ballrooms
balsa
bamboo *noun*
bamboos
ban *verb*
bans
banning
banned
banana *noun*
bananas

band *noun*
bands
band *verb*
bands
banding
banded
bandage *noun*
bandages
bandit *noun*
bandits
bandstand *noun*
bandstands
bandwagon *noun*
bandwagons
bandy *adjective*
bandier
bandiest
bang *noun*
bangs
bang *verb*
bangs
banging
banged
banger *noun*
bangers
banish *verb*
banishes
banishing
banished
banishment
banisters
banjo *noun*
banjos
bank *noun*
banks
bank *verb*
banks
banking
banked
banknote *noun*
banknotes

. . . .

★ **Bail** means 'money paid to let a prisoner out of prison' and 'a piece of wood put on the stumps in cricket'. ! bale.
☆ **Bail** means 'to pay money to let a prisoner out of prison' and 'to scoop water out of a boat'. ! bale.
✪ **Bale** means 'a large bundle'. ! bail.
✲ **Bale** means 'to jump out of an aircraft'. ! bail.

bankrupt
bankruptcy
banner *noun*
  banners
banquet *noun*
  banquets
baptism *noun*
  baptisms
★ Baptist *noun*
  Baptists
baptize *verb*
  baptizes
  baptizing
  baptized
bar *noun*
  bars
bar *verb*
  bars
  barring
  barred
barb *noun*
  barbs
barbarian *noun*
  barbarians
barbaric
barbarism
barbarity *noun*
  barbarities
barbarous *adjective*
barbecue *noun*
  barbecues
barber *noun*
  barbers
bar code *noun*
  bar codes
bard *noun*
  bards
☆ bare *adjective*
  barer
  barest
bareback

barely
bargain *noun*
  bargains
bargain *verb*
  bargains
  bargaining
  bargained
barge *noun*
  barges
barge *verb*
  barges
  barging
  barged
baritone *noun*
  baritones
bark *noun*
  barks
bark *verb*
  barks
  barking
  barked
barley
barman *noun*
  barmen
bar mitzvah *noun*
  bar mitzvahs
barnacle *noun*
  barnacles
barnyard *noun*
  barnyards
barometer *noun*
  barometers
barometric
baron *noun*
  barons
baroness *noun*
  baronesses
baronial
barrack *verb*
  barracks
  barracking

  barracked
○ barracks *plural noun*
barrage *noun*
  barrages
barrel *noun*
  barrels
barren
barricade *noun*
  barricades
barricade *verb*
  barricades
  barricading
  barricaded
barrier *noun*
  barriers
barrister *noun*
  barristers
barrow *noun*
  barrows
barter *verb*
  barters
  bartering
  bartered
✳ base *noun*
  bases
base *verb*
  bases
  basing
  based
baseball *noun*
  baseballs
basement *noun*
  basements
bash *verb*
  bashes
  bashing
  bashed
bash *noun*
  bashes
bashful
  bashfully

. . . .

★ You use a capital B when you mean a member of the Christian Church.

☆ **Bare** means 'naked' or 'not covered'. ! **bear.**

○ **Barracks** is plural but sometimes has a singular verb, e.g. *The Barracks is over there.*

✳ **Base** means 'a place where things are controlled'. ! **bass.**

ba - be

basic
basically
basin noun
basins
basis noun
bases
bask verb
basks
basking
basked
basket noun
baskets
basketball noun
basketballs
basketful noun
basketfuls
★ **bass** noun
basses
bassoon noun
bassoons
bastard noun
bastards
bat noun
bats
bat verb
bats
batting
batted
batch noun
batches
bath noun
baths
bath verb
baths
bathing
bathed
bathe verb
bathes
bathing
bathed
bathroom noun
bathrooms

☆ **baton** noun
batons
batsman noun
batsmen
battalion noun
battalions
◎ **batten** noun
battens
batter verb
batters
battering
battered
batter noun
battery noun
batteries
battle noun
battles
battlefield noun
battlefields
battlements
battleship noun
battleships
bawl verb
bawls
bawling
bawled
bay noun
bays
bayonet noun
bayonets
bazaar noun
bazaars
✻ **beach** noun
beaches
beacon noun
beacons
bead noun
beads
beady adjective
beadier
beadiest

beagle noun
beagles
beak noun
beaks
beaker noun
beakers
beam noun
beams
beam verb
beams
beaming
beamed
✽ **bean** noun
beans
✽ **bear** verb
bears
bearing
bore
borne
✽ **bear** noun
bears
bearable
beard noun
beards
bearded
bearing noun
bearings
beast noun
beasts
beastly
beat verb
beats
beating
beat
beaten
beat noun
beats
beautiful
beautifully

★ **Bass** means 'a singer with a low voice'. ! **base**.
☆ A **baton** is a stick used by a conductor in an orchestra. ! **batten**.
◎ A **batten** is a flat strip of wood. ! **baton**.
✻ **Beach** means 'sandy part of the seashore'. ! **beech**.
✽ A **bean** is a vegetable. ! **been**.
✽ To **bear** something is to carry it and a **bear** is an animal. ! **bare**.

beautify verb
beautifies
beautifying
beautified
beauty noun
beauties
beaver noun
beavers
becalmed
became see become
because
beckon verb
beckons
beckoning
beckoned
become verb
becomes
becoming
became
become
bedclothes
bedding
bedlam
bedraggled
bedridden
bedroom noun
bedrooms
bedside
bedspread noun
bedspreads
bedstead noun
bedsteads
bedtime
bee noun
bees
★ **beech** noun
beeches
beef
beefburger noun
beefburgers

beefeater noun
beefeaters
beefy adjective
beefier
beefiest
beehive noun
beehives
beeline
☆ **been** see be
beer noun
beers
beet noun
beet or beets
beetle noun
beetles
beetroot noun
beetroot
before
beforehand
beg verb
begs
begging
begged
began see begin
beggar noun
beggars
begin verb
begins
beginning
began
begun
beginner noun
beginners
beginning noun
beginnings
begrudge verb
begrudges
begrudging
begrudged
begun see begin

behalf
behave verb
behaves
behaving
behaved
behaviour
behead verb
beheads
beheading
beheaded
behind adverb and
preposition
behind noun
behinds
beige noun
being noun
beings
belch verb
belches
belching
belched
belch noun
belches
belfry noun
belfries
belief noun
beliefs
believe verb
believes
believing
believed
believable
believer
bellow verb
bellows
bellowing
bellowed
bellows
belly noun
bellies

· ·

★ Beech means 'a tree'. ! beach.
☆ You use been in e.g. I've been to the zoo. ! bean.

belong verb
  belongs
  belonging
  belonged
belongings
beloved
below
belt noun
  belts
belt verb
  belts
  belting
  belted
bench noun
  benches
bend verb
  bends
  bending
  bent
bend noun
  bends
beneath
benefaction
benefactor noun
  benefactors
benefit noun
  benefits
beneficial
  beneficially
benevolence
benevolent
bent see **bend**
bequeath verb
  bequeaths
  bequeathing
  bequeathed
bequest
★ **bereaved**
  bereavement
☆ **bereft**
beret noun

  berets
berry noun
  berries
berserk
berth noun
  berths
beside
besides
besiege verb
  besieges
  besieging
  besieged
bestseller noun
  bestsellers
bet noun
  bets
bet verb
  bets
  betting
  bet
  betted
betray verb
  betrays
  betraying
  betrayed
betrayal
better adjective and
  adverb
better verb
  betters
  bettering
  bettered
between
❍ **beware** verb
bewilder verb
  bewilders
  bewildering
  bewildered
bewilderment
bewitch verb
  bewitches

  bewitching
  bewitched
beyond

bi-
bi- at the beginning of a word means 'two', e.g. **bicycle** (= a machine with two wheels), **bilateral** (= having two sides).

bias noun
  biases
biased
bib noun
  bibs
Bible noun
  Bibles
biblical
bicycle noun
  bicycles
bid noun
  bids
bid verb
  bids
  bidding
  bid
bide verb
  bides
  biding
  bided
big adjective
  bigger
  biggest
bigamist
bigamous
bigamy
bike noun
  bikes
bikini noun
  bikinis

- -

★ You use **bereaved** when you mean a person with a close relative who has died. **! bereft.**

☆ You use **bereft** when you mean 'deprived of something', e.g. *bereft of hope*. **! bereaved.**

❍ **Beware** has no other forms.

bile
bilge *noun*
  bilges
bilingual
billiards
billion *noun*
  billions
billionth
billow *noun*
  billows
billow *verb*
  billows
  billowing
  billowed
billy goat *noun*
  billy goats
binary
bind *verb*
  binds
  binding
  bound
bingo
binoculars

bio-
bio- at the beginning of a word means 'life', e.g. **biography** (= a story of a person's life), **biology** (= the study of living things).

biodegradable
biographer
biographical
biography *noun*
  biographies
biological
biologist
biology
bionic

biosphere
birch *noun*
  birches
bird *noun*
  birds
birdseed
Biro *noun*
  Biros
birth *noun*
  births
birth control
birthday *noun*
  birthdays
birthmark *noun*
  birthmarks
birthplace *noun*
  birthplaces
biscuit *noun*
  biscuits
bisect *verb*
  bisects
  bisecting
  bisected
bishop *noun*
  bishops
bison *noun*
  bison
bit *noun*
  bits
bit see bite
bitch *noun*
  bitches
bitchy *adjective*
  bitchier
  bitchiest
bite *verb*
  bites
  biting
  bit
  bitten
★ bite *noun*

bites
bitter
black *adjective*
  blacker
  blackest
black *noun*
  blacks
blackberry *noun*
  blackberries
blackbird *noun*
  blackbirds
blackboard *noun*
  blackboards
blacken *verb*
  blackens
  blackening
  blackened
blackmail *verb*
  blackmails
  blackmailing
  blackmailed
blackout *noun*
  blackouts
blacksmith *noun*
  blacksmiths
bladder *noun*
  bladders
blade *noun*
  blades
blame *verb*
  blames
  blaming
  blamed
blame *noun*
blancmange *noun*
  blancmanges
blank *adjective* and *noun*
  blanks
blanket *noun*
  blankets

★ A bite is an act of biting. ! byte.

blare verb
blares
blaring
blared
blaspheme verb
blasphemes
blaspheming
blasphemed
blasphemous
blasphemy
blast noun
blasts
blast verb
blasts
blasting
blasted
blast-off
blaze noun
blazes
blaze verb
blazes
blazing
blazed
blazer noun
blazers
bleach noun
bleaches
bleach verb
bleaches
bleaching
bleached
bleak adjective
bleaker
bleakest
bleary adjective
blearier
bleariest
blearily
bleat noun
bleats

bleat verb
bleats
bleating
bleated
bleed verb
bleeds
bleeding
bled
bleep noun
bleeps
blemish noun
blemishes
blend verb
blends
blending
blended
blend noun
blends
bless verb
blesses
blessing
blessed
blessing noun
blessings
★ **blew** see blow
blight noun
blights
blind adjective
blinder
blindest
blind verb
blinds
blinding
blinded
blind noun
blinds
blindfold noun
blindfolds
blindfold verb
blindfolds
blindfolding
blindfolded

blindfold
blink verb
blinks
blinking
blinked
bliss
blissful
blissfully
blister noun
blisters
blitz noun
blitzes
blizzard noun
blizzards
bloated
block noun
blocks
block verb
blocks
blocking
blocked
blockade noun
blockades
blockage noun
blockages
blond adjective
blonder
blondest
☆ **blonde** noun
blondes
blood
bloodhound noun
bloodhounds
bloodshed
bloodshot
bloodstream
bloodthirsty
adjective
bloodthirstier
bloodthirstiest

. . . .

★ You use **blew** in e.g. *the wind blew hard*. **!** blue.
☆ You use **blonde** when you are talking about a girl or woman.

bloody *adjective*
bloodier
bloodiest
bloom *verb*
blooms
blooming
bloomed
bloom *noun*
blooms
blossom *noun*
blossoms
blossom *verb*
blossoms
blossoming
blossomed
blot *noun*
blots
blot *verb*
blots
blotting
blotted
blotch *noun*
blotches
blotchy *adjective*
blotchier
blotchiest
blouse *noun*
blouses
blow *noun*
blows
blow *verb*
blows
blowing
blew
blown
blowlamp *noun*
blowlamps
blowtorch *noun*
blowtorches
blue *adjective*
bluer
bluest

★ **blue** *noun*
blues
bluebell *noun*
bluebells
bluebottle *noun*
bluebottles
blueprint *noun*
blueprints
bluff *verb*
bluffs
bluffing
bluffed
bluff *noun*
bluffs
blunder *verb*
blunders
blundering
blundered
blunder *noun*
blunders
blunt *adjective*
blunter
bluntest
blur *verb*
blurs
blurring
blurred
blur *noun*
blurs
blush *verb*
blushes
blushing
blushed
bluster *verb*
blusters
blustering
blustered
blustery
boa constrictor
noun
boa constrictors

☆ **boar** *noun*
boars
✪ **board** *noun*
boards
board *verb*
boards
boarding
boarded
boarder *noun*
boarders
board game *noun*
board games
boast *verb*
boasts
boasting
boasted
boastful
boastfully
boat *noun*
boats
boating
bob *verb*
bobs
bobbing
bobbed
bobble *noun*
bobbles
bobsled *noun*
bobsleds
bobsleigh *noun*
bobsleighs
bodice *noun*
bodices
bodily
body *noun*
bodies
bodyguard *noun*
bodyguards

· ·

★ **Blue** is the colour. **!** **blew**.
☆ A **boar** is a wild pig. **!** **bore**.
✪ A **board** is a piece of wood. **!** **bored**.

bo

boggy *adjective*
 boggier
 boggiest
bogus
boil *verb*
 boils
 boiling
 boiled
boil *noun*
 boils
boiler *noun*
 boilers
boisterous
 boisterously
bold *adjective*
 bolder
 boldest
bollard *noun*
 bollards
bolster *verb*
 bolsters
 bolstering
 bolstered
bolster *noun*
 bolsters
bolt *noun*
 bolts
bolt *verb*
 bolts
 bolting
 bolted
bomb *noun*
 bombs
bomb *verb*
 bombs
 bombing
 bombed
bombard *verb*
 bombards
 bombarding
 bombarded

bombardment
bomber *noun*
 bombers
bond *noun*
 bonds
bondage
bone *noun*
 bones
bonfire *noun*
 bonfires
bonnet *noun*
 bonnets
bonus *noun*
 bonuses
bony *adjective*
 bonier
 boniest
boo *verb*
 boos
 booing
 booed
booby *noun*
 boobies
book *noun*
 books
book *verb*
 books
 booking
 booked
bookcase *noun*
 bookcases
booklet *noun*
 booklets
bookmaker *noun*
 bookmakers
bookmark *noun*
 bookmarks
boom *noun*
 booms
boom *verb*

 booms
 booming
 boomed
boomerang *noun*
 boomerangs
boost *verb*
 boosts
 boosting
 boosted
booster *noun*
 boosters
boot *noun*
 boots
boot *verb*
 boots
 booting
 booted
booth *noun*
 booths
border *noun*
 borders
borderline
bore *verb*
 bores
 boring
 bored
★ **bore** *noun*
 bores
boredom
boring
☆ **born**
✪ **borne** see **bear**
borough *noun*
 boroughs
borrow *verb*
 borrows
 borrowing
 borrowed
bosom *noun*
 bosoms

· ·

★ **Bore** means 'something boring'. ! **boar**.
☆ You use **born** in e.g. *He was born in June.* ! **borne**.
✪ You use **borne** in e.g. *She has borne three children* and *The cost is borne by the government.* ! **born**.

boss *noun*
  bosses
boss *verb*
  bosses
  bossing
  bossed
bossy *adjective*
  bossier
  bossiest
botanical
botanist
botany
both
bother *verb*
  bothers
  bothering
  bothered
bother *noun*
bottle *noun*
  bottles
bottle *verb*
  bottles
  bottling
  bottled
bottleneck *noun*
  bottlenecks
bottom *noun*
  bottoms
bottomless
★ **bough** *noun*
  boughs
bought
boulder *noun*
  boulders
bounce *verb*
  bounces
  bouncing
  bounced
bounce *noun*
  bounces

bouncing
bouncy *adjective*
  bouncier
  bounciest
bound *verb*
  bounds
  bounding
  bounded
bound *adjective* and *noun*
  bounds
bound see **bind**
boundary *noun*
  boundaries
bounds
bouquet *noun*
  bouquets
bout *noun*
  bouts
boutique *noun*
  boutiques
☆ **bow** *noun*
  bows
○ **bow** *verb*
  bows
  bowing
  bowed
bowels
bowl *noun*
  bowls
bowl *verb*
  bowls
  bowling
  bowled
bow-legged
bowler *noun*
  bowlers
bowling
bowls
bow tie *noun*

bow ties
box *noun*
  boxes
box *verb*
  boxes
  boxing
  boxed
boxer *noun*
  boxers
Boxing Day *noun*
boy *noun*
  boys
boycott *verb*
  boycotts
  boycotting
  boycotted
boyfriend *noun*
  boyfriends
boyhood
boyish
bra *noun*
  bras
brace *noun*
  braces
bracelet *noun*
  bracelets
braces
bracken
bracket *noun*
  brackets
bracket *verb*
  brackets
  bracketing
  bracketed
brag *verb*
  brags
  bragging
  bragged

. . . .

★ A **bough** is a part of a tree. **!** bow.
☆ A **bow** is a knot with loops and rhymes with 'go'. A **bow** is also the front of a ship or a bending of the body and rhymes with 'cow'.
○ To **bow** is to bend the body and rhymes with 'cow'.

braid *noun*
braids
braille
brain *noun*
brains
brainy *adjective*
brainier
brainiest
★ **brake** *noun*
brakes
bramble *noun*
brambles
branch *noun*
branches
branch *verb*
branches
branching
branched
brand *noun*
brands
brand *verb*
brands
branding
branded
brandish *verb*
brandishes
brandishing
brandished
brand-new
brandy *noun*
brandies
brass
brassière *noun*
brassières
brassy *adjective*
brassier
brassiest
brave *adjective*
braver
bravest
brave *noun*

braves
bravery
brawl *noun*
brawls
brawn
brawny *adjective*
brawnier
brawniest
bray *verb*
brays
braying
brayed
brazen
brazier *noun*
braziers
☆ **breach** *noun*
breaches
bread
breadth *noun*
breadths
breadwinner *noun*
breadwinners
✪ **break** *verb*
breaks
breaking
broke
broken
break *noun*
breaks
breakable
breakage *noun*
breakages
breakdown *noun*
breakdowns
breaker *noun*
breakers
breakfast *noun*
breakfasts
breakneck
breakthrough *noun*

breakthroughs
breakwater *noun*
breakwaters
breast *noun*
breasts
breaststroke
breath *noun*
breaths
breathalyse
breathalyses
breathalysing
breathalysed
breathalyser *noun*
breathalysers
breathe *verb*
breathes
breathing
breathed
breather *noun*
breathers
breathless
breathtaking
bred see **breed**
✳ **breech** *noun*
breeches
breeches
breed *verb*
breeds
breeding
bred
breed *noun*
breeds
breeder *noun*
breeders
breeze *noun*
breezes
breezy *adjective*
breezier
breeziest
brethren

. . . .

★ A **brake** is what makes a car stop. ! **break**.
☆ A **breach** is a gap or a breaking of a rule. ! **breech**.
✪ To **break** something is to make it go into pieces. ! **brake**.
✳ A **breech** is a part of a gun. ! **breach**.

brevity
brew verb
  brews
  brewing
  brewed
brewer noun
  brewers
brewery noun
  breweries
★ **briar** noun
  briars
bribe noun
  bribes
bribe verb
  bribes
  bribing
  bribed
bribery
brick noun
  bricks
bricklayer noun
  bricklayers
bride noun
  brides
☆ **bridal**
bridegroom noun
  bridegrooms
bridesmaid noun
  bridesmaids
bridge noun
  bridges
○ **bridle** noun
  bridles
brief adjective
  briefer
  briefest
brief noun
  briefs
brief verb
  briefs

briefing
briefed
briefcase noun
  briefcases
brigade noun
  brigades
brigadier noun
  brigadiers
brigand noun
  brigands
bright adjective
  brighter
  brightest
brighten verb
  brightens
  brightening
  brightened
brilliance
brilliant
brim noun
  brims
brimming
brine
bring verb
  brings
  bringing
  brought
brink
brisk adjective
  brisker
  briskest
bristle noun
  bristles
bristly
  bristlier
  bristliest
British
Briton noun
  Britons
brittle adjective

brittler
brittlest
✶ **broach** verb
  broaches
  broaching
  broached
broad adjective
  broader
  broadest
  broadly
broadcast noun
  broadcasts
broadcast verb
  broadcasts
  broadcasting
  broadcast
broadcaster
broaden verb
  broadens
  broadening
  broadened
broad-minded
broadside noun
  broadsides
brochure noun
  brochures
brogue noun
  brogues
broke see **break**
broken see **break**
bronchitis
bronze
✱ **brooch** noun
  brooches
brood noun
  broods
brood verb
  broods
  brooding
  brooded

· ·

★ **Briar** means 'a prickly bush' and 'a pipe'. You will sometimes see it spelt _brier_.
☆ **Bridal** means 'to do with a **bride**'. ! **bridle**.
○ A **bridle** is part of a horse's harness. ! **bridal**.
✶ **Broach** means 'to mention something'. ! **brooch**.
✱ A **brooch** is an ornament you wear. ! **broach**.

broody adjective
broodier
broodiest
brook noun
brooks
broom noun
brooms
broomstick noun
broomsticks
broth noun
broths
brother noun
brothers
brotherly
brother-in-law noun
brothers-in-law
brought see bring
brow noun
brows
brown adjective
browner
brownest
★ **brownie** noun
brownies
☆ **Brownie** noun
Brownies
browse verb
browses
browsing
browsed
bruise noun
bruises
bruise verb
bruises
bruising
bruised
brunette noun
brunettes
brush noun
brushes

brush verb
brushes
brushing
brushed
Brussels sprout noun
Brussels sprouts
brutal
brutally
brutality
brutalities
brute noun
brutes
bubble noun
bubbles
bubble verb
bubbles
bubbling
bubbled
bubble gum
bubbly adjective
bubblier
bubbliest
buccaneer noun
buccaneers
buck noun
bucks
buck verb
bucks
bucking
bucked
bucket noun
buckets
bucketful noun
bucketfuls
buckle noun
buckles
buckle verb
buckles
buckling
buckled

bud noun
buds
Buddhism
Buddhist
budding
budge verb
budges
budging
budged
budgerigar noun
budgerigars
budget noun
budgets
budget verb
budgets
budgeting
budgeted
budgie noun
budgies
buff
buffalo noun
buffalo or
buffaloes
buffer noun
buffers
buffet noun
buffets
bug noun
bugs
bug verb
bugs
bugging
bugged
bugle noun
bugles
bugler
build verb
builds
building
built

. . . .

★ A **brownie** is a chocolate cake.
☆ A **Brownie** is a junior Guide.

builder *noun*
　builders
building *noun*
　buildings
built-in
built-up
bulb *noun*
　bulbs
bulge *noun*
　bulges
bulge *verb*
　bulges
　bulging
　bulged
bulk
bulky *adjective*
　bulkier
　bulkiest
bull *noun*
　bulls
bulldog *noun*
　bulldogs
bulldoze *verb*
　bulldozes
　bulldozing
　bulldozed
bulldozer *noun*
　bulldozers
bullet *noun*
　bullets
bulletin *noun*
　bulletins
bulletproof
bullfight *noun*
　bullfights
bullfighter
bullion
bullock *noun*
　bullocks
bull's-eye *noun*
　bull's-eyes

bully *verb*
　bullies
　bullying
　bullied
bully *noun*
　bullies
bulrush *noun*
　bulrushes
★ **bulwark** *noun*
　bulwarks
☆ **bulwarks** *plural noun*
bum *noun*
　bums
bumble-bee *noun*
　bumble-bees
bump *verb*
　bumps
　bumping
　bumped
bump *noun*
　bumps
bumper *adjective*
　and *noun*
　bumpers
bumpy *adjective*
　bumpier
　bumpiest
bunch *noun*
　bunches
bundle *noun*
　bundles
bundle *verb*
　bundles
　bundling
　bundled
bung *verb*
　bungs
　bunging
　bunged
bung *noun*
　bungs

bungalow *noun*
　bungalows
bungle *verb*
　bungles
　bungling
　bungled
bungler
bunk *noun*
　bunks
bunk bed *noun*
　bunk beds
bunker *noun*
　bunkers
bunny *noun*
　bunnies
bunsen burner *noun*
　bunsen burners
buoy *noun*
　buoys
buoyancy
buoyant
burden *noun*
　burdens
burdensome
✪ **bureau** *noun*
　bureaux
burglar *noun*
　burglars
burglary *noun*
　burglaries
burgle *verb*
　burgles
　burgling
　burgled
burial *noun*
　burials
burly *adjective*
　burlier
　burliest

- -

★ A **bulwark** is a strong wall.
☆ **Bulwarks** are the sides of a ship.
✪ **Bureau** is a French word used in English. It means 'a writing desk' or 'an office'.

★ **burn** verb
burns
burning
burnt or burned
burn noun
burns
burner noun
burners
burning
burp noun
burps
burp verb
burps
burping
burped
burr noun
burrs
burrow noun
burrows
burrow verb
burrows
burrowing
burrowed
burst verb
bursts
bursting
burst
burst noun
bursts
bury verb
buries
burying
buried
bus noun
buses
bus stop noun
bus stops
bush noun
bushes
bushy adjective
bushier

bushiest
busily
business noun
businesses
businesslike
busker noun
buskers
bust verb
busts
busting
bust
bust noun
busts
bust adjective
bustle verb
bustles
bustling
bustled
busy adjective
busier
busiest
busybody noun
busybodies
☆ **but**
butcher noun
butchers
butchery
butler noun
butlers
❍ **butt** noun
butts
✳ **butt** verb
butts
butting
butted
butter
buttercup noun
buttercups
butterfingers noun
butterfingers

butterfly noun
butterflies
butterscotch noun
butterscotches
buttocks
button noun
buttons
button verb
buttons
buttoning
buttoned
buttonhole noun
buttonholes
buttress noun
buttresses
buy verb
buys
buying
bought
buy noun
buys
buyer
buzz noun
buzzes
buzz verb
buzzes
buzzing
buzzed
buzzard noun
buzzards
buzzer noun
buzzers
✳ **by** preposition
✳ **bye** noun
byes
bye-bye
by-election noun
by-elections
by-law noun
by-laws

. . . .

★ You use **burned** in e.g. *I burned the cakes.* You use **burnt** in e.g. *I can smell burnt cakes.* You use **burned** or **burnt** in e.g. *I have burned/burnt the cakes.*
☆ You use **but** in e.g. *I like fish but I'm not hungry.* ! **butt**.
❍ A **butt** is a barrel or part of a gun. ! **but**.
✳ **Butt** means 'to hit with your head'. ! **but**.
✳ You use **by** in e.g. *a book by J. K. Rowling.* ! **bye**.
✳ You use **bye** in e.g *bye for now.* ! **by**.

bypass noun
　bypasses
by-product noun
　by-products
bystander noun
　bystanders
★ **byte** noun

Cc

CAB abbreviation
cab noun
　cabs
cabaret noun
　cabarets
cabbage noun
　cabbages
cabin noun
　cabins
cabinet noun
　cabinets
cable noun
　cables
cackle verb
　cackles
　cackling
　cackled
cackle noun
　cackles
cactus noun
　cacti
☆ **caddie** noun
　caddies
✪ **caddy** noun
　caddies
cadet noun
　cadets

cadge verb
　cadges
　cadging
　cadged
café noun
　cafés
cafeteria noun
　cafeterias
caffeine
caftan noun
　caftans use **kaftan**
cage noun
　cages
cagey adjective
　cagier
　cagiest
cagoule noun
　cagoules
cake noun
　cakes
caked
calamine
calamitous
calamity noun
　calamities
calcium
calculate verb
　calculates
　calculating
　calculated
calculation
~calculator noun
　calculators
calendar noun
　calendars
✳ **calf** noun
　calves
calico
call noun
　calls

call verb
　calls
　calling
　called
calling noun
　callings
callipers
callous
calm adjective
　calmer
　calmest
　calmly
calmness
calorie noun
　calories
✴ **calves** see **calf**
calypso noun
　calypsos
camcorder noun
　camcorders
came see **come**
camel noun
　camels
camera noun
　cameras
cameraman
camouflage
camp noun
　camps
camp verb
　camps
　camping
　camped
campaign noun
　campaigns
camper noun
　campers

- -

★ A **byte** is a unit in computing. ! **bite**.
☆ A **caddie** is a person who helps a golfer. ! **caddy**.
✪ A **caddy** is a container for tea. ! **caddie**.
✳ **Calf** means 'a young cow' and 'a part of your leg'.
✴ **Calves** is the plural of calf. ! **carves**.

campaign verb
campaigns
campaigning
campaigned
campsite noun
campsites
campus noun
campuses
can verb
could
★ **can** verb
cans
canning
canned
can noun
cans
canal noun
canals
canary noun
canaries
cancel verb
cancels
cancelling
cancelled
cancellation noun
cancellations
cancer noun
cancers
candidate noun
candidates
candle noun
candles
candlelight
candlestick noun
candlesticks
candy noun
candies
candyfloss
cane noun
canes

cane verb
canes
caning
caned
canine
cannabis
canned music
cannibal noun
cannibals
cannibalism
☆ **cannon** noun
cannon or
cannons
cannonball noun
cannonballs
cannot
canoe noun
canoes
canoe verb
canoes
canoeing
canoed
canoeist
✪ **canon** noun
canons
canopy noun
canopies
can't verb
canteen noun
canteens
canter verb
canters
cantering
cantered
canton noun
cantons
✳ **canvas** noun
canvases
✱ **canvass** verb
canvasses
canvassing

canvassed
canyon noun
canyons
cap verb
caps
capping
capped
cap noun
caps
capable
capably
capability
capacity noun
capacities
cape noun
capes
caper verb
capers
capering
capered
caper noun
capers
capital noun
capitals
capitalism
capitalist
capsize verb
capsizes
capsizing
capsized
capsule noun
capsules
captain noun
captains
caption noun
captions
captivating
captive adjective and noun
captives

- -

★ This verb **can** means 'to put food in a can', and it has normal forms.
☆ A **cannon** is a gun. **! canon.** You use **cannons** in e.g. *There are ten cannons on the walls* and **cannon** in e.g. *They use all their cannon.*
✪ A **canon** is a member of the clergy. **! cannon.**
✳ **Canvas** means 'a strong cloth'. **! canvass.**
✱ **Canvass** means 'to ask people for their support'. **! canvas.**

captivity
captor *noun*
  captors
capture *verb*
  captures
  capturing
  captured
capture *noun*
car *noun*
  cars
caramel *noun*
  caramels
carat *noun*
  carats
caravan *noun*
  caravans
carbohydrate *noun*
  carbohydrates
carbon
car-boot sale *noun*
  car-boot sales
carburettor *noun*
  carburettors
carcass *noun*
  carcasses
card *noun*
  cards
cardboard
cardigan *noun*
  cardigans
cardinal *noun*
  cardinals
cardphone *noun*
  cardphones
care *noun*
  cares
care *verb*
  cares
  caring
  cared

career *noun*
  careers
career *verb*
  careers
  careering
  careered
carefree
careful *adjective*
  carefully
careless *adjective*
  carelessly
  carelessness
caress *verb*
  caresses
  caressing
  caressed
caress *noun*
  caresses
caretaker *noun*
  caretakers
cargo *noun*
  cargoes
Caribbean
caricature *noun*
  caricatures
carnation *noun*
  carnations
carnival *noun*
  carnivals
carnivore *noun*
  carnivores
carnivorous
carol *noun*
  carols
caroller
carolling
carp *noun*
  carp
carpenter *noun*
  carpenters
carpentry

carpet *noun*
  carpets
carriage *noun*
  carriages
carriageway *noun*
  carriageways
carrier *noun*
  carriers
carrot *noun*
  carrots
carry *verb*
  carries
  carrying
  carried
cart *noun*
  carts
cart *verb*
  carts
  carting
  carted
carthorse *noun*
  carthorses
cartilage
carton *noun*
  cartons
cartoon *noun*
  cartoons
cartoonist
cartridge *noun*
  cartridges
cartwheel *noun*
  cartwheels
★ **carve** *verb*
  carves
  carving
  carved
cascade *noun*
  cascades
case *noun*
  cases

★ You use **carves** in e.g. *He carves the meat with a knife.* ! **calves.**

cash verb
cashes
cashing
cashed
cash noun
cashier noun
cashiers
cash register noun
cash registers
cask noun
casks
casket noun
caskets
casserole noun
casseroles
cassette noun
cassettes
cast verb
casts
casting
cast
cast noun
casts
castanets plural noun
castaway noun
castaways
castle noun
castles
castor noun
castors
castor sugar
casual adjective
casually
casualty noun
casualties
cat noun
cats
catalogue noun
catalogues

catalyst noun
catalysts
catamaran noun
catamarans
catapult noun
catapults
catastrophe noun
catastrophes
catastrophic
catch verb
catches
catching
caught
catch noun
catches
catching
catchphrase noun
catchphrases
catchy adjective
catchier
catchiest
category noun
categories
cater verb
caters
catering
catered
caterer noun
caterers
caterpillar noun
caterpillars
cathedral noun
cathedrals
Catherine wheel noun
Catherine wheels
cathode noun
cathodes
Catholic adjective and noun
Catholics

catkin noun
catkins
Cat's-eye noun
Cat's-eyes
cattle
caught see catch
cauldron noun
cauldrons
cauliflower noun
cauliflowers
cause verb
causes
causing
caused
cause noun
causes
caution noun
cautions
cautious adjective
cautiously
cavalier noun
cavaliers
cavalry noun
cavalries
cave noun
caves
cave verb
caves
caving
caved
caveman noun
cavemen
cavern noun
caverns
cavity noun
cavities
CD
CD-ROM noun

cease verb
ceases
ceasing
ceased
ceasefire noun
ceasefires
ceaseless adjective
ceaselessly
cedar noun
cedars
ceiling noun
ceilings
celebrate verb
celebrates
celebrating
celebrated
celebration noun
celebrations
celebrity noun
celebrities
celery
★ **cell** noun
cells
cellar noun
cellars
cello noun
cellos
cellular
celluloid
cellulose
Celsius
Celt noun
Celts
Celtic
cement
cemetery noun
cemeteries
censor verb
censors
censoring
censored

☆ **censor** noun
censors
censorship
censure verb
censures
censured
censuring
○ **censure** noun
census noun
censuses
★ **cent** noun
cents
centenary noun
centenaries
centigrade
centimetre noun
centimetres
centipede noun
centipedes
central adjective
centrally
centre noun
centres
centrifugal force
centurion noun
centurions
century noun
centuries
ceramic adjective
ceramics plural noun
✳ **cereal** noun
cereals
ceremony noun
ceremonies
ceremonial adjective
ceremonially
certain
certainly
certainty noun
certainties

certificate noun
certificates
certify verb
certifies
certifying
certified
chaffinch noun
chaffinches
chain noun
chains
chair noun
chairs
chairlift noun
chairlifts
chairman noun
chairmen
chairperson noun
chairpersons
chalet noun
chalets
chalk noun
chalks
chalky adjective
chalkier
chalkiest
challenge verb
challenges
challenging
challenged
challenge noun
challenges
challenger noun
challengers
chamber noun
chambers
champagne
champion noun
champions
championship noun
championships

- -

★ A **cell** is a small room or a part of an organism. ! **sell**.
☆ A **censor** is someone who makes sure books and films are suitable for people to see. ! **censure**.
○ **Censure** means 'harsh criticism'. ! **censor**.
✶ A **cent** is a coin used in America. ! **scent, sent**.
✳ A **cereal** is something you eat. ! **serial**.

chance *noun*
chances
chancel *noun*
chancels
chancellor *noun*
chancellors
Chancellor of the Exchequer
chandelier *noun*
chandeliers
change *verb*
changes
changing
changed
change *noun*
changes
changeable
channel *noun*
channels
chant *noun*
chants
chant *verb*
chants
chanting
chanted
chaos
chaotic *adjective*
chaotically
chap *noun*
chaps
chapatti *noun*
chapattis
chapel *noun*
chapels
chapped
chapter *noun*
chapters
char *verb*
chars
charring
charred

character *noun*
characters
characteristic *adjective*
characteristically
characteristic *noun*
characteristics
characterize *verb*
characterizes
characterizing
characterized
charades *plural noun*
charcoal
charge *verb*
charges
charging
charged
charge *noun*
charges
chariot *noun*
chariots
charioteer *noun*
charioteers
charitable *adjective*
charitably
charity *noun*
charities
charm *verb*
charms
charming
charmed
charm *noun*
charms
charming
chart *noun*
charts
charter *noun*
charters
charter *verb*
charters
chartering
chartered

charwoman *noun*
charwomen
chase *verb*
chases
chasing
chased
chase *noun*
chases
chasm *noun*
chasms
chassis *noun*
chassis
chat *verb*
chats
chatting
chatted
chat *noun*
chats
chatty *adjective*
chattier
chattiest
★ **château** *noun*
châteaux
chatter *verb*
chatters
chattering
chattered
chauffeur *noun*
chauffeurs
chauvinism
chauvinist
☆ **cheap** *adjective*
cheaper
cheapest
cheat *verb*
cheats
cheating
cheated
cheat *noun*
cheats

- -

★ **Château** is a French word used in English. It means 'a castle or large house'.
☆ **Cheap** means 'not costing much'. ! ~~cheep~~.

check *verb*
checks
checking
checked
check *noun*
checks
checkmate *noun*
checkmates
checkout *noun*
checkouts
check-up *noun*
check-ups
cheek *noun*
cheeks
cheek *verb*
cheeks
cheeking
cheeked
cheeky *adjective*
cheekier
cheekiest
cheekily
★ cheep *verb*
cheeps
cheeping
cheeped
cheer *verb*
cheers
cheering
cheered
cheer *noun*
cheers
cheerful *adjective*
cheerfully
cheerio
cheese *noun*
cheeses
cheesy *adjective*
cheesier
cheesiest
cheetah *noun*
cheetahs

chef *noun*
chefs
chemical *adjective*
chemically
chemical *noun*
chemicals
chemist *noun*
chemists
chemistry
cheque *noun*
cheques
chequebook *noun*
chequebooks
chequered
cherish *verb*
cherishes
cherishing
cherished
cherry *noun*
cherries
chess
chest *noun*
chests
chestnut *noun*
chestnuts
chest of drawers
noun
chests of drawers
chew *verb*
chews
chewing
chewed
chewy *adjective*
chewier
chewiest
☆ chic
chick *noun*
chicks
chicken *noun*
chickens

chicken *verb*
chickens
chickening
chickened
chickenpox
chief *adjective*
chiefly
chief *noun*
chiefs
chieftain *noun*
chieftains
chilblain *noun*
chilblains
child *noun*
children
childhood *noun*
childhoods
childish
childminder *noun*
childminders
childproof
chill *noun*
chills
chill *verb*
chills
chilling
chilled
○ chilli *noun*
chillies
✳ chilly *adjective*
chillier
chilliest
chime *noun*
chimes
chime *verb*
chimes
chiming
chimed
chimney *noun*
chimneys

· ·

★ Cheep is the noise a bird makes. ! cheap.
☆ Chic is a French word and means 'smart or elegant'. There is no word *chicly*.
○ A chilli is a type of hot pepper, added to meat or vegetable dishes. ! chilly.
✳ You use chilly to describe cold, bleak weather or atmosphere. ! chilli.

chimpanzee *noun*
chimpanzees
chin *noun*
chins
china
chink *noun*
chinks
chip *noun*
chips
chip *verb*
chips
chipping
chipped
chirp *verb*
chirps
chirping
chirped
chirpy *adjective*
chirpier
chirpiest
chisel *noun*
chisels
chisel *verb*
chisels
chiselling
chiselled
chivalrous *adjective*
chivalrously
chivalry
chlorine
chlorophyll
choc ice *noun*
choc ices
chock-a-block
chock-full
chocolate *noun*
chocolates
choice *noun*
choices
choir *noun*
choirs

choirboy *noun*
choirboys
choirgirl *noun*
choirgirls
choke *verb*
chokes
choking
choked
choke *noun*
chokes
cholera
cholesterol
choose *verb*
chooses
choosing
chose
chosen
choosy *adjective*
choosier
choosiest
chop *verb*
chops
chopping
chopped
chop *noun*
chops
chopper *noun*
choppers
choppy *adjective*
choppier
choppiest
chopsticks
choral
★ **chord** *noun*
chords
chore *noun*
chores
chorister *noun*
choristers
chorus *noun*
choruses

chose see choose
chosen see choose
christen *verb*
christens
christening
christened
christening
Christian *adjective*
and *noun*
Christians
Christianity
Christmas *noun*
Christmases
chrome
chromium
chromosome *noun*
chromosomes
chronic *adjective*
chronically
chronicle *noun*
chronicles
chronological
adjective
chronologically
chronology
chrysalis *noun*
chrysalises
chrysanthemum
noun
chrysanthemums
chubby *adjective*
chubbier
chubbiest
chuck *verb*
chucks
chucking
chucked
chuckle *verb*
chuckles
chuckling
chuckled

· ·

★ A **chord** is a number of musical notes played together. ! cord.

chuckle *noun*
 chuckles
chug *verb*
 chugs
 chugging
 chugged
chum *noun*
 chums
chummy *adjective*
 chummier
 chummiest
chunk *noun*
 chunks
chunky *adjective*
 chunkier
 chunkiest
church *noun*
 churches
churchyard *noun*
 churchyards
churn *noun*
 churns
churn *verb*
 churns
 churning
 churned
★ **chute** *noun*
 chutes
chutney *noun*
 chutneys
cider *noun*
 ciders
cigar *noun*
 cigars
cigarette *noun*
 cigarettes
cinder *noun*
 cinders
cine camera *noun*
 cine cameras
cinema *noun*
 cinemas

cinnamon
circle *noun*
 circles
circle *verb*
 circles
 circling
 circled
circuit *noun*
 circuits
circular *adjective*
 and *noun*
 circulars
circulate *verb*
 circulates
 circulating
 circulated
circulation *noun*
 circulations
circumference *noun*
 circumferences
circumstance *noun*
 circumstances
circus *noun*
 circuses
cistern *noun*
 cisterns
citizen *noun*
 citizens
citizenship
citric acid
citrus
city *noun*
 cities
civic
civil
civilian *noun*
 civilians
civilization *noun*
 civilizations

civilize *verb*
 civilizes
 civilizing
 civilized
clad
claim *verb*
 claims
 claiming
 claimed
claim *noun*
 claims
claimant *noun*
 claimants
clam *noun*
 clams
clamber *verb*
 clambers
 clambering
 clambered
clammy *adjective*
 clammier
 clammiest
clamp *noun*
 clamps
clamp *verb*
 clamps
 clamping
 clamped
clan *noun*
 clans
clang *verb*
 clangs
 clanging
 clanged
clanger *noun*
 clangers
clank *verb*
 clanks
 clanking
 clanked

· ·

★ A **chute** is a funnel for sending things down. **! shoot.**

clap *verb*
  claps
  clapping
  clapped
clap *noun*
  claps
clapper *noun*
  clappers
clarification
clarify *verb*
  clarifies
  clarifying
  clarified
clarinet *noun*
  clarinets
clarinettist
clarity
clash *verb*
  clashes
  clashing
  clashed
clash *noun*
  clashes
clasp *verb*
  clasps
  clasping
  clasped
clasp *noun*
  clasps
class *noun*
  classes
class *verb*
  classes
  classing
  classed
classic *noun*
  classics
classic
classical *adjective*
  classically
classification

classified
classify *verb*
  classifies
  classifying
  classified
classmate *noun*
  classmates
classroom *noun*
  classrooms
clatter *noun*
clatter *verb*
  clatters
  clattering
  clattered
★ clause *noun*
  clauses
☆ claw *noun*
  claws
✪ claw *verb*
  claws
  clawing
  clawed
clay
clayey
clean *adjective*
  cleaner
  cleanest
  cleanly
clean *verb*
  cleans
  cleaning
  cleaned
cleaner *noun*
  cleaners
cleanliness
cleanse *verb*
  cleanses
  cleansing
  cleansed
cleanser

clear *adjective*
  clearer
  clearest
  clearly
clear *verb*
  clears
  clearing
  cleared
clearance *noun*
  clearances
clearing *noun*
  clearings
clef *noun*
  clefs
clench *verb*
  clenches
  clenching
  clenched
clergy
clergyman *noun*
  clergymen
clergywoman *noun*
  clergywomen
clerical
clerk *noun*
  clerks
clever *adjective*
  cleverer
  cleverest
cliché *noun*
  clichés
click *noun*
  clicks
client *noun*
  clients
cliff *noun*
  cliffs
cliffhanger *noun*
  cliffhangers
climate *noun*
  climates

★ A clause is a part of a sentence or contract. ! claws.
☆ Claws are the hard sharp nails that some animals have on their feet. ! clause.
✪ To claw is to scratch, maul, or pull a person or thing.

climatic
climax *noun*
 climaxes
climb *verb*
 climbs
 climbing
 climbed
climb *noun*
 climbs
climber *noun*
 climbers
cling *verb*
 clings
 clinging
 clung
clingfilm
clinic *noun*
 clinics
clink *verb*
 clinks
 clinking
 clinked
clip *verb*
 clips
 clipping
 clipped
clip *noun*
 clips
clipboard *noun*
 clipboards
clipper *noun*
 clippers
clippers *plural noun*
clipping *noun*
 clippings
cloak *noun*
 cloaks
cloakroom *noun*
 cloakrooms
clobber *verb*
 clobbers

 clobbering
 clobbered
clock *noun*
 clocks
clockwise
clockwork
clog *verb*
 clogs
 clogging
 clogged
clog *noun*
 clogs
cloister *noun*
 cloisters
clone *noun*
 clones
clone *verb*
 clones
 cloning
 cloned
close *verb*
 closes
 closing
 closed
close *adjective* and
 noun
 closer
 closest
 closely
close *noun*
 closes
close-up *noun*
 close-ups
closure *noun*
 closures
clot *noun*
 clots
clot *verb*
 clots
 clotting
 clotted

cloth *noun*
 cloths
clothe *verb*
 clothes
 clothing
 clothed
clothes
clothing
cloud *noun*
 clouds
cloud *verb*
 clouds
 clouding
 clouded
cloudless
cloudy *adjective*
 cloudier
 cloudiest
clout *verb*
 clouts
 clouting
 clouted
clove *noun*
 cloves
clover
clown *noun*
 clowns
clown *verb*
 clowns
 clowning
 clowned
club *noun*
 clubs
club *verb*
 clubs
 clubbing
 clubbed
cluck *verb*
 clucks
 clucking
 clucked

clue noun
  clues
clueless
clump noun
  clumps
clumsiness
clumsy adjective
  clumsier
  clumsiest
  clumsily
clung see **ding**
cluster noun
  clusters
clutch verb
  clutches
  clutching
  clutched
clutch noun
  clutches
clutter verb
  clutters
  cluttering
  cluttered
clutter noun

co-
co- makes words meaning 'together', e.g. a **co-pilot** is another pilot who sits together with the chief pilot. You often need a hyphen, e.g. **co-author, co-driver**, but some words are spelt joined up, e.g. **cooperate, coordinate**.

coach verb
  coaches
  coaching
  coached

coach noun
  coaches
coal
★ **coarse** adjective
  coarser
  coarsest
  coarsely
coast noun
  coasts
coast verb
  coasts
  coasting
  coasted
coastal
coastguard noun
  coastguards
coastline
coat noun
  coats
coat verb
  coats
  coating
  coated
coating noun
  coatings
coax verb
  coaxes
  coaxing
  coaxed
cobalt
cobbled
cobbler noun
  cobblers
cobbles plural noun
cobblestone noun
  cobblestones
cobra noun
  cobras
cobweb noun
  cobwebs

cock noun
  cocks
cock verb
  cocks
  cocking
  cocked
cockerel noun
  cockerels
cocker spaniel noun
  cocker spaniels
cockle noun
  cockles
cockney noun
  cockneys
cockpit noun
  cockpits
cockroach noun
  cockroaches
cocky adjective
  cockier
  cockiest
cocoa noun
  cocoas
coconut noun
  coconuts
cocoon noun
  cocoons
☆ **cod** noun
  cod
code noun
  codes
code verb
  codes
  coding
  coded
coeducation
coeducational
coffee noun
  coffees
coffin noun
  coffins

. . . .

★ **Coarse** means 'rough' or 'crude'. ! **course**.
☆ You use **cod** for the plural: *The sea is full of cod.*

cog noun
  cogs
cohort noun
  cohorts
coil verb
  coils
  coiling
  coiled
coil noun
  coils
coin noun
  coins
coin verb
  coins
  coining
  coined
coinage noun
  coinages
coincide verb
  coincides
  coinciding
  coincided
coincidence noun
  coincidences
coincidentally
coke
cola noun
  colas
colander noun
  colanders
cold adjective
  colder
  coldest
  coldly
cold noun
  colds
cold-blooded
coldness
coleslaw
collaborate verb
  collaborates

  collaborating
  collaborated
collaboration
collaborator
collage noun
  collages
collapse verb
  collapses
  collapsing
  collapsed
collapse noun
  collapses
collapsible
collar noun
  collars
collate verb
  collates
  collating
  collated
colleague noun
  colleagues
collect verb
  collects
  collecting
  collected
collection noun
  collections
collective
collector
college noun
  colleges
collide verb
  collides
  colliding
  collided
collie noun
  collies
collision noun
  collisions
colloquial adjective
  colloquially

colon noun
  colons
★ **colonel** noun
  colonels
colonial
colonist noun
  colonists
colony noun
  colonies
colossal adjective
  colossally
colour noun
  colours
colour verb
  colours
  colouring
  coloured
colour-blind
coloured
colourful adjective
  colourfully
colouring
colourless
colt noun
  colts
column noun
  columns
coma noun
  comas
comb noun
  combs
comb verb
  combs
  combing
  combed
combat noun
  combats
combat verb
  combats
  combating
  combated

· ·

★ A **colonel** is an army officer. **!** kernel

combatant noun
  combatants
combination noun
  combinations
combine verb
  combines
  combining
  combined
combine noun
  combines
combustion
come verb
  comes
  coming
  came
comeback noun
  comebacks
comedian noun
  comedians
comedy noun
  comedies
comet noun
  comets
comfort verb
  comforts
  comforting
  comforted
comfort noun
  comforts
comfortable
  adjective
  comfortably
comic adjective and
  noun
  comics
comical adjective
  comically
comma noun
  commas
command verb
  commands

commanding
commanded
command noun
  commands
commander noun
  commanders
commandment
  noun
  commandments
commando noun
  commandos
commemorate verb
  commemorates
  commemorating
  commemorated
commemoration
commence verb
  commences
  commencing
  commenced
commencement
commend verb
  commends
  commending
  commended
commendable
commendation
comment verb
  comments
  commenting
  commented
comment noun
  comments
commentary noun
  commentaries
commentate
commentator noun
  commentators
commerce
commercial
  adjective

commercially
commercial noun
  commercials
commercialized
commit verb
  commits
  committing
  committed
commitment noun
  commitments
committee noun
  committees
commodity noun
  commodities
common adjective
  commoner
  commonest
common noun
  commons
commonplace
commonwealth
  noun
  commonwealths
commotion noun
  commotions
communal adjective
  communally
commune noun
  communes
communicate verb
  communicates
  communicating
  communicated
communication
  noun
  communications
communicative
communion noun
  communions
communism

communist *noun*
  communists
community *noun*
  communities
commute
commuter *noun*
  commuters
compact *adjective*
  compactly
compact *noun*
  compacts
compact disc *noun*
  compact discs
companion *noun*
  companions
companionship
company *noun*
  companies
comparable
  adjective
  comparably
comparative
  adjective
  comparatively
comparative *noun*
  comparatives
compare *verb*
  compares
  comparing
  compared
comparison *noun*
  comparisons
compartment *noun*
  compartments
compass *noun*
  compasses
compassion
compassionate
  adjective
  compassionately

compatible *adjective*
  compatibly
compel *verb*
  compels
  compelling
  compelled
compensate *verb*
  compensates
  compensating
  compensated
compensation *noun*
  compensations
compère *noun*
  compères
compete *verb*
  competes
  competing
  competed
competence
competent *adjective*
  competently
competition *noun*
  competitions
competitive
  adjective
  competitively
competitor *noun*
  competitors
compilation *noun*
  compilations
compile *verb*
  compiles
  compiling
  compiled
compiler *noun*
  compilers
complacent
  adjective
  complacently
complain *verb*
  complains

complaining
complained
complaint *noun*
  complaints
★ complement *noun*
  complements
☆ complementary
complete *adjective*
  completely
complete *verb*
  completes
  completing
  completed
completion
complex *adjective*
  and *noun*
  complexes
complexion *noun*
  complexions
complexity *noun*
  complexities
complicated
complication *noun*
  complications
✪ compliment *noun*
  compliments
✻ complimentary
component *noun*
  components
compose *verb*
  composes
  composing
  composed
composer *noun*
  composers
composition *noun*
  compositions
compost
compound *noun*
  compounds

· ·

★ A **complement** is a thing that completes something. ! compliment.
☆ Something **complementary** completes something. ! complimentary.
✪ A **compliment** is something good you say about someone. ! complement.
✻ Something **complimentary** praises someone. ! complementary.

comprehend verb
comprehends
comprehending
comprehended
comprehension
noun
comprehensions
comprehensive
adjective
comprehensively
comprehensive
noun
comprehensives
compress verb
compresses
compressing
compressed
compression
comprise verb
comprises
comprising
comprised
compromise noun
compromises
compromise verb
compromises
compromising
compromised
compulsory
computation
compute verb
computes
computing
computed
computer noun
computers
comrade noun
comrades
comradeship
con verb
cons

conning
conned
concave
conceal verb
conceals
concealing
concealed
concealment
conceit
conceited
conceive verb
conceives
conceiving
conceived
concentrate verb
concentrates
concentrating
concentrated
concentrated
concentration noun
concentrations
concentric
concept noun
concepts
conception noun
conceptions
concern verb
concerns
concerning
concerned
concern noun
concerns
concerning
concert noun
concerts
concertina noun
concertinas
concerto noun
concertos
concession noun

concessions
concise adjective
concisely
conclude verb
concludes
concluding
concluded
conclusion noun
conclusions
concrete adjective
and noun
concussion
condemn verb
condemns
condemning
condemned
condemnation
condensation
condense verb
condenses
condensing
condensed
condition noun
conditions
condom noun
condoms
conduct verb
conducts
conducting
conducted
conduct noun
conduction
conductor noun
conductors
cone noun
cones
confectioner noun
confectioners
confectionery

confer *verb*
confers
conferring
conferred
conference *noun*
conferences
confess *verb*
confesses
confessing
confessed
confession *noun*
confessions
confetti
confide *verb*
confides
confiding
confided
confidence *noun*
confidences
confident *adjective*
confidently
confidential
adjective
confidentially
confine *verb*
confines
confining
confined
confinement
confirm *verb*
confirms
confirming
confirmed
confirmation
confiscate *verb*
confiscates
confiscating
confiscated
confiscation *noun*
confiscations

conflict *verb*
conflicts
conflicting
conflicted
conflict *noun*
conflicts
conform *verb*
conforms
conforming
conformed
conformity
confront *verb*
confronts
confronting
confronted
confrontation *noun*
confrontations
confuse *verb*
confuses
confusing
confused
confusion *noun*
confusions
congested
congestion
congratulate *verb*
congratulates
congratulating
congratulated
congratulations
plural noun
congregation *noun*
congregations
congress *noun*
congresses
congruence
congruent
conical
conifer *noun*
conifers
coniferous

conjunction *noun*
conjunctions
conjure *verb*
conjures
conjuring
conjured
conjuror *noun*
conjurors
★ **conker** *noun*
conkers
connect *verb*
connects
connecting
connected
connection *noun*
connections
conning tower *noun*
conning towers
☆ **conquer** *verb*
conquers
conquering
conquered
conqueror *noun*
conquerors
conquest *noun*
conquests
conscience
conscientious
adjective
conscientiously
conscious *adjective*
consciously
consciousness
conscription
consecutive *adjective*
consecutively
consensus
consent *verb*
consents
consenting
consented

★ A **conker** is the fruit of a horse chestnut tree. **!** conquer.
☆ To **conquer** means 'to invade or take over'. **!** conker.

consent *noun*
consequence *noun*
  consequences
consequently
conservation
conservationist
conservative
★ **Conservative** *noun*
  Conservatives
conservatory *noun*
  conservatories
conserve *verb*
  conserves
  conserving
  conserved
consider *verb*
  considers
  considering
  considered
considerable
  adjective
  considerably
considerate
  adjective
  considerately
consideration *noun*
  considerations
consist *verb*
  consists
  consisting
  consisted
consistency *noun*
  consistencies
consistent *adjective*
  consistently
consolation *noun*
  consolations
console *verb*
  consoles
  consoling
  consoled

consonant *noun*
  consonants
conspicuous
  adjective
  conspicuously
conspiracy *noun*
  conspiracies
conspirator
conspire *verb*
  conspires
  conspiring
  conspired
constable *noun*
  constables
constancy
constant *adjective*
  constantly
constant *noun*
  constants
constellation *noun*
  constellations
constipated
constipation
constituency *noun*
  constituencies
constituent *noun*
  constituents
constitute *verb*
  constitutes
  constituting
  constituted
constitution *noun*
  constitutions
constitutional
construct *verb*
  constructs
  constructing
  constructed
construction *noun*
  constructions

constructive
consul *noun*
  consuls
consult *verb*
  consults
  consulting
  consulted
consultant *noun*
  consultants
consultation *noun*
  consultations
consume *verb*
  consumes
  consuming
  consumed
consumer *noun*
  consumers
consumption
contact *noun*
  contacts
contact *verb*
  contacts
  contacting
  contacted
contagious
contain *verb*
  contains
  containing
  contained
container *noun*
  containers
contaminate *verb*
  contaminates
  contaminating
  contaminated
contamination
contemplate *verb*
  contemplates
  contemplating
  contemplated
contemplation

★ Use a capital C when you mean a member of the political party.

contemporary
  adjective and noun
  contemporaries
contempt
contemptible
  adjective
  contemptibly
contemptuous
  adjective
  contemptuously
contend verb
  contends
  contending
  contended
contender noun
  contenders
content adjective and
  noun
contented adjective
  contentedly
contentment
contents plural noun
contest verb
  contests
  contesting
  contested
contest noun
  contests
contestant noun
  contestants
context noun
  contexts
continent noun
  continents
continental
continual adjective
  continually
continuation

continue verb
  continues
  continuing
  continued
continuous adjective
  continuously
continuity
contour noun
  contours
contraception
contraceptive noun
  contraceptives
contract verb
  contracts
  contracting
  contracted
contract noun
  contracts
contraction noun
  contractions
contractor noun
  contractors
contradict verb
  contradicts
  contradicting
  contradicted
contradiction noun
  contradictions
contradictory
contraflow noun
  contraflows
contraption noun
  contraptions
contrary adjective
  and noun
contrast verb
  contrasts
  contrasting
  contrasted
contrast noun
  contrasts

contribute verb
  contributes
  contributing
  contributed
contribution noun
  contributions
contributor noun
  contributors
contrivance noun
  contrivances
contrive verb
  contrives
  contriving
  contrived
control verb
  controls
  controlling
  controlled
control noun
  controls
controller noun
  controllers
controversial
  adjective
  controversially
controversy noun
  controversies
conundrum noun
  conundrums
convalescence
convalescent
convection
convector noun
  convectors
convenience noun
  conveniences
convenient adjective
  conveniently
convent noun
  convents
convention noun
  conventions

conventional adjective
conventionally
converge verb
converges
converging
converged
conversation noun
conversations
conversational adjective
conversationally
converse verb
converses
conversing
conversed
converse noun
conversion noun
conversions
convert verb
converts
converting
converted
convert noun
converts
convertible
convex
convey verb
conveys
conveying
conveyed
conveyor belt noun
conveyor belts
convict verb
convicts
convicting
convicted
convict noun
convicts
conviction noun
convictions

convince verb
convinces
convincing
convinced
convoy noun
convoys
cook verb
cooks
cooking
cooked
cook noun
cooks
cooker noun
cookers
cookery
cool adjective
cooler
coolest
coolly
cool verb
cools
cooling
cooled
cooler
coolness
coop noun
coops
cooperate verb
cooperates
cooperating
cooperated
cooperation
cooperative
coordinate verb
coordinates
coordinating
coordinated
coordinate noun
coordinates
coordination
coordinator noun
coordinators

coot noun
coots
cop verb
cops
copping
copped
cop noun
cops
cope verb
copes
coping
coped
copier noun
copiers
copper noun
coppers
copper sulphate
copy verb
copies
copying
copied
copy noun
copies
coral
★ **cord** noun
cords
cordial adjective
cordially
cordial noun
cordials
cordiality
corduroy
core noun
cores
corgi noun
corgis
cork noun
corks
corkscrew noun
corkscrews

· ·

★ A **cord** is a piece of thin rope. ! chord.

cormorant noun
  cormorants
corn noun
  corns
corned beef
corner noun
  corners
corner verb
  corners
  cornering
  cornered
cornet noun
  cornets
cornfield noun
  cornfields
cornflakes
cornflour
cornflower noun
  cornflowers
Cornish
Cornish pasty noun
  Cornish pasties
corny adjective
  cornier
  corniest
coronation noun
  coronations
coroner noun
  coroners
corporal noun
  corporals
corporal adjective
corporation noun
  corporations
★ **corps** noun
  corps
☆ **corpse** noun
  corpses
corpuscle noun
  corpuscles

corral noun
  corrals
correct adjective
  correctly
correct verb
  corrects
  correcting
  corrected
correction noun
  corrections
correctness
correspond verb
  corresponds
  corresponding
  corresponded
correspondence
correspondent noun
  correspondents
corridor noun
  corridors
corrode verb
  corrodes
  corroding
  corroded
corrosion
corrosive
corrugated
corrupt
corruption
corset noun
  corsets
cosmetics plural
  noun
cosmic
cosmonaut noun
  cosmonauts
cost verb
  costs
  costing
  cost

cost noun
  costs
costly adjective
  costlier
  costliest
costume noun
  costumes
cosy adjective
  cosier
  cosiest
cosy noun
  cosies
cot noun
  cots
cottage noun
  cottages
cotton
couch noun
  couches
cough verb
  coughs
  coughing
  coughed
cough noun
  coughs
could see can
couldn't
✿ **council** noun
  councils
✳ **councillor** noun
  councillors
✴ **counsel** noun
  counsels
counsel verb
  counsels
  counselling
  counselled
✳ **counsellor** noun
  counsellors

· ·

★ A **corps** is a unit of soldiers. ! **corpse**.
☆ A **corpse** is a dead body. ! **corps**.
✿ A **council** is a group of people who run the affairs of a town. ! **counsel**.
✳ A **councillor** is a member of a council. ! **counsellor**.
✴ **Counsel** means 'advice'. ! **council**.
✳ A **counsellor** is someone who gives advice. ! **councillor**.

count *verb*
counts
counting
counted
count *noun*
counts
countdown *noun*
countdowns
countenance *noun*
countenances

counter-
counter- makes words meaning 'opposite', e.g. a **counter-claim** is a claim someone makes in response to a claim from someone else. You often need a hyphen, but some words are spelt joined up, e.g. **counteract**, **counterbalance**.

counter *noun*
counters
counterfeit
countess *noun*
countesses
countless
country *noun*
countries
countryman *noun*
countrymen
countryside
countrywoman *noun*
countrywomen
county *noun*
counties
couple *noun*
couples

couple *verb*
couples
coupling
coupled
coupling *noun*
couplings
coupon *noun*
coupons
courage
courageous *adjective*
courageously
courgette *noun*
courgettes
courier *noun*
couriers
★ **course** *noun*
courses
court *noun*
courts
court *verb*
courts
courting
courted
courteous *adjective*
courteously
courtesy *noun*
courtesies
court martial *noun*
courts martial
courtship
courtyard *noun*
courtyards
cousin *noun*
cousins
cove *noun*
coves
cover *verb*
covers
covering
covered

cover *noun*
covers
coverage
cover-up *noun*
cover-ups
cow *noun*
cows
coward *noun*
cowards
cowardice
cowardly
cowboy *noun*
cowboys
cowslip *noun*
cowslips
cox *noun*
coxes
coxswain *noun*
coxswains
coy *adjective*
coyly
coyness
crab *noun*
crabs
crack *verb*
cracks
cracking
cracked
crack *noun*
cracks
cracker *noun*
crackers
crackle *verb*
crackles
crackling
crackled
crackling
cradle *noun*
cradles
craft *noun*
crafts

★ You use **course** in e.g. *a French course.* **!** coarse.

craftsman noun
 craftsmen
craftsmanship
crafty adjective
 craftier
 craftiest
 craftily
craftiness
crag noun
 crags
craggy adjective
 craggier
 craggiest
cram verb
 crams
 cramming
 crammed
cramp verb
 cramps
 cramping
 cramped
cramp noun
 cramps
crane noun
 cranes
crane verb
 cranes
 craning
 craned
crane-fly noun
 crane-flies
crank verb
 cranks
 cranking
 cranked
crank noun
 cranks
cranky adjective
 crankier
 crankiest

cranny noun
 crannies
crash verb
 crashes
 crashing
 crashed
crash noun
 crashes
crate noun
 crates
crater noun
 craters
crave verb
 craves
 craving
 craved
crawl verb
 crawls
 crawling
 crawled
crawl noun
 crawls
crayon noun
 crayons
craze noun
 crazes
craziness
crazy adjective
 crazier
 craziest
 crazily
creak verb
 creaks
 creaking
 creaked
creak noun
 creaks
creaky adjective
 creakier
 creakiest
cream noun
 creams

creamy adjective
 creamier
 creamiest
crease verb
 creases
 creasing
 creased
crease noun
 creases
create verb
 creates
 creating
 created
creation noun
 creations
creative adjective
 creatively
creativity
creator noun
 creators
creature noun
 creatures
crèche noun
 crèches
credibility
credible adjective
 credibly
credit verb
 credits
 crediting
 credited
credit noun
creditable adjective
 creditably
creditor noun
 creditors
creed noun
 creeds
creek noun
 creeks

creep verb
creeps
creeping
crept
creep noun
creeps
creeper noun
creepers
creepy adjective
creepier
creepiest
cremate verb
cremates
cremating
cremated
cremation noun
cremations
crematorium noun
crematoria
creosote
crêpe noun
crêpes
crept see creep
crescendo noun
crescendos
crescent noun
crescents
cress
crest noun
crests
crevice noun
crevices
crew noun
crews
crib verb
cribs
cribbing
cribbed
crib noun
cribs
★ **cricket** noun

crickets
cricketer noun
cricketers
cried see cry
crime noun
crimes
criminal adjective
and noun
criminals
crimson
crinkle verb
crinkles
crinkling
crinkled
crinkly adjective
crinklier
crinkliest
cripple verb
cripples
crippling
crippled
cripple noun
cripples
crisis noun
crises
crisp adjective
crisper
crispest
crisp noun
crisps
criss-cross adjective
critic noun
critics
critical adjective
critically
criticism noun
criticisms
criticize verb
criticizes
criticizing
criticized

croak verb
croaks
croaking
croaked
croak noun
croaks
☆ **crochet**
crock noun
crocks
crockery
crocodile noun
crocodiles
crocus noun
crocuses
croft noun
crofts
crofter
croissant noun
croissants
crook noun
crooks
crook verb
crooks
crooking
crooked
crooked
croon verb
croons
crooning
crooned
crop noun
crops
crop verb
crops
cropping
cropped

- -

★ **Cricket** means 'a game' and 'an insect like a grasshopper'.
☆ **Crochet** is a kind of needlework. ! crotchet.

cross-
cross- makes words meaning 'across', e.g. a *cross-channel ferry* is one that goes across the English Channel. You usually need a hyphen, but some words are spelt joined up, e.g. **crossroads** and **crosswind.**

cross *adjective*
  crossly
cross *verb*
  crosses
  crossing
  crossed
cross *noun*
  crosses
crossbar *noun*
  crossbars
crossbow *noun*
  crossbows
cross-country
cross-examine *verb*
  cross-examines
  cross-examining
  cross-examined
cross-examination *noun*
  cross-examinations
cross-eyed
crossing *noun*
  crossings
cross-legged
crossness
crossroads *noun*
  crossroads
cross-section *noun*
  cross-sections

crosswise
crossword *noun*
  crosswords
★ **crotchet** *noun*
  crotchets
crouch *verb*
  crouches
  crouching
  crouched
crow *noun*
  crows
crow *verb*
  crows
  crowing
  crowed
crowbar *noun*
  crowbars
crowd *noun*
  crowds
crowd *verb*
  crowds
  crowding
  crowded
crown *noun*
  crowns
crown *verb*
  crowns
  crowning
  crowned
crow's-nest *noun*
  crow's-nests
crucial *adjective*
  crucially
crucifix *noun*
  crucifixes
☆ **crucifixion** *noun*
  crucifixions
crucify *verb*
  crucifies
  crucifying
  crucified

crude *adjective*
  cruder
  crudest
cruel *adjective*
  crueller
  cruellest
  cruelly
cruelty *noun*
  cruelties
cruise *verb*
  cruises
  cruising
  cruised
cruise *noun*
  cruises
cruiser *noun*
  cruisers
crumb *noun*
  crumbs
crumble *verb*
  crumbles
  crumbling
  crumbled
crumbly *adjective*
  crumblier
  crumbliest
crumpet *noun*
  crumpets
crumple *verb*
  crumples
  crumpling
  crumpled
crunch *noun*
  crunches
crunch *verb*
  crunches
  crunching
  crunched
crunchy *adjective*
  crunchier
  crunchiest

★ A **crotchet** is a note in music. ! ~~crochet~~
☆ Use a capital C when you are talking about Christ.

crusade noun
  crusades
crusader noun
  crusaders
crush verb
  crushes
  crushing
  crushed
crush noun
  crushes
crust noun
  crusts
crustacean noun
  crustaceans
crutch noun
  crutches
cry verb
  cries
  crying
  cried
cry noun
  cries
crypt noun
  crypts
crystal noun
  crystals
crystalline
crystallize verb
  crystallizes
  crystallizing
  crystallized
cub noun
  cubs
cubbyhole noun
  cubbyholes
cube noun
  cubes
cube verb
  cubes
  cubing
  cubed

cubic
cubicle noun
  cubicles
cuboid noun
  cuboids
cuckoo noun
  cuckoos
cucumber noun
  cucumbers
cud
cuddle verb
  cuddles
  cuddling
  cuddled
cuddly
★ **cue** noun
  cues
cuff verb
  cuffs
  cuffing
  cuffed
cuff noun
  cuffs
cul-de-sac noun
  cul-de-sacs or
  culs-de-sac
culminate verb
  culminates
  culminating
  culminated
culmination
culprit noun
  culprits
cult noun
  cults
cultivate verb
  cultivates
  cultivating
  cultivated
cultivation

cultivated
culture noun
  cultures
cultural adjective
  culturally
cultured
cunning
cup noun
  cups
cup verb
  cups
  cupping
  cupped
cupboard noun
  cupboards
cupful noun
  cupfuls
curate noun
  curates
curator noun
  curators
☆ **curb** verb
  curbs
  curbing
  curbed
curd noun
  curds
curdle verb
  curdles
  curdling
  curdled
cure verb
  cures
  curing
  cured
cure noun
  cures
curfew noun
  curfews

- -

★ A **cue** is a signal for action or a stick used in snooker. ! queue.
☆ To **curb** a feeling is to restrain it. ! kerb.

curiosity noun
curiosities
curious adjective
curiously
curl verb
curls
curling
curled
curl noun
curls
curly adjective
curlier
curliest
★ **currant** noun
currants
currency noun
currencies
☆ **current** noun
currents
current adjective
currently
curriculum noun
curriculums or
curricula
curry verb
curries
currying
curried
curry noun
curries
curse verb
curses
cursing
cursed
curse noun
curses
cursor noun
cursors
curtain noun
curtains

curtsy verb
curtsies
curtsying
curtsied
curtsy noun
curtsies
curvature noun
curvatures
curve verb
curves
curving
curved
curve noun
curves
cushion noun
cushions
cushion verb
cushions
cushioning
cushioned
custard
custom noun
customs
customary adjective
customarily
customer noun
customers
customize noun
customizes
customizing
customized
cut verb
cuts
cutting
cut
cut noun
cuts
cute adjective
cuter
cutest

cutlass noun
cutlasses
cutlery
cutlet noun
cutlets
cut-out noun
cut-outs
cut-price
cutter noun
cutters
cutting noun
cuttings
cycle noun
cycles
cycle verb
cycles
cycling
cycled
cyclist noun
cyclists
cyclone noun
cyclones
cyclonic
○ **cygnet** noun
cygnets
cylinder noun
cylinders
cylindrical
cymbal noun
cymbals
cynic noun
cynics
cynical adjective
cynically
cynicism
cypress noun
cypresses

. . . .

★ A **currant** is a small dried grape. ! current.
☆ A **current** is a flow of water, air, or electricity. ! currant.
○ A **cygnet** is a young swan. ! signet.

Dd

dab *verb*
dabs
dabbing
dabbed
dab *noun*
dabs
dabble *verb*
dabbles
dabbling
dabbled
dachshund *noun*
dachshunds
dad *noun*
dads
daddy *noun*
daddies
daddy-long-legs
noun
daddy-long-legs
daffodil *noun*
daffodils
daft *adjective*
dafter
daftest
dagger *noun*
daggers
dahlia *noun*
dahlias
daily *adjective* and
adverb
daintiness
dainty *adjective*
daintier
daintiest
daintily
dairy *noun*
dairies

daisy *noun*
daisies
dale *noun*
dales
Dalmatian *noun*
Dalmatians
dam *noun*
dams
★ **dam** *verb*
dams
damming
dammed
damage *verb*
damages
damaging
damaged
damage *noun*
damages *plural noun*
☆ **Dame** *noun*
Dames
✪ **dame** *noun*
dames
✳ **damn** *verb*
damns
damning
damned
damned
damp *adjective* and
noun
damper
dampest
dampen *verb*
dampens
dampening
dampened
damson *noun*
damsons
dance *verb*
dances
dancing
danced

dance *noun*
dances
dancer *noun*
dancers
dandelion *noun*
dandelions
dandruff
danger *noun*
dangers
dangerous *adjective*
dangerously
dangle *verb*
dangles
dangling
dangled
dappled
dare *verb*
dares
daring
dared
dare *noun*
dares
daredevil *noun*
daredevils
daring
dark *adjective* and
noun
darker
darkest
darken *verb*
darkens
darkening
darkened
darkness
darkroom *noun*
darkrooms
darling *noun*
darlings
darn *verb*
darns
darning
darned

. . . .

★ **Dam** means 'to build a dam across water'. **!** damn.
☆ Use a capital D when it is a title, e.g. *Dame Jane Smith*.
✪ Use a small d when you mean a pantomime woman played by a man.
✳ **Damn** means 'to say that something is very bad'. **!** dam.

dart *noun*
  darts
dartboard *noun*
  dartboards
dash *verb*
  dashes
  dashing
  dashed
dash *noun*
  dashes
dashboard *noun*
  dashboards
★ data *plural noun*
database *noun*
  databases
date *noun*
  dates
date *verb*
  dates
  dating
  dated
daughter *noun*
  daughters
dawdle *verb*
  dawdles
  dawdling
  dawdled
dawn *noun*
  dawns
dawn *verb*
  dawns
  dawning
  dawned
day *noun*
  days
daybreak
daydream *verb*
  daydreams
  daydreaming
  daydreamed
daylight

day-to-day
daze *verb*
  dazes
  dazing
  dazed
daze *noun*
dazzle *verb*
  dazzles
  dazzling
  dazzled

de-
de- makes verbs with
an opposite meaning,
e.g. **deactivate** means
'to stop something
working'. You need a
hyphen when the
word begins with an e
or *i*, e.g. **de-escalate**,
de-ice.

dead
deaden *verb*
  deadens
  deadening
  deadened
dead end *noun*
  dead ends
deadline *noun*
  deadlines
deadlock
deadly *adjective*
  deadlier
  deadliest
deaf *adjective*
  deafer
  deafest
deafness
deafen *verb*
  deafens
  deafening
  deafened

deal *verb*
  deals
  dealing
  dealt
deal *noun*
  deals
dealer *noun*
  dealers
dean *noun*
  deans
☆ dear *adjective*
  dearer
  dearest
death *noun*
  deaths
deathly
debatable
debate *noun*
  debates
debate *verb*
  debates
  debating
  debated
debris
debt *noun*
  debts
debtor *noun*
  debtors
debug *verb*
  debugs
  debugging
  debugged
début *noun*
  débuts
decade *noun*
  decades
decay *verb*
  decays
  decaying
  decayed

. . . .

★ **Data** is strictly a plural noun, but is often used as a singular noun: *Here is
     the data.*
☆ **Dear** means 'loved' or 'expensive'. **! deer.**

decay *noun*
deceased
deceit
deceitful *adjective*
deceitfully
deceive *verb*
deceives
deceiving
deceived
December
decency
decent *adjective*
decently
deception *noun*
deceptions
deceptive
decibel *noun*
decibels
decide *verb*
decides
deciding
decided
deciduous
decimal *noun*
decimals
decimalization
decimalize *verb*
decimalizes
decimalizing
decimalized
decipher *verb*
deciphers
deciphering
deciphered
decision *noun*
decisions
decisive *adjective*
decisively
deck *noun*
decks

deckchair *noun*
deckchairs
declaration *noun*
declarations
declare *verb*
declares
declaring
declared
decline *verb*
declines
declining
declined
decode *verb*
decodes
decoding
decoded
decompose *verb*
decomposes
decomposing
decomposed
decorate *verb*
decorates
decorating
decorated
decoration *noun*
decorations
decorative
decorator *noun*
decorators
decoy *noun*
decoys
decrease *verb*
decreases
decreasing
decreased
decrease *noun*
decreases
decree *noun*
decrees
decree *verb*
decrees

decreeing
decreed
decrepit
dedicate *verb*
dedicates
dedicating
dedicated
dedication
deduce *verb*
deduces
deducing
deduced
deduct *verb*
deducts
deducting
deducted
deductible
deduction *noun*
deductions
deed *noun*
deeds
deep *adjective*
deeper
deepest
deeply
deepen *verb*
deepens
deepening
deepened
deep-freeze *noun*
deep-freezes
★ deer *noun*
deer
deface *verb*
defaces
defacing
defaced
default *noun*
defaults

. . . .

★ A **deer** is an animal. ! **dear**.

defeat verb
defeats
defeating
defeated
defeat noun
defeats
defect noun
defects
defect verb
defects
defecting
defected
defective adjective
defectively
defence noun
defences
defenceless
defend verb
defends
defending
defended
defendant noun
defendants
defender noun
defenders
defensible
defensive adjective
defensively
defer verb
defers
deferring
deferred
deferment
defiance
defiant adjective
defiantly
deficiency noun
deficiencies
deficient
deficit noun
deficits

defile verb
defiles
defiling
defiled
define verb
defines
defining
defined
definite adjective
definitely
definition noun
definitions
deflate verb
deflates
deflating
deflated
deflect verb
deflects
deflecting
deflected
deflection
deforestation
deformed
deformity noun
deformities
defrost verb
defrosts
defrosting
defrosted
deft adjective
defter
deftest
deftly
defuse verb
defuses
defusing
defused
defy verb
defies
defying
defied

degenerate verb
degenerates
degenerating
degenerated
degeneration
degradation
degrade verb
degrades
degrading
degraded
degree noun
degrees
dehydrated
dehydration
de-ice verb
de-ices
de-icing
de-iced
de-icer
deity noun
deities
dejected
dejection
delay verb
delays
delaying
delayed
delay noun
delays
delegate noun
delegates
delegate verb
delegates
delegating
delegated
delegation
delete verb
deletes
deleting
deleted
deletion

deliberate *adjective*
  deliberately
deliberate *verb*
  deliberates
  deliberating
  deliberated
deliberation
delicacy *noun*
  delicacies
delicate *adjective*
  delicately
delicatessen *noun*
  delicatessens
delicious *adjective*
  deliciously
delight *verb*
  delights
  delighting
  delighted
delight *noun*
  delights
delightful *adjective*
  delightfully
delinquency
delinquent *noun*
  delinquents
delirious *adjective*
  deliriously
delirium *noun*
deliver *verb*
  delivers
  delivering
  delivered
delivery *noun*
  deliveries
delta *noun*
  deltas
delude *verb*
  deludes
  deluding
  deluded

deluge *noun*
  deluges
deluge *verb*
  deluges
  deluging
  deluged
delusion *noun*
  delusions
de luxe
demand *verb*
  demands
  demanding
  demanded
demand *noun*
  demands
demanding
demerara
demist *verb*
  demists
  demisting
  demisted
demo *noun*
  demos
democracy *noun*
  democracies
democrat *noun*
  democrats
democratic *adjective*
  democratically
demolish *verb*
  demolishes
  demolishing
  demolished
demolition
demon *noun*
  demons
demonstrate *verb*
  demonstrates
  demonstrating
  demonstrated

demonstration *noun*
  demonstrations
demonstrator *noun*
  demonstrators
demoralize *verb*
  demoralizes
  demoralizing
  demoralized
demote *verb*
  demotes
  demoting
  demoted
den *noun*
  dens
denial *noun*
  denials
denim
denominator *noun*
  denominators
denote *verb*
  denotes
  denoting
  denoted
denounce *verb*
  denounces
  denouncing
  denounced
denunciation
dense *adjective*
  denser
  densest
  densely
density *noun*
dent *noun*
  dents
dental
dentist *noun*
  dentists
dentistry
denture *noun*
  dentures

deny *verb*
  denies
  denying
  denied
deodorant *noun*
  deodorants
depart *verb*
  departs
  departing
  departed
department *noun*
  departments
departure *noun*
  departures
depend *verb*
  depends
  depending
  depended
dependable
★ **dependant** *noun*
  dependants
dependence
☆ **dependent** *adjective*
depict *verb*
  depicts
  depicting
  depicted
deplorable *adjective*
  deplorably
deplore *verb*
  deplores
  deploring
  deplored
deport *verb*
  deports
  deporting
  deported
deposit *verb*
  deposits
  depositing
  deposited

deposit *noun*
  deposits
depot *noun*
  depots
depress *verb*
  depresses
  depressing
  depressed
depression *noun*
  depressions
deprivation
deprive *verb*
  deprives
  depriving
  deprived
depth *noun*
  depths
deputize *verb*
  deputizes
  deputizing
  deputized
deputy *noun*
  deputies
derail *verb*
  derails
  derailing
  derailed
derby *noun*
  derbies
derelict
deride *verb*
  derides
  deriding
  derided
derision
derive *verb*
  derives
  deriving
  derived
derrick *noun*
  derricks

derv
✪ **descant** *noun*
  descants
descend *verb*
  descends
  descending
  descended
descendant *noun*
  descendants
✳ **descent**
describe *verb*
  describes
  describing
  described
description *noun*
  descriptions
descriptive *adjective*
  descriptively
✴ **desert** *noun*
  deserts
desert *verb*
  deserts
  deserting
  deserted
deserter *noun*
  deserters
desertion
deserve *verb*
  deserves
  deserving
  deserved
design *verb*
  designs
  designing
  designed
design *noun*
  designs
designate *verb*
  designates
  designating
  designated

· ·

★ **Dependant** is a noun: *She has three dependants.* ! dependent.
☆ **Dependent** is an adjective: *She has three dependent children.* ! dependant.
✪ **Descant** is a term in music. ! descent.
✳ **Descent** is a way down. ! descant.
✴ A **desert** is a very dry area of land. ! dessert.

designer noun
  designers
desirable
desire verb
  desires
  desiring
  desired
desire noun
  desires
desk noun
  desks
desktop
desolate
desolation
despair verb
  despairs
  despairing
  despaired
despair noun
despatch verb
  use dispatch
desperate adjective
  desperately
desperation
despicable adjective
  despicably
despise verb
  despises
  despising
  despised
despite
★ **dessert** noun
  desserts
dessertspoon noun
  dessertspoons
destination noun
  destinations
destined
destiny noun
  destinies

destroy verb
  destroys
  destroying
  destroyed
destroyer noun
  destroyers
destruction
destructive
detach verb
  detaches
  detaching
  detached
detachable
detached
detachment noun
  detachments
detail noun
  details
detain verb
  detains
  detaining
  detained
detect verb
  detects
  detecting
  detected
detection
detector
detective noun
  detectives
detention noun
  detentions
deter verb
  deters
  deterring
  deterred
detergent noun
  detergents
deteriorate verb
  deteriorates
  deteriorating
  deteriorated

deterioration
determination
determine verb
  determines
  determining
  determined
determined
deterrence
deterrent noun
  deterrents
detest verb
  detests
  detesting
  detested
detestable
detonate verb
  detonates
  detonating
  detonated
detonation
detonator
detour noun
  detours
☆ **deuce**
devastate verb
  devastates
  devastating
  devastated
devastation
develop verb
  develops
  developing
  developed
development noun
  developments
device noun
  devices
devil noun
  devils

. . . .

★ A **dessert** is a sweet pudding. ! desert.
☆ **Deuce** is a score in tennis. ! juice.

devilish
devilment
devious adjective
  deviously
devise verb
  devises
  devising
  devised
devolution
devote verb
  devotes
  devoting
  devoted
devotee
devotion
devour verb
  devours
  devouring
  devoured
devout
★ **dew**
dewy
☆ **dhoti** noun
  dhotis
diabetes
diabetic
diabolical adjective
  diabolically
diagnose verb
  diagnoses
  diagnosing
  diagnosed
diagnosis noun
  diagnoses
diagonal adjective
  diagonally
diagonal noun
  diagonals
diagram noun
  diagrams

dial noun
  dials
dial verb
  dials
  dialling
  dialled
dialect noun
  dialects
dialogue noun
  dialogues
diameter noun
  diameters
diamond noun
  diamonds
diaphragm noun
  diaphragms
diarrhoea
diary noun
  diaries
dice noun
  dice
dictate verb
  dictates
  dictating
  dictated
dictation
dictator noun
  dictators
dictatorial adjective
  dictatorially
dictionary noun
  dictionaries
did see **do**
diddle verb
  diddles
  diddling
  diddled
didn't verb

die verb
  dies
  dying
  died
diesel noun
  diesels
diet noun
  diets
diet verb
  diets
  dieting
  dieted
differ verb
  differs
  differing
  differed
difference noun
  differences
different adjective
  differently
difficult
difficulty noun
  difficulties
dig verb
  digs
  digging
  dug
dig noun
  digs
digest verb
  digests
  digesting
  digested
digestible
digestion
digestive
digger
digit noun
  digits
digital adjective
  digitally

. . . .

★ **Dew** is moisture on grass and plants. ! **due**.
☆ A **dhoti** is a piece of clothing worn by Hindus.

dignified
dignity
dike *noun*
  use dyke
dilemma *noun*
  dilemmas
dilute *verb*
  dilutes
  diluting
  diluted
dilution
dim *adjective*
  dimmer
  dimmest
  dimly
dimension *noun*
  dimensions
diminish *verb*
  diminishes
  diminishing
  diminished
dimple *noun*
  dimples
din *noun*
  dins
dine *verb*
  dines
  dining
  dined
★ diner *noun*
  diners
☆ dinghy *noun*
  dinghies
✪ dingy *adjective*
  dingier
  dingiest
✷ dinner *noun*
  dinners
dinosaur *noun*
  dinosaurs

dioxide *noun*
  dioxides
dip *verb*
  dips
  dipping
  dipped
dip *noun*
  dips
diphtheria
diploma *noun*
  diplomas
diplomacy
diplomat
diplomatic *adjective*
  diplomatically
dire *adjective*
  direr
  direst
direct *adjective*
  directly
direct *verb*
  directs
  directing
  directed
direction *noun*
  directions
director *noun*
  directors
directory *noun*
  directories
dirt
dirtiness
dirty *adjective*
  dirtier
  dirtiest
  dirtily

dis-
dis- makes a word with an opposite meaning, e.g. **disobey** means 'to refuse to obey' and **disloyal** means 'not loyal'. These words are spelt joined up.

disability *noun*
  disabilities
disabled
disadvantage *noun*
  disadvantages
disagree *verb*
  disagrees
  disagreeing
  disagreed
disagreeable *adjective*
  disagreeably
disagreement *noun*
  disagreements
disappear *verb*
  disappears
  disappearing
  disappeared
disappearance *noun*
  disappearances
disappoint *verb*
  disappoints
  disappointing
  disappointed
disappointing
disappointment *noun*
  disappointments
disapproval

- -

★ A **diner** is someone who eats dinner. ! **dinner**.
☆ A **dinghy** is a small sailing boat. ! **dingy**.
✪ **Dingy** means 'dirty-looking, drab, dull-coloured'. ! **dinghy**.
✷ **Dinner** is a meal. ! **diner**.

disapprove *verb*
  disapproves
  disapproving
  disapproved
disarm *verb*
  disarms
  disarming
  disarmed
disarmament
disaster *noun*
  disasters
disastrous *adjective*
  disastrously
★ **disc** *noun*
  discs
discard *verb*
  discards
  discarding
  discarded
discharge *verb*
  discharges
  discharging
  discharged
disciple *noun*
  disciples
discipline
disc jockey *noun*
  disc jockeys
disclose *verb*
  discloses
  disclosing
  disclosed
disclosure
disco *noun*
  discos
discomfort
disconnect *verb*
  disconnects
  disconnecting
  disconnected
disconnection

discontent
discontented
discotheque *noun*
  discotheques
discount *noun*
  discounts
discourage *verb*
  discourages
  discouraging
  discouraged
discouragement
discover *verb*
  discovers
  discovering
  discovered
discovery *noun*
  discoveries
discreet *adjective*
  discreetly
discriminate *verb*
  discriminates
  discriminating
  discriminated
discrimination
discus *noun*
  discuses
discuss *verb*
  discusses
  discussing
  discussed
discussion *noun*
  discussions
disease *noun*
  diseases
diseased
disgrace *verb*
  disgraces
  disgracing
  disgraced
disgrace *noun*
disgraceful *adjective*
  disgracefully

disguise *verb*
  disguises
  disguising
  disguised
disguise *noun*
  disguises
disgust *verb*
  disgusts
  disgusting
  disgusted
disgust *noun*
disgusting
dish *noun*
  dishes
dish *verb*
  dishes
  dishing
  dished
dishcloth *noun*
  dishcloths
dishevelled
dishonest *adjective*
  dishonestly
dishonesty
dishwasher *noun*
  dishwashers
disinfect *verb*
  disinfects
  disinfecting
  disinfected
disinfectant *noun*
  disinfectants
disintegrate *verb*
  disintegrates
  disintegrating
  disintegrated
disintegration
disinterested
☆ **disk** *noun*
  disks

. . . .

★ A **disc** is a flat round object. ! **disk**.
☆ A **disk** is what you put in a computer. ! **disc**.

dislike verb
 dislikes
 disliking
 disliked
dislike noun
 dislikes
dislocate verb
 dislocates
 dislocating
 dislocated
dislodge verb
 dislodges
 dislodging
 dislodged
disloyal adjective
 disloyally
disloyalty
dismal adjective
 dismally
dismantle verb
 dismantles
 dismantling
 dismantled
dismay
dismayed
dismiss verb
 dismisses
 dismissing
 dismissed
dismissal
dismount verb
 dismounts
 dismounting
 dismounted
disobedience
disobedient
disobey verb
 disobeys
 disobeying
 disobeyed
disorder noun
 disorders

disorderly
dispatch verb
 dispatches
 dispatching
 dispatched
dispense verb
 dispenses
 dispensing
 dispensed
dispenser noun
 dispensers
dispersal
disperse verb
 disperses
 dispersing
 dispersed
display verb
 displays
 displaying
 displayed
display noun
 displays
displease verb
 displeases
 displeasing
 displeased
disposable
disposal
dispose verb
 disposes
 disposing
 disposed
disprove verb
 disproves
 disproving
 disproved
dispute noun
 disputes
disqualification
disqualify verb
 disqualifies

 disqualifying
 disqualified
disregard verb
 disregards
 disregarding
 disregarded
disrespect
disrespectful
 adjective
 disrespectfully
disrupt verb
 disrupts
 disrupting
 disrupted
disruption
disruptive
dissatisfaction
dissatisfied
dissect verb
 dissects
 dissecting
 dissected
dissection
dissolve verb
 dissolves
 dissolving
 dissolved
dissuade verb
 dissuades
 dissuading
 dissuaded
distance noun
 distances
distant adjective
 distantly
distil verb
 distils
 distilling
 distilled
distillery noun
 distilleries

distinct *adjective*
distinctly
distinction *noun*
distinctions
distinctive
distinguish *verb*
distinguishes
distinguishing
distinguished
distinguished
distort *verb*
distorts
distorting
distorted
distortion *noun*
distortions
distract *verb*
distracts
distracting
distracted
distraction *noun*
distractions
distress *verb*
distresses
distressing
distressed
distress *noun*
distribute *verb*
distributes
distributing
distributed
distribution
distributor
district *noun*
districts
distrust
distrustful
disturb *verb*
disturbs
disturbing
disturbed

disturbance *noun*
disturbances
disused
ditch *noun*
ditches
dither *verb*
dithers
dithering
dithered
divan *noun*
divans
dive *verb*
dives
diving
dived
diver *noun*
divers
diverse
diversify *verb*
diversifies
diversifying
diversified
diversion *noun*
diversions
diversity
divert *verb*
diverts
diverting
diverted
divide *verb*
divides
dividing
divided
dividend *noun*
dividends
dividers *plural noun*
divine *adjective*
divinely
divine *verb*
divines
divining
divined

divinity
divisible
division *noun*
divisions
divorce *verb*
divorces
divorcing
divorced
divorce *noun*
divorces
★ **Diwali**
dizziness
dizzy *adjective*
dizzier
dizziest
dizzily
do *verb*
does
doing
did
done
docile *adjective*
docilely
dock *noun*
docks
dock *verb*
docks
docking
docked
dock *noun*
docks
docker *noun*
dockers
dockyard *noun*
dockyards
doctor *noun*
doctors
doctrine *noun*
doctrines

★ **Diwali** is a Hindu festival.

document noun
documents
documentary noun
documentaries
doddery
dodge verb
dodges
dodging
dodged
dodge noun
dodges
dodgem noun
dodgems
dodgy adjective
dodgier
dodgiest
★ **doe** noun
does
doesn't abbreviation
dog noun
dogs
dog-eared
dogged adjective
doggedly
doldrums plural noun
dole verb
doles
doling
doled
dole noun
doll noun
dolls
dollar noun
dollars
dolly noun
dollies
dolphin noun
dolphins

-dom
-dom makes nouns,
e.g. kingdom. Other
noun suffixes are
-hood, -ment, -ness,
and -ship.

domain noun
domains
dome noun
domes
domestic adjective
domestically
domesticated
dominance
dominant adjective
dominantly
dominate verb
dominates
dominating
dominated
domination
dominion noun
dominions
domino noun
dominoes
donate verb
donates
donating
donated
donation noun
donations
done see do
donkey noun
donkeys
donor noun
donors
don't abbreviation
doodle verb
doodles
doodling
doodled

doodle noun
doodles
doom verb
dooms
dooming
doomed
doom noun
door noun
doors
doorstep noun
doorsteps
doorway noun
doorways
dope noun
dopes
dopey adjective
dopier
dopiest
dormitory noun
dormitories
dose noun
doses
dossier noun
dossiers
dot verb
dots
dotting
dotted
dot noun
dots
dottiness
dotty adjective
dottier
dottiest
dottily
double adjective
doubly
double noun
doubles

· ·

★ A **doe** is a female deer. ! dough.

double verb
doubles
doubling
doubled
double-cross verb
double-crosses
double-crossing
double-crossed
double-decker noun
double-deckers
doubt verb
doubts
doubting
doubted
doubt noun
doubts
doubtful adjective
doubtfully
doubtless
★ **dough**
doughnut noun
doughnuts
doughy adjective
doughier
doughiest
dove noun
doves
dowel noun
dowels
down
downcast
downfall noun
downfalls
downhill
downpour noun
downpours
downright adjective
downs plural noun
downstairs
downstream

downward adjective
and adverb
downwards adverb
downy adjective
downier
downiest
doze verb
dozes
dozing
dozed
dozen noun
dozens
dozy adjective
dozier
doziest
drab adjective
drabber
drabbest
draft verb
drafts
drafting
drafted
draft noun
drafts
drag verb
drags
dragging
dragged
drag noun
dragon noun
dragons
dragonfly noun
dragonflies
drain verb
drains
draining
drained
drain noun
drains
drainage
drake noun
drakes

drama noun
dramas
dramatic adjective
dramatically
dramatist noun
dramatists
dramatization
dramatize verb
dramatizes
dramatizing
dramatized
drank see drink
drape verb
drapes
draping
draped
drastic adjective
drastically
draught noun
draughts
draughty adjective
draughtier
draughtiest
draughts noun
draughtsman noun
draughtsmen
☆ **draw** verb
draws
drawing
drew
drawn
draw noun
draws
drawback noun
drawbacks
drawbridge noun
drawbridges
✪ **drawer** noun
drawers

. . . .

★ **Dough** is a mixture of flour and water used for baking. ! doe.
☆ To **draw** is to make a picture with a pencil, pen, or crayon. ! drawer.
✪ A **drawer** is part of a cupboard. ! draw.

drawing *noun*
drawings
drawl *verb*
drawls
drawling
drawled
dread *verb*
dreads
dreading
dreaded
dread *noun*
dreadful *adjective*
dreadfully
dreadlocks
dream *noun*
dreams
dream *verb*
dreams
dreaming
dreamt *or* dreamed
dreamy *adjective*
dreamier
dreamiest
dreariness
dreary *adjective*
drearier
dreariest
drearily
dredge *verb*
dredges
dredging
dredged
dredger
drench *verb*
drenches
drenching
drenched
dress *verb*
dresses
dressing
dressed

dress *noun*
dresses
dresser *noun*
dressers
dressing *noun*
dressings
dressmaker *noun*
dressmakers
drew see draw
dribble *verb*
dribbles
dribbling
dribbled
dried see dry
drier *noun*
driers
drift *verb*
drifts
drifting
drifted
drift *noun*
drifts
driftwood
drill *verb*
drills
drilling
drilled
drill *noun*
drills
drink *verb*
drinks
drinking
drank
drunk
drink *noun*
drinks
drinker *noun*
drinkers
drip *noun*
drips

drip *verb*
drips
dripping
dripped
dripping
drive *verb*
drives
driving
drove
driven
drive *noun*
drives
driver *noun*
drivers
drizzle *verb*
drizzles
drizzling
drizzled
drizzle *noun*
drone *verb*
drones
droning
droned
drone *noun*
drones
drool *verb*
drools
drooling
drooled
droop *verb*
droops
drooping
drooped
drop *verb*
drops
dropping
dropped
drop *noun*
drops
droplet *noun*
droplets

drought noun
  droughts
drove see **drive**
drown verb
  drowns
  drowning
  drowned
drowsiness
drowsy adjective
  drowsier
  drowsiest
  drowsily
drug noun
  drugs
drug verb
  drugs
  drugging
  drugged
Druid noun
  Druids
drum noun
  drums
drum verb
  drums
  drumming
  drummed
drummer noun
  drummers
drumstick noun
  drumsticks
drunk see **drink**
drunk adjective and
  noun
  drunks
drunkard noun
  drunkards
dry adjective
  drier
  driest
  drily

dry verb
  dries
  drying
  dried
dryness
★ **dual** adjective
  dually
dub verb
  dubs
  dubbing
  dubbed
duchess noun
  duchesses
duck noun
  ducks
duck verb
  ducks
  ducking
  ducked
duckling noun
  ducklings
duct noun
  ducts
dud noun
  duds
☆ **due**
✿ **duel** noun
  duels
duet noun
  duets
duff
duffel coat noun
  duffel coats
dug see **dig**
dugout noun
  dugouts
duke noun
  dukes
dull adjective
  duller

dullest
  dully
dullness
duly
dumb adjective
  dumber
  dumbest
dumbfounded
dummy noun
  dummies
dump verb
  dumps
  dumping
  dumped
dump noun
  dumps
dumpling noun
  dumplings
dumpy adjective
  dumpier
  dumpiest
dune noun
  dunes
dung
dungarees
dungeon noun
  dungeons
duo noun
  duos
duplicate noun
  duplicates
duplicate verb
  duplicates
  duplicating
  duplicated
duplication
durability
durable
duration
during

. . . .

★ **Dual** means 'having two parts'. ! **duel**
☆ **Due** means 'expected'. ! **dew**.
✿ A **duel** is a fight between two people. ! **dual**

dusk
dust
dust *verb*
  dusts
  dusting
  dusted
dustbin *noun*
  dustbins
duster *noun*
  dusters
dustman *noun*
  dustmen
dustpan *noun*
  dustpans
dusty *adjective*
  dustier
  dustiest
dutiful *adjective*
  dutifully
duty *noun*
  duties
duvet *noun*
  duvets
dwarf *noun*
  dwarfs *or* dwarves
dwarf *verb*
  dwarfs
  dwarfing
  dwarfed
dwell *verb*
  dwells
  dwelling
  dwelt
dwelling *noun*
  dwellings
dwindle *verb*
  dwindles
  dwindling
  dwindled
★ dye *verb*
  dyes

dyeing
dyed
dye *noun*
  dyes
dying *see* die
dyke *noun*
  dykes
dynamic *adjective*
  dynamically
dynamite
dynamo *noun*
  dynamos
dynasty *noun*
  dynasties
dyslexia
dyslexic
dystrophy *noun*

Ee

e-
e- stands for 'electronic' and makes words about computers and the Internet, e.g. **email** (spelt joined up), **e-commerce** and **e-shopping** (spelt with hyphens).

each
eager *adjective*
  eagerly
eagerness
eagle *noun*
  eagles
ear *noun*
  ears

earache
eardrum *noun*
  eardrums
earl *noun*
  earls
early *adjective* and *adverb*
  earlier
  earliest
earmark *verb*
  earmarks
  earmarking
  earmarked
earn *verb*
  earns
  earning
  earned
earnest *adjective*
  earnestly
earnings *plural noun*
earphones
earring *noun*
  earrings
earth *noun*
  earths
earthenware
earthly
earthquake *noun*
  earthquakes
earthworm *noun*
  earthworms
earthy *adjective*
  earthier
  earthiest
earwig *noun*
  earwigs
ease *verb*
  eases
  easing
  eased
ease *noun*

★ Dye means 'to change the colour of something'. ! die.

easel *noun*
easels
east *adjective*
and *adverb*
★ east *noun*
Easter
easterly *adjective*
and *noun*
easterlies
eastern
eastward *adjective*
and *adverb*
eastwards *adverb*
easy *adjective* and
adverb
easier
easiest
easily
eat *verb*
eats
eating
ate
eaten
eatable
eaves
ebb *verb*
ebbs
ebbing
ebbed
ebb
ebony
eccentric
eccentricity *noun*
eccentricities
echo *verb*
echoes
echoing
echoed
echo *noun*
echoes
éclair *noun*
éclairs

eclipse *noun*
eclipses
ecological
ecology
economic
economical *adjective*
economically
economics
economist *noun*
economists
economize *verb*
economizes
economizing
economized
economy *noun*
economies
ecstasy *noun*
ecstasies
ecstatic *adjective*
ecstatically
eczema

-ed and -t
Some verbs ending in
l, m, n, and *p* have
past forms and past
participles ending in
-ed and *-t*, e.g.
**burned/burnt, leaped/
leapt**. Both forms are
correct, and the *-t*
form is especially
common when it
comes before a noun,
e.g. *burnt cakes*.

edge *noun*
edges
edge *verb*
edges
edging
edged
edgeways

edgy *adjective*
edgier
edgiest
edible
edit *verb*
edits
editing
edited
edition *noun*
editions
editor *noun*
editors
editorial *noun*
editorials
educate *verb*
educates
educating
educated
education
educational
educator
eel *noun*
eels
eerie *adjective*
eerier
eeriest
eerily
eeriness
☆ effect *noun*
effects
effective *adjective*
effectively
effectiveness
effeminate
effervescence
effervescent
efficiency
efficient *adjective*
efficiently

· ·

★ You use a capital E in **the East**, meaning China, Japan, etc.
☆ An **effect** is something that is caused by something else. ! **affect**.

effort *noun*
  efforts
effortless *adjective*
  effortlessly
egg *noun*
  eggs
egg *verb*
  eggs
  egging
  egged

-ei- and -ie-
The rule 'i before e except after c' is true when it is pronounced -ee-, e.g. **thief**, **ceiling**. There are a few exceptions, of which the most important are **seize** and **protein**.

★ **Eid**
eiderdown *noun*
  eiderdowns
☆ **eight**
eighteen
eighteenth
✪ **eighth** *adjective* and *noun*
  eighthly
eightieth
eighty *noun*
  eighties
either
eject *verb*
  ejects
  ejecting
  ejected
ejection
elaborate *adjective*
  elaborately

elaborate *verb*
  elaborates
  elaborating
  elaborated
elaboration
elastic
elated
elation
elbow *noun*
  elbows
elbow *verb*
  elbows
  elbowing
  elbowed
elder *adjective* and *noun*
  elders
elderberry *noun*
  elderberries
elderly
eldest
elect *verb*
  elects
  electing
  elected
election *noun*
  elections
electorate
electric
electrical *adjective*
  electrically
electrician *noun*
  electricians
electricity
electrification
electrify *verb*
  electrifies
  electrifying
  electrified
electrocute *verb*
  electrocutes

  electrocuting
  electrocuted
electrocution
electromagnet *noun*
  electromagnets
electron *noun*
  electrons
electronic *adjective*
  electronically
electronics
elegance
elegant *adjective*
  elegantly
element *noun*
  elements
elementary
elephant *noun*
  elephants
elevate *verb*
  elevates
  elevating
  elevated
elevation *noun*
  elevations
eleven
eleventh
elf *noun*
  elves
eligibility
eligible
eliminate *verb*
  eliminates
  eliminating
  eliminated
elimination
élite *noun*
  élites
elk *noun*
  elk *or* elks

- -

★ **Eid** is a Muslim festival.
☆ **Eight** is the number. ! ate.
✪ Note that there are two h's in **eighth**.

ellipse *noun*
  ellipses
elliptical *adjective*
  elliptically
elm *noun*
  elms
elocution
eloquence
eloquent
else
elsewhere
elude *verb*
  eludes
  eluding
  eluded
elusive *adjective*
  elusively
elves see **elf**
★ email *noun*
  emails
email *verb*
  emails
  emailing
  emailed
emancipate *verb*
  emancipates
  emancipating
  emancipated
emancipation
embankment *noun*
  embankments
embark *verb*
  embarks
  embarking
  embarked
embarkation
☆ embarrass *verb*
  embarrasses
  embarrassing
  embarrassed

embarrassment
embassy *noun*
  embassies
embedded
embers *plural noun*
emblem *noun*
  emblems
embrace *verb*
  embraces
  embracing
  embraced
embroider *verb*
  embroiders
  embroidering
  embroidered
embroidery *noun*
  embroideries
embryo *noun*
  embryos
emerald *noun*
  emeralds
emerge *verb*
  emerges
  emerging
  emerged
emergence
emergency *noun*
  emergencies
emery paper
emigrant *noun*
  emigrants
emigrate *verb*
  emigrates
  emigrating
  emigrated
emigration
eminence
eminent
○ emission *noun*
  emissions

emit *verb*
  emits
  emitting
  emitted
emotion *noun*
  emotions
emotional *adjective*
  emotionally
emperor *noun*
  emperors
emphasis *noun*
  emphases
emphasize *verb*
  emphasizes
  emphasizing
  emphasized
emphatic *adjective*
  emphatically
empire *noun*
  empires
employ *verb*
  employs
  employing
  employed
employee *noun*
  employees
employer *noun*
  employers
employment
empress *noun*
  empresses
empties *plural noun*
emptiness
empty *adjective*
  emptier
  emptiest
empty *verb*
  empties
  emptying
  emptied
emu *noun*
  emus

★ Email is short for electronic mail.
☆ Note that there are two rs in embarrass and embarrassment.
○ An emission is something that escapes, like fumes. ! omission.

emulsion noun
 emulsions
enable verb
 enables
 enabling
 enabled
enamel noun
 enamels
encampment noun
 encampments

-ence
See the note at -ance.

enchant verb
 enchants
 enchanting
 enchanted
enchantment
encircle verb
 encircles
 encircling
 encircled
enclose verb
 encloses
 enclosing
 enclosed
enclosure
encore noun
 encores
encounter verb
 encounters
 encountering
 encountered
encourage verb
 encourages
 encouraging
 encouraged
encouragement
encyclopedia noun
 encyclopedias
encyclopedic

end verb
 ends
 ending
 ended
end noun
 ends
endanger verb
 endangers
 endangering
 endangered
endeavour verb
 endeavours
 endeavouring
 endeavoured
ending noun
 endings
endless adjective
 endlessly
endurance
endure verb
 endures
 enduring
 endured
enemy noun
 enemies
energetic adjective
 energetically
energy noun
 energies
enforce verb
 enforces
 enforcing
 enforced
enforceable
enforcement
engage verb
 engages
 engaging
 engaged
engagement noun
 engagements

engine noun
 engines
engineer noun
 engineers
engineering
engrave verb
 engraves
 engraving
 engraved
engraver
engrossed
engulf verb
 engulfs
 engulfing
 engulfed
enhance verb
 enhances
 enhancing
 enhanced
enhancement
enjoy verb
 enjoys
 enjoying
 enjoyed
enjoyable
enjoyment
enlarge verb
 enlarges
 enlarging
 enlarged
enlargement noun
 enlargements
enlist verb
 enlists
 enlisting
 enlisted
enmity noun
 enmities
★ **enormity** noun
 enormities

★ An **enormity** is a wicked act. If you mean 'large size', use **enormousness**.

enormous *adjective*
  enormously
enormousness
enough
enquire *verb*
  enquires
  enquiring
  enquired
★ **enquiry** *noun*
  enquiries
enrage *verb*
  enrages
  enraging
  enraged
enrich *verb*
  enriches
  enriching
  enriched
enrichment
enrol *verb*
  enrols
  enrolling
  enrolled
enrolment
ensemble *noun*
  ensembles
ensue *verb*
  ensues
  ensuing
  ensued
ensure *verb*
  ensures
  ensuring
  ensured

-ent
See the note at -ant.

entangle *verb*
  entangles
  entangling
  entangled

entanglement
enter *verb*
  enters
  entering
  entered
enterprise *noun*
  enterprises
enterprising
entertain *verb*
  entertains
  entertaining
  entertained
entertainer *noun*
  entertainers
entertainment
  noun
  entertainments
enthusiasm *noun*
  enthusiasms
enthusiast *noun*
  enthusiasts
enthusiastic
  adjective
  enthusiastically
entire *adjective*
  entirely
entirety
entitle *verb*
  entitles
  entitling
  entitled
entrance *noun*
  entrances
entrance *verb*
  entrances
  entrancing
  entranced
entrant *noun*
  entrants
entreat *verb*
  entreats

  entreating
  entreated
entreaty *noun*
  entreaties
entrust *verb*
  entrusts
  entrusting
  entrusted
entry *noun*
  entries
envelop *verb*
  envelops
  enveloping
  enveloped
envelope *noun*
  envelopes
envious *adjective*
  enviously
environment *noun*
  environments
environmental
environmentalist
  noun
  environmentalists
envy *verb*
  envies
  envying
  envied
envy *noun*
enzyme *noun*
  enzymes
epic *noun*
  epics
epidemic *noun*
  epidemics
epilepsy
epileptic *adjective*
  and *noun*
  epileptics
epilogue *noun*
  epilogues

• •

★ An **enquiry** is a question. ! inquiry.

episode *noun*
  episodes
epistle *noun*
  epistles
epitaph *noun*
  epitaphs
epoch *noun*
  epochs
equal *adjective*
  equally
equal *verb*
  equals
  equalling
  equalled
equal *noun*
  equals
equality
equalize *verb*
  equalizes
  equalizing
  equalized
equalizer *noun*
  equalizers
equation *noun*
  equations
equator
equatorial
equestrian
equilateral
equilibrium *noun*
  equilibria
equinox *noun*
  equinoxes
equip *verb*
  equips
  equipping
  equipped

equipment
equivalence
equivalent

-er and -est
-er and -est make adjectives and adverbs meaning 'more' or 'most', e.g. faster, slowest. You can do this when the word has one syllable, and when a consonant comes at the end of the word after a single vowel you double it, e.g. fatter, bigger. You can use -er and -est with some two-syllable adjectives, e.g. commoner, pleasantest, and words ending in *y*, which change to -ier and -iest, e.g. angrier, happiest.

-er and -or
-er makes nouns meaning 'a person or thing that does something', e.g. a helper is a person who helps and an opener is a tool that opens things. You can make new words this way, e.g. complainer, repairer. Some words end in -or, e.g. actor, visitor, but you can't use -or to make new words.

era *noun*
  eras

erase *verb*
  erases
  erasing
  erased
eraser
erect *adjective*
erect *verb*
  erects
  erecting
  erected
erection *noun*
  erections
ermine *noun*
  ermine
erode *verb*
  erodes
  eroding
  eroded
erosion
errand *noun*
  errands
erratic *adjective*
  erratically
erroneous *adjective*
  erroneously
error *noun*
  errors
erupt *verb*
  erupts
  erupting
  erupted
eruption
escalate *verb*
  escalates
  escalating
  escalated
escalation
escalator *noun*
  escalators
escape *verb*
  escapes
  escaping
  escaped

escape noun
  escapes
escort verb
  escorts
  escorting
  escorted
escort noun
  escorts
Eskimo noun
  Eskimos or Eskimo
especially
espionage
esplanade noun
  esplanades

-ess
makes nouns for
female people and
animals, e.g.
manageress, lioness.

essay noun
  essays
essence noun
  essences
essential adjective
  essentially
essential noun
  essentials
establish verb
  establishes
  establishing
  established
establishment noun
  establishments
estate noun
  estates
esteem verb
  esteems
  esteeming
  esteemed
estimate noun
  estimates

estimate verb
  estimates
  estimating
  estimated
estuary noun
  estuaries
etch verb
  etches
  etching
  etched
etching noun
  etchings
eternal adjective
  eternally
eternity
ether
ethnic
etymology noun
  etymologies
eucalyptus noun
  eucalyptuses
euphemism noun
  euphemisms
euphemistic
  adjective
  euphemistically
Eurasian
European adjective
  and noun
  Europeans
euthanasia
evacuate verb
  evacuates
  evacuating
  evacuated
evacuation
evacuee
evade verb
  evades
  evading
  evaded

evaluate verb
  evaluates
  evaluating
  evaluated
evaluation
evangelical
evangelism
evangelist noun
  evangelists
evaporate verb
  evaporates
  evaporating
  evaporated
evaporation
evasion noun
  evasions
evasive
eve noun
  eves
even adjective
  evenly
even adverb
even verb
  evens
  evening
  evened
evening noun
  evenings
evenness
event noun
  events
eventful adjective
  eventfully
eventual adjective
  eventually
ever
evergreen adjective
  and noun
  evergreens
everlasting

every
everybody
everyday
everyone
everything
everywhere
evict verb
  evicts
  evicting
  evicted
eviction
evidence
evident adjective
  evidently
evil adjective
  evilly
evil noun
  evils
evolution
evolutionary
evolve verb
  evolves
  evolving
  evolved
★ **ewe** noun
  ewes

ex-
ex- makes nouns with the meaning 'former' or 'who used to be', e.g. **ex-president**, **ex-wife**. You use a hyphen to make these words.

exact adjective
  exactly
exactness

exaggerate verb
  exaggerates
  exaggerating
  exaggerated
exaggeration
exalt verb
  exalts
  exalting
  exalted
exam noun
  exams
examination noun
  examinations
examine verb
  examines
  examining
  examined
examiner noun
  examiners
example noun
  examples
exasperate verb
  exasperates
  exasperating
  exasperated
exasperation
excavate verb
  excavates
  excavating
  excavated
excavation noun
  excavations
excavator noun
  excavators
exceed verb
  exceeds
  exceeding
  exceeded
exceedingly
excel verb
  excels

excelling
excelled
excellence
excellent adjective
  excellently
☆ **except**
exception noun
  exceptions
exceptional adjective
  exceptionally
excerpt noun
  excerpts
excess noun
  excesses
excessive adjective
  excessively
exchange verb
  exchanges
  exchanging
  exchanged
exchange noun
  exchanges
excitable adjective
  excitably
excite verb
  excites
  exciting
  excited
excitedly
excitement noun
  excitements
exclaim verb
  exclaims
  exclaiming
  exclaimed
exclamation noun
  exclamations

. . . .

★ A **ewe** is a female sheep. ! **yew, you**.
☆ You use **except** in e.g. *everyone except me*. ! **accept**.

exclude *verb*
  excludes
  excluding
  excluded
exclusion
exclusive *adjective*
  exclusively
excrement
excrete *verb*
  excretes
  excreting
  excreted
excretion
excursion *noun*
  excursions
excusable
excuse *verb*
  excuses
  excusing
  excused
excuse *noun*
  excuses
execute *verb*
  executes
  executing
  executed
execution *noun*
  executions
executioner *noun*
  executioners
executive *noun*
  executives
exempt *adjective*
exemption *noun*
exercise *noun*
  exercises
★ **exercise** *verb*
  exercises
  exercising
  exercised

exert *verb*
  exerts
  exerting
  exerted
exertion *noun*
  exertions
exhale *verb*
  exhales
  exhaling
  exhaled
exhalation
exhaust *verb*
  exhausts
  exhausting
  exhausted
exhaust *noun*
  exhausts
exhaustion
exhibit *verb*
  exhibits
  exhibiting
  exhibited
exhibit *noun*
  exhibits
exhibition *noun*
  exhibitions
exhibitor *noun*
  exhibitors
exile *verb*
  exiles
  exiling
  exiled
exile *noun*
  exiles
exist *verb*
  exists
  existing
  existed
existence *noun*
  existences
exit *verb*
  exits

  exiting
  exited
exit *noun*
  exits
exorcism
exorcist
☆ **exorcize** *verb*
  exorcizes
  exorcizing
  exorcized
exotic *adjective*
  exotically
expand *verb*
  expands
  expanding
  expanded
expanse *noun*
  expanses
expansion
expect *verb*
  expects
  expecting
  expected
expectant *adjective*
  expectantly
expectation *noun*
  expectations
expedition *noun*
  expeditions
expel *verb*
  expels
  expelling
  expelled
expenditure
expense *noun*
  expenses
expensive
experience *verb*
  experiences
  experiencing
  experienced

· ·

★ To **exercise** is to keep your body fit. ! exorcise.
☆ To **exorcise** is to get rid of evil spirits. ! exercise.

experience *noun*
experiences
experienced
experiment *verb*
experiments
experimenting
experimented
experiment *noun*
experiments
experimental
adjective
experimentally
experimentation
expert *adjective* and
noun
experts
expertise
expire *verb*
expires
expiring
expired
expiry
explain *verb*
explains
explaining
explained
explanation *noun*
explanations
explanatory
explode *verb*
explodes
exploding
exploded
exploit *noun*
exploits
exploit *verb*
exploits
exploiting
exploited
exploitation
exploration *noun*
explorations

exploratory
explore *verb*
explores
exploring
explored
explorer *noun*
explorers
explosion *noun*
explosions
explosive *adjective*
and *noun*
explosives
export *verb*
exports
exporting
exported
export *noun*
exports
exporter *noun*
exporters
expose *verb*
exposes
exposing
exposed
exposure *noun*
exposures
express *adjective* and
noun
expresses
express *verb*
expresses
expressing
expressed
expression *noun*
expressions
expressive *adjective*
expressively
expulsion *noun*
expulsions
exquisite *adjective*
exquisitely

extend *verb*
extends
extending
extended
extension *noun*
extensions
extensive *adjective*
extensively
extent *noun*
extents
exterior *noun*
exteriors
exterminate *verb*
exterminates
exterminating
exterminated
extermination
external *adjective*
externally
extinct
extinction
extinguish *verb*
extinguishes
extinguishing
extinguished
extinguisher *noun*
extinguishers
extra *adjective* and
noun
extras
extract *verb*
extracts
extracting
extracted
extract *noun*
extracts
extraction *noun*
extractions
extraordinary
adjective
extraordinarily

extrasensory
extraterrestrial
  adjective and *noun*
  extraterrestrials
extravagance
extravagant
  adjective
  extravagantly
extreme *adjective*
  extremely
extreme *noun*
  extremes
extremity *noun*
  extremities
exuberance
exuberant *adjective*
  exuberantly
exult *verb*
  exults
  exulting
  exulted
exultant
exultation
eye *noun*
  eyes
eye *verb*
  eyes
  eyeing
  eyed
eyeball *noun*
  eyeballs
eyebrow *noun*
  eyebrows
eyelash *noun*
  eyelashes
eyelid *noun*
  eyelids
eyepiece *noun*
  eyepieces
eyesight

eyesore *noun*
  eyesores
eyewitness *noun*
  eyewitnesses

Ff

-f
Most nouns ending in
-f have plurals ending
in -ves, e.g. shelf -
shelves, but some
have plurals ending in
-fs, e.g. chiefs. Nouns
ending in -ff have
plurals ending in -ffs,
e.g. cuffs.

fable *noun*
  fables
fabric *noun*
  fabrics
fabricate *verb*
  fabricates
  fabricating
  fabricated
fabulous *adjective*
  fabulously
face *noun*
  faces
face *verb*
  faces
  facing
  faced
facet *noun*
  facets
facetious *adjective*
  facetiously

facial *adjective*
  facially
facilitate *verb*
  facilitates
  facilitating
  facilitated
facility *noun*
  facilities
fact *noun*
  facts
factor *noun*
  factors
factory *noun*
  factories
factual *adjective*
  factually
fad *noun*
  fads
fade *verb*
  fades
  fading
  faded
faeces
fag *noun*
  fags
fagged
faggot *noun*
  faggots
Fahrenheit
fail *verb*
  fails
  failing
  failed
fail *noun*
  fails
failing *noun*
  failings
failure *noun*
  failures

faint *adjective*
fainter
faintest
faintly
faint *verb*
faints
fainting
fainted
faint-hearted
faintness
fair *adjective*
fairer
fairest
★ **fair** *noun*
fairs
fairground *noun*
fairgrounds
fairly
fairness
fairy *noun*
fairies
fairyland
faith *noun*
faiths
faithful *adjective*
faithfully
faithfulness
fake *noun*
fakes
fake *verb*
fakes
faking
faked
faker
falcon *noun*
falcons
falconry
fall *verb*
falls
falling
fell
fallen

fall *noun*
falls
fallacious *adjective*
fallaciously
fallacy *noun*
fallacies
fallen see fall
fallout
fallow
falls *plural noun*
false *adjective*
falser
falsest
falsely
falsehood *noun*
falsehoods
falseness
falter *verb*
falters
faltering
faltered
fame
famed
familiar *adjective*
familiarly
familiarity
family *noun*
families
famine *noun*
famines
famished
famous *adjective*
famously
fan *verb*
fans
fanning
fanned
fan *noun*
fans
fanatic *noun*
fanatics

fanatical *adjective*
fanatically
fanciful *adjective*
fancifully
fancy *adjective*
fancier
fanciest
fancy *verb*
fancies
fancying
fancied
fancy *noun*
fancies
fanfare *noun*
fanfares
fang *noun*
fangs
fantastic *adjective*
fantastically
fantasy *noun*
fantasies
far *adjective* and
adverb
farther
farthest
far-away
farce *noun*
farces
farcical *adjective*
farcically
fare *verb*
fares
faring
fared
☆ **fare** *noun*
fares
farewell
far-fetched

- -

★ A **fair** is a group of outdoor entertainments or an exhibition. ! **fare**.
☆ A **fare** is money you pay, for example on a bus. ! **fair**.

farm *noun*
  farms
farm *verb*
  farms
  farming
  farmed
farmer *noun*
  farmers
farmhouse *noun*
  farmhouses
farmyard *noun*
  farmyards
★ **farther**
☆ **farthest**
farthing *noun*
  farthings
fascinate *verb*
  fascinates
  fascinating
  fascinated
fascination
fascism
fascist *noun*
  fascists
fashion *noun*
  fashions
fashion *verb*
  fashions
  fashioning
  fashioned
fashionable
fast *adjective* and
  adverb
  faster
  fastest
fast *verb*
  fasts
  fasting
  fasted
fasten *verb*
  fastens

fastening
fastened
fastener
fastening
fat *adjective*
  fatter
  fattest
fat *noun*
  fats
fatal *adjective*
  fatally
fatality *noun*
  fatalities
❍ **fate** *noun*
  fates
father *noun*
  fathers
father-in-law *noun*
  fathers-in-law
fathom *noun*
  fathoms
fathom *verb*
  fathoms
  fathoming
  fathomed
fatigue
fatigued
fatten *verb*
  fattens
  fattening
  fattened
fattening
fatty *adjective*
  fattier
  fattiest
fault *noun*
  faults
fault *verb*
  faults
  faulting
  faulted

faultless *adjective*
  faultlessly
faulty *adjective*
  faultier
  faultiest
fauna
favour *noun*
  favours
favour *verb*
  favours
  favouring
  favoured
favourable *adjective*
  favourably
favourite *adjective*
  and *noun*
  favourites
favouritism
fawn *noun*
  fawns
fax *noun*
  faxes
fax *verb*
  faxes
  faxing
  faxed

-fe
Most nouns ending
in -*fe* have plurals
ending in -ves,
e.g. life - lives.

fear *noun*
  fears
fear *verb*
  fears
  fearing
  feared
fearful *adjective*
  fearfully

. . . .

★ You can use **farther** or **further** in e.g. *farther up the road.* See **further.**
☆ You can use **farthest** or **furthest** in e.g. *the place farthest from here.* See
   furthest.
❍ **Fate** is a power that is thought to make things happen. ! **fête.**

fearless *adjective*
  fearlessly
fearsome
feasible
feast *noun*
  feasts
feast *verb*
  feasts
  feasting
  feasted
★ **feat** *noun*
  feats
feather *noun*
  feathers
feathery
feature *noun*
  features
feature *verb*
  features
  featuring
  featured
☆ **February** *noun*
  Februaries
fed see **feed**
federal
federation
fee *noun*
  fees
feeble *adjective*
  feebler
  feeblest
  feebly
feed *verb*
  feeds
  feeding
  fed
feed *noun*
  feeds
feedback

feel *verb*
  feels
  feeling
  felt
feel *noun*
feeler *noun*
  feelers
feeling *noun*
  feelings
○ **feet** see **foot**
feline
fell see **fall**
fell *verb*
  fells
  felling
  felled
fell *noun*
  fells
fellow *noun*
  fellows
fellowship *noun*
  fellowships
felt see **feel**
felt *noun*
felt-tip pen *or*
felt-tipped pen
  noun
  felt-tip pens *or*
  felt-tipped pens
female *adjective* and
  noun
  females
feminine
femininity
feminism
feminist *noun*
  feminists
fen *noun*
  fens
fence *noun*
  fences

fence *verb*
  fences
  fencing
  fenced
fencer *adjective*
  fencers
fencing
fend *verb*
  fends
  fending
  fended
fender *noun*
  fenders
ferment *verb*
  ferments
  fermenting
  fermented
fermentation
ferment
fern *noun*
  ferns
ferocious *adjective*
  ferociously
ferocity
ferret *noun*
  ferrets
ferret *verb*
  ferrets
  ferreting
  ferreted
ferry *noun*
  ferries
ferry *verb*
  ferries
  ferrying
  ferried
fertile
fertility
fertilization

· ·

★ A **feat** is an achievement. ! **feet**.
☆ Note that **February** has two rs.
○ **Feet** is the plural of foot. ! **feat**.

fertilize verb
 fertilizes
 fertilizing
 fertilized
fertilizer noun
 fertilizers
fervent adjective
 fervently
fervour
festival noun
 festivals
festive
festivity
festoon verb
 festoons
 festooning
 festooned
fetal
fetch verb
 fetches
 fetching
 fetched
★ **fête** noun
 fêtes
fetlock noun
 fetlocks
fetters plural noun
☆ **fetus** noun
 fetuses
feud noun
 feuds
feudal
feudalism
fever noun
 fevers
fevered
feverish adjective
 feverishly
few adjective
 fewer

 fewest
fez noun
 fezzes
✪ **fiancé** noun
 fiancés
✳ **fiancée** noun
 fiancées
fiasco noun
 fiascos
fib noun
 fibs
fibber noun
 fibbers
fibre noun
 fibres
fibreglass
fibrous
fickle
fiction noun
 fictions
fictional adjective
 fictionally
fictitious adjective
 fictitiously
fiddle verb
 fiddles
 fiddling
 fiddled
fiddle noun
 fiddles
fiddler noun
 fiddlers
fiddling
fiddly
fidelity
fidget verb
 fidgets
 fidgeting
 fidgeted
fidgety

field noun
 fields
field verb
 fields
 fielding
 fielded
fielder noun
 fielders
field Marshal noun
 field Marshals
fieldwork
fiend noun
 fiends
fiendish adjective
 fiendishly
fierce adjective
 fiercer
 fiercest
 fiercely
fierceness
fiery adjective
 fierier
 fieriest
fife noun
 fifes
fifteen
fifteenth
fifth
fifthly
fiftieth
fifty noun
 fifties
fig noun
 figs
fight verb
 fights
 fighting
 fought
fight noun
 fights

- -

★ A **fête** is an outdoor entertainment with stalls. **!** fate.
☆ You will also see this word spelt **foetus**.
✪ A woman's **fiancé** is the man who is going to marry her.
✳ A man's **fiancée** is the woman who is going to marry him.

fighter noun
  fighters
figurative adjective
  figuratively
figure noun
  figures
figure verb
  figures
  figuring
  figured
filament noun
  filaments
file verb
  files
  filing
  filed
file noun
  files
filings plural noun
fill verb
  fills
  filling
  filled
fill noun
  fills
filler noun
  fillers
fillet noun
  fillets
filling noun
  fillings
filly noun
  fillies
film noun
  films
film verb
  films
  filming
  filmed
filter noun
  filters

filter verb
  filters
  filtering
  filtered
filth
filthy adjective
  filthier
  filthiest
fin noun
  fins
final adjective
  finally
final noun
  finals
finale noun
  finales
finalist noun
  finalists
finality
finance
finance verb
  finances
  financing
  financed
finances plural noun
financial adjective
  financially
financier noun
  financiers
finch noun
  finches
find verb
  finds
  finding
  found
finder noun
  finders
findings plural noun
fine adjective
  finer
  finest

  finely
fine noun
  fines
fine verb
  fines
  fining
  fined
finger noun
  fingers
finger verb
  fingers
  fingering
  fingered
fingernail noun
  fingernails
fingerprint noun
  fingerprints
finicky
finish verb
  finishes
  finishing
  finished
finish noun
  finishes
★ **fir** noun
  firs
fire noun
  fires
fire verb
  fires
  firing
  fired
firearm noun
  firearms
firefighter noun
  firefighters
fireman noun
  firemen
fireplace noun
  fireplaces
fireproof

. . . .

★ A **fir** is a tree. ! **fur**.

fireside noun
  firesides
firewood
firework noun
  fireworks
firm adjective
  firmer
  firmest
  firmly
firm noun
  firms
firmness
first adjective and
  adverb
  firstly
first-class
first floor noun
  first floors
first-hand adjective
first-rate
fish noun
  fish or fishes
fish verb
  fishes
  fishing
  fished
fisherman noun
  fishermen
fishmonger noun
  fishmongers
fishy adjective
  fishier
  fishiest
fission
fist noun
  fists
fit adjective
  fitter
  fittest

fit verb
  fits
  fitting
  fitted
fit noun
  fits
fitness
fitter noun
  fitters
fitting adjective
fitting noun
  fittings
five
fiver noun
  fivers
fix verb
  fixes
  fixing
  fixed
fix noun
  fixes
fixture noun
  fixtures
fizz verb
  fizzes
  fizzing
  fizzed
fizzy adjective
  fizzier
  fizziest
fizzle verb
  fizzles
  fizzling
  fizzled
fjord noun
  fjords
flabbergasted
flabby adjective
  flabbier
  flabbiest

flag noun
  flags
flag verb
  flags
  flagging
  flagged
flagpole noun
  flagpoles
flagship noun
  flagships
flagstaff noun
  flagstaffs
flagstone noun
  flagstones
★ **flair** noun
flake noun
  flakes
flake verb
  flakes
  flaking
  flaked
flaky adjective
  flakier
  flakiest
flame noun
  flames
flame verb
  flames
  flaming
  flamed
flamingo noun
  flamingos
flan noun
  flans
flank noun
  flanks
flannel noun
  flannels
flap noun
  flaps

. . . .

★ **Flair** is a special talent. ! flare.

flap verb
flaps
flapping
flapped
flapjack noun
flapjacks
★ **flare** noun
flares
flare verb
flares
flaring
flared
flash noun
flashes
flash verb
flashes
flashing
flashed
flashback noun
flashbacks
flashy adjective
flashier
flashiest
flask noun
flasks
flat adjective
flatter
flattest
flatly
flat noun
flats
flatness
flatten verb
flattens
flattening
flattened
flatter verb
flatters
flattering
flattered
flatterer noun

flatterers
flattery
flaunt verb
flaunts
flaunting
flaunted
flavour noun
flavours
flavour verb
flavours
flavouring
flavoured
flavouring
flaw noun
flaws
flawed
flawless adjective
flawlessly
flax
☆ **flea** noun
fleas
fleck noun
flecks
● **flee** verb
flees
fleeing
fled
fleece noun
fleeces
fleece verb
fleeces
fleecing
fleeced
fleecy adjective
fleecier
fleeciest
fleet noun
fleets
fleeting
flesh

fleshy adjective
fleshier
fleshiest
✳ **flew** see **fly**
flex noun
flexes
flex verb
flexes
flexing
flexed
flexibility
flexible adjective
flexibly
flick verb
flicks
flicking
flicked
flick noun
flicks
flicker verb
flickers
flickering
flickered
flight noun
flights
flimsy adjective
flimsier
flimsiest
flinch verb
flinches
flinching
flinched
fling verb
flings
flinging
flung
flint noun
flints
flinty adjective
flintier
flintiest

. . . .

★ A **flare** is a bright light. ! **flair**.
☆ A **flea** is an insect. ! **flee**.
● To **flee** is to run away. ! **flea**.
✳ **Flew** is the past of **fly**. ! **flu**, **flue**.

flip verb
flips
flipping
flipped
flippancy
flippant adjective
flippantly
flipper noun
flippers
flirt verb
flirts
flirting
flirted
flirtation
flit verb
flits
flitting
flitted
float verb
floats
floating
floated
float noun
floats
flock verb
flocks
flocking
flocked
flock noun
flocks
flog verb
flogs
flogging
flogged
flood verb
floods
flooding
flooded
flood noun
floods
floodlight noun
floodlights

floodlit
floor noun
floors
floor verb
floors
flooring
floored
floorboard noun
floorboards
flop verb
flops
flopping
flopped
flop noun
flops
floppy adjective
floppier
floppiest
floppy disk noun
floppy disks
flora
floral
florist noun
florists
floss
flounder verb
flounders
floundering
floundered
★ **flour**
flourish verb
flourishes
flourishing
flourished
floury adjective
flourier
flouriest
flow verb
flows
flowing
flowed

flow noun
flows
☆ **flower** noun
flowers
flower verb
flowers
flowering
flowered
flowerpot noun
flowerpots
flowery
flown
◎ **flu**
fluctuate verb
fluctuates
fluctuating
fluctuated
fluctuation
✳ **flue** noun
flues
fluency
fluent adjective
fluently
fluff
fluffy adjective
fluffier
fluffiest
fluid noun
fluids
fluke noun
flukes
flung see **fling**
fluorescent
fluoridation
fluoride
flurry noun
flurries
flush verb
flushes
flushing
flushed

- -

★ **Flour** is powder used in making bread. ! **flower**.
☆ A **flower** is a part of a plant. ! **flour**.
◎ **Flu** is an illness. ! **flew**, **flue**.
✳ A **flue** is a pipe for smoke and fumes. ! **flew**, **flu**.

flush *noun*
flushes
flush *adjective*
flustered
flute *noun*
flutes
flutter *verb*
flutters
fluttering
fluttered
flutter *noun*
flutters
fly *verb*
flies
flying
flew
flown
fly *noun*
flies
flyleaf *noun*
flyleaves
flyover *noun*
flyovers
flywheel *noun*
flywheels
foal *noun*
foals
foam *noun*
foam *verb*
foams
foaming
foamed
foamy *adjective*
foamier
foamiest
focal
focus *verb*
focuses
focusing
focused
focus *noun*
focuses *or* foci

fodder
foe *noun*
foes
foetus *noun* use fetus
fog *noun*
fogs
★ foggy *adjective*
foggier
foggiest
foghorn *noun*
foghorns
☆ fogy *noun*
fogies
foil *verb*
foils
foiling
foiled
foil *noun*
foils
fold *verb*
folds
folding
folded
fold *noun*
folds
folder *noun*
folders
foliage
folk
folklore
follow *verb*
follows
following
followed
follower *noun*
followers
fond *adjective*
fonder
fondest
fondly
fondness

font *noun*
fonts
food *noun*
foods
fool *noun*
fools
fool *verb*
fools
fooling
fooled
foolhardiness
foolhardy
 adjective
foolhardier
foolhardiest
foolish *adjective*
foolishly
foolishness
foolproof
○ foot *noun*
feet
football *noun*
footballs
footballer *noun*
footballers
foothill *noun*
foothills
foothold *noun*
footholds
footing
footlights
footnote *noun*
footnotes
footpath *noun*
footpaths
footprint *noun*
footprints
footstep *noun*
footsteps

★ **Foggy** means 'covered in fog'. ! fogy.
☆ A **fogy** is someone with old-fashioned ideas. ! foggy.
○ The plural is **foot** in e.g. *a six-foot pole*.

★ **for** *preposition*
   and *conjunction*
forbid *verb*
   forbids
   forbidding
   forbade
   forbidden
force *verb*
   forces
   forcing
   forced
force *noun*
   forces
forceful *adjective*
   forcefully
forceps *plural noun*
forcible *adjective*
   forcibly
ford *verb*
   fords
   fording
   forded
ford *noun*
   fords
☆ **fore** *adjective* and
   noun
forecast *verb*
   forecasts
   forecasting
   forecast
   forecasted
forecast *noun*
   forecasts
forecourt *noun*
   forecourts
forefathers *plural*
   noun
forefinger *noun*
   forefingers
○ **foregone** *adjective*
foreground *noun*

   foregrounds
forehead *noun*
   foreheads
foreign
foreigner *noun*
   foreigners
foreman *noun*
   foremen
foremost
forename *noun*
   forenames
foresee *verb*
   foresees
   foreseeing
   foresaw
   foreseen
foreseeable
foresight
forest *noun*
   forests
forester *noun*
   foresters
forestry
foretell *verb*
   foretells
   foretelling
   foretold
✳ **forever** *adverb*
forfeit *verb*
   forfeits
   forfeiting
   forfeited
forfeit *noun*
   forfeits
forgave see **forgive**
forge *verb*
   forges
   forging
   forged
forge *noun*

   forges
forgery *noun*
   forgeries
forget *verb*
   forgets
   forgetting
   forgot
   forgotten
forgetful
forgetfulness
forget-me-not *noun*
   forget-me-nots
forgive *verb*
   forgives
   forgiving
   forgave
   forgiven
forgiveness
fork *noun*
   forks
fork *verb*
   forks
   forking
   forked
fork-lift truck *noun*
   fork-lift trucks
forlorn
form *verb*
   forms
   forming
   formed
form *noun*
   forms
formal *adjective*
   formally
formality *noun*
   formalities
format *noun*
   formats
formation *noun*
   formations

- -

★ You use **for** in phrases like *a present for you.* ! **fore**.
☆ You use **fore** in phrases like *come to the fore.* ! **for**.
○ You can use **foregone** in *a foregone conclusion.*
✳ You use **forever** in e.g. *They are forever complaining.* You can also use **for ever** in e.g. *The rain seemed to go on for ever.*

former *adjective*
formerly
formidable *adjective*
formidably
formula *noun*
formulas *or*
formulae
formulate *verb*
formulates
formulating
formulated
forsake *verb*
forsakes
forsaking
forsook
forsaken
fort *noun*
forts
★ **forth**
fortieth
fortification *noun*
fortifications
fortify *verb*
fortifies
fortifying
fortified
fortnight *noun*
fortnights
fortnightly
fortress *noun*
fortresses
fortunate *adjective*
fortunately
fortune *noun*
fortunes
fortune-teller *noun*
fortune-tellers
forty *noun*
forties
forward *adjective*
and *adverb*

forward *noun*
forwards
forwards *adverb*
fossil *noun*
fossils
fossilized
foster *verb*
fosters
fostering
fostered
foster child *noun*
foster children
foster parent *noun*
foster parents
fought see fight
☆ **foul** *adjective*
fouler
foulest
foully
○ **foul** *verb*
fouls
fouling
fouled
✳ **foul** *noun*
fouls
foulness
found *verb*
founds
founding
founded
found see find
foundation *noun*
foundations
founder *noun*
founders
founder *verb*
founders
foundering
foundered
foundry *noun*
foundries

fountain *noun*
fountains
four *noun*
fours
fourteen *noun*
fourteens
fourteenth
✳ **fourth**
fourthly
✳ **fowl** *noun*
fowl *or* fowls
fox *noun*
foxes
fox *verb*
foxes
foxing
foxed
foxglove *noun*
foxgloves
foxy *adjective*
foxier
foxiest
foyer *noun*
foyers
fraction *noun*
fractions
fractionally
fracture *verb*
fractures
fracturing
fractured
fracture *noun*
fractures
fragile *adjective*
fragilely
fragility
fragment *noun*
fragments
fragmentary
fragmentation

★ You use forth in e.g. *to go forth.* ! fourth.
☆ Foul means 'dirty' or 'disgusting'. ! fowl.
○ To foul is to break a rule in a game. ! fowl.
✳ A foul is breaking a rule in a game. ! fowl.
✳ You use fourth in e.g. *for the fourth time.* ! forth.
✳ A fowl is a kind of bird. ! foul.

fragrance noun
  fragrances
fragrant
frail adjective
  frailer
  frailest
  frailly
frailty noun
  frailties
frame verb
  frames
  framing
  framed
frame noun
  frames
framework noun
  frameworks
★ **franc** noun
  francs
franchise noun
  franchises
☆ **frank** adjective
  franker
  frankest
  frankly
○ **frank** verb
  franks
  franking
  franked
frankness
frantic adjective
  frantically
fraud noun
  frauds
fraudulent adjective
  fraudulently
fraught
frayed
freak noun
  freaks

freakish
freckle noun
  freckles
freckled
free adjective
  freer
  freest
  freely
free verb
  frees
  freeing
  freed
freedom noun
  freedoms
freehand adjective
freewheel verb
  freewheels
  freewheeling
  freewheeled
✳ **freeze** verb
  freezes
  freezing
  froze
  frozen
freezer noun
  freezers
freight
freighter noun
  freighters
frenzied
frenzy noun
  frenzies
frequency noun
  frequencies
frequent adjective
  frequently
frequent verb
  frequents
  frequenting
  frequented

fresh adjective
  fresher
  freshest
  freshly
freshness
freshen verb
  freshens
  freshening
  freshened
freshwater
fret verb
  frets
  fretting
  fretted
fretful adjective
  fretfully
fretsaw noun
  fretsaws
fretwork
friar noun
  friars
friary noun
  friaries
friction
Friday noun
  Fridays
fridge noun
  fridges
friend noun
  friends
friendless
friendliness
friendly adjective
  friendlier
  friendliest
friendship noun
  friendships
✴ **frieze** noun
  friezes
frigate noun
  frigates

- -

★ A **franc** is a French unit of money. ! **frank**.
☆ **Frank** means 'speaking honestly'. ! **franc**.
○ To **frank** is to mark a letter with a postmark. ! **franc**.
✳ To **freeze** is to be very cold. ! **frieze**.
✴ A **frieze** is a strip of designs along a wall. ! **freeze**.

fright noun
 frights
frighten verb
 frightens
 frightening
 frightened
frightful adjective
 frightfully
frill noun
 frills
frilled
frilly adjective
 frillier
 frilliest
fringe noun
 fringes
fringed
frisk verb
 frisks
 frisking
 frisked
friskiness
frisky adjective
 friskier
 friskiest
 friskily
fritter verb
 fritters
 frittering
 frittered
fritter noun
 fritters
frivolous adjective
 frivolously
frivolity noun
 frivolities
frizzy adjective
 frizzier
 frizziest
★ **fro**
frock noun

 frocks
frog noun
 frogs
frogman noun
 frogmen
frolic noun
 frolics
frolicsome
frolic verb
 frolics
 frolicking
 frolicked
front noun
 fronts
frontier noun
 frontiers
frost
 noun
 frosts
frost verb
 frosts
 frosting
 frosted
frostbite
frostbitten
frosty adjective
 frostier
 frostiest
froth noun
froth verb
 froths
 frothing
 frothed
frothy adjective
 frothier
 frothiest
froth verb
 froths
 frothing
 frothed

frown verb
 frowns
 frowning
 frowned
frown noun
 frowns
froze see freeze
frozen see freeze
frugal adjective
 frugally
frugality
fruit noun
 fruit or fruits
fruitful adjective
 fruitfully
fruitless adjective
 fruitlessly
fruity adjective
 fruitier
 fruitiest
frustrate verb
 frustrates
 frustrating
 frustrated
frustration noun
 frustrations
fry verb
 fries
 frying
 fried
fudge
fuel noun
 fuels
fuel verb
 fuels
 fuelling
 fuelled
fug noun
 fugs
fuggy adjective
 fuggier
 fuggiest

★ You use **fro** in to and fro.

fugitive *noun*
  fugitives

-ful
-ful makes nouns for amounts, e.g. **handful**, **spoonful**. The plural of these words ends in *-fuls*, e.g. **handfuls**. *-ful* also makes adjectives, e.g. **graceful**, and when the adjective ends in *-y* following a consonant, you change the *y* to *i*, e.g. **beauty - beautiful**.

fulcrum *noun*
  fulcra *or* fulcrums
fulfil *verb*
  fulfils
  fulfilling
  fulfilled
fulfilment
full *adjective*
  fully
fullness
fumble *verb*
  fumbles
  fumbling
  fumbled
fume *verb*
  fumes
  fuming
  fumed
fumes *plural noun*
fun
function *verb*
  functions
  functioning
  functioned
function *noun*
  functions

functional *adjective*
  functionally
fund *noun*
  funds
fundamental
  adjective
  fundamentally
funeral *noun*
  funerals
fungus *noun*
  fungi
funk *verb*
  funks
  funking
  funked
funnel *noun*
  funnels
funny *adjective*
  funnier
  funniest
  funnily
★ **fur** *noun*
  furs
furious *adjective*
  furiously
furl *verb*
  furls
  furling
  furled
furlong *noun*
  furlongs
furnace *noun*
  furnaces
furnish *verb*
  furnishes
  furnishing
  furnished
furniture
furrow *noun*
  furrows
furry *adjective*

  furrier
  furriest
☆ **further** *adjective*
✪ **further** *verb*
  furthers
  furthering
  furthered
furthermore
✷ **furthest**
furtive *adjective*
  furtively
fury *noun*
  furies
fuse *verb*
  fuses
  fusing
  fused
fuse *noun*
  fuses
fuselage *noun*
  fuselages
fusion *noun*
  fusions
fuss *verb*
  fusses
  fussing
  fussed
fuss *noun*
  fusses
fussiness
fussy *adjective*
  fussier
  fussiest
  fussily
futile *adjective*
  futilely
futility
futon *noun*
  futons

★ **Fur** is the hair of animals. ! **fir**.
☆ You use **further** in e.g. *We need further information.* See **farther**.
✪ To **further** something is to make it progress.
✷ You use **furthest** in e.g. *Who has read the furthest?* See **farthest**.

future
fuzz
fuzziness *noun*
fuzzy *adjective*
　fuzzier
　fuzziest
　fuzzily

Gg

gabardine *noun*
　gabardines
gabble *verb*
　gabbles
　gabbling
　gabbled
gable *noun*
　gables
gabled
gadget *noun*
　gadgets
Gaelic
gag *verb*
　gags
　gagging
　gagged
gag *noun*
　gags
gaiety
gaily
gain *verb*
　gains
　gaining
　gained
gain *noun*
　gains
gala *noun*
　galas

galactic
galaxy *noun*
　galaxies
gale *noun*
　gales
gallant *adjective*
　gallantly
gallantry
★ galleon *noun*
　galleons
gallery *noun*
　galleries
galley *noun*
　galleys
☆ gallon *noun*
　gallons
gallop *verb*
　gallops
　galloping
　galloped
gallop *noun*
　gallops
gallows
galore
galvanize *verb*
　galvanizes
　galvanizing
　galvanized
gamble *verb*
　gambles
　gambling
　gambled
gamble *noun*
　gambles
gambler *noun*
　gamblers
game *noun*
　games
gamekeeper *noun*
　gamekeepers

gammon
gander *noun*
　ganders
gang *noun*
　gangs
gang *verb*
　gangs
　ganging
　ganged
gangplank *noun*
　gangplanks
gangster *noun*
　gangsters
gangway *noun*
　gangways
gaol *noun* use jail
gaoler *noun* use jailer
gap *noun*
　gaps
gape *verb*
　gapes
　gaping
　gaped
garage *noun*
　garages
garbage
garden *noun*
　gardens
gardener *noun*
　gardeners
gardening
gargle *verb*
　gargles
　gargling
　gargled
gargoyle *noun*
　gargoyles
garland *noun*
　garlands
garlic

. . . .

★ A **galleon** is a type of ship. ! gallon.
☆ A **gallon** is a measurement of liquid. ! galleon.

garment noun
  garments
garnish verb
  garnishes
  garnishing
  garnished
garrison noun
  garrisons
garter noun
  garters
gas noun
  gases
gas verb
  gasses
  gassing
  gassed
gaseous
gash noun
  gashes
gasket noun
  gaskets
gasoline
gasometer noun
  gasometers
gasp verb
  gasps
  gasping
  gasped
gasp noun
  gasps
gastric
gate noun
  gates
★ **gateau** noun
  gateaux
gateway noun
  gateways
gather verb
  gathers
  gathering
  gathered

gathering noun
  gatherings
gaudy adjective
  gaudier
  gaudiest
gauge verb
  gauges
  gauging
  gauged
gauge noun
  gauges
gaunt
gauntlet noun
  gauntlets
gauze
gave see give
gay adjective
  gayer
  gayest
gaze verb
  gazes
  gazing
  gazed
gaze noun
  gazes
gazetteer noun
  gazetteers
gear noun
  gears
geese see goose
Geiger counter noun
  Geiger counters
gel noun
  gels
gelatine
gelding noun
  geldings
gem noun
  gems

gender noun
  genders
gene noun
  genes
genealogy noun
  genealogies
general adjective
  generally
general noun
  generals
generalization noun
  generalizations
generalize verb
  generalizes
  generalizing
  generalized
generate verb
  generates
  generating
  generated
generation noun
  generations
generator noun
  generators
generosity
generous adjective
  generously
genetic adjective
  genetically
genetics plural noun
genial adjective
  genially
genie noun
  genies
genitals plural noun
genius noun
  geniuses
gent noun
  gents

★ **Gateau** is a French word used in English. It means 'a rich cream cake'.

gentle *adjective*
gentler
gentlest
gently
gentleman *noun*
gentlemen
gentlemanly
gentleness
genuine *adjective*
genuinely
genus *noun*
genera

geo-
geo- means 'earth',
e.g. **geography** (= the
study of the earth).

geographer
geographical
adjective
geographically
geography
geological *adjective*
geologically
geologist
geology
geometric *adjective*
geometrically
geometrical
adjective
geometrically
geometry
geranium *noun*
geraniums
gerbil *noun*
gerbils
germ *noun*
germs
germinate *verb*
germinates

germinating
germinated
germination
gesticulate *verb*
gesticulates
gesticulating
gesticulated
gesture *noun*
gestures
get *verb*
gets
getting
got
getaway *noun*
getaways
geyser *noun*
geysers
ghastly *adjective*
ghastlier
ghastliest
ghetto *noun*
ghettos
ghost *noun*
ghosts
ghostly *adjective*
ghostlier
ghostliest
ghoulish *adjective*
ghoulishly
giant *noun*
giants
giddiness
giddy *adjective*
giddier
giddiest
giddily
gift *noun*
gifts
gifted
gigantic *adjective*
gigantically

giggle *verb*
giggles
giggling
giggled
giggle *noun*
giggles
★ **gild** *verb*
gilds
gilding
gilded
gills *plural noun*
gimmick *noun*
gimmicks
gin
ginger
gingerbread
gingerly
gingery
gipsy *noun* use **gypsy**
giraffe *noun*
giraffes
girder *noun*
girders
girdle *noun*
girdles
girl *noun*
girls
girlfriend *noun*
girlfriends
girlhood
girlish
☆ **giro** *noun*
giros
girth *noun*
girths
gist
give *verb*
gives
giving
gave
given

- -

★ To **gild** something is to cover it with gold. ! **guild**.
☆ A **giro** is a system of paying money. ! **gyro**.

given see give
giver noun
  givers
glacial
glacier noun
  glaciers
glad adjective
  gladder
  gladdest
  gladly
gladden verb
  gladdens
  gladdening
  gladdened
gladiator noun
  gladiators
gladness
glamorize verb
  glamorizes
  glamorizing
  glamorized
glamorous adjective
  glamorously
glamour
glance verb
  glances
  glancing
  glanced
glance noun
  glances
gland noun
  glands
glandular
glare verb
  glares
  glaring
  glared
glare noun
  glares
glass noun
  glasses

glassful noun
  glassfuls
glassy adjective
  glassier
  glassiest
glaze verb
  glazes
  glazing
  glazed
glaze noun
  glazes
glazier noun
  glaziers
gleam noun
  gleams
gleam verb
  gleams
  gleaming
  gleamed
glee
gleeful adjective
  gleefully
glen noun
  glens
glide verb
  glides
  gliding
  glided
glider noun
  gliders
glimmer verb
  glimmers
  glimmering
  glimmered
glimmer noun
  glimmers
glimpse verb
  glimpses
  glimpsing
  glimpsed
glimpse noun

  glimpses
glint verb
  glints
  glinting
  glinted
glint noun
  glints
glisten verb
  glistens
  glistening
  glistened
glitter verb
  glitters
  glittering
  glittered
gloat verb
  gloats
  gloating
  gloated
global adjective
  globally
globe noun
  globes
gloom
gloominess
gloomy adjective
  gloomier
  gloomiest
  gloomily
glorification
glorify verb
  glorifies
  glorifying
  glorified
glorious adjective
  gloriously
glory noun
  glories
gloss noun
  glosses

glossary *noun*
glossaries
glossy *adjective*
glossier
glossiest
glove *noun*
gloves
glow *verb*
glows
glowing
glowed
glow *noun*
glows
glower *verb*
glowers
glowering
glowered
glow-worm *noun*
glow-worms
glucose
glue *noun*
glues
glue *verb*
glues
gluing
glued
gluey *adjective*
gluier
gluiest
glum *adjective*
glummer
glummest
glumly
glutton *noun*
gluttons
gluttonous
gluttony
gnarled
★ **gnash** *verb*
gnashes
gnashing
gnashed

★ **gnat** *noun*
gnats
★ **gnaw** *verb*
gnaws
gnawing
gnawed
★ **gnome** *noun*
gnomes
go *verb*
goes
going
went
gone
go *noun*
goes
goal *noun*
goals
goalie *noun*
goalies
goalkeeper *noun*
goalkeepers
goalpost *noun*
goalposts
goat *noun*
goats
gobble *verb*
gobbles
gobbling
gobbled
gobbledegook
goblet *noun*
goblets
goblin *noun*
goblins
☆ **God**
✪ **god** *noun*
gods
godchild *noun*
godchildren

goddess *noun*
goddesses
godparent *noun*
godparents
goggles *plural noun*
gold
golden
goldfinch *noun*
goldfinches
goldfish *noun*
goldfish
golf
golfer *noun*
golfers
golfing
gondola *noun*
gondolas
gondolier *noun*
gondoliers
gone see go
gong *noun*
gongs
good *adjective*
better
best
goodbye *interjection*
Good Friday
good-looking
good-natured
goodness
goods *plural noun*
goodwill
gooey *adjective*
gooier
gooiest
goose *noun*
geese
gooseberry *noun*
gooseberries

- -

★ In these words beginning with gn- the 'g' is silent.
☆ You use a capital G when you mean the Christian, Jewish, and Muslim creator.
✪ You use a small g when you mean any male divine being.

gore verb
gores
goring
gored
gorge noun
gorges
gorgeous adjective
gorgeously
★ **gorilla** noun
gorillas
gorse
gory adjective
gorier
goriest
gosling noun
goslings
gospel noun
gospels
gossip verb
gossips
gossiping
gossiped
gossip noun
gossips
got see get
gouge verb
gouges
gouging
gouged
gourd noun
gourds
govern verb
governs
governing
governed
government noun
governments
governor noun
governors
gown noun
gowns

grab verb
grabs
grabbing
grabbed
grace noun
graces
graceful adjective
gracefully
gracefulness
gracious adjective
graciously
grade noun
grades
grade verb
grades
grading
graded
gradient noun
gradients
gradual adjective
gradually
graduate noun
graduates
graduate verb
graduates
graduating
graduated
graduation
graffiti plural noun
grain noun
grains
grainy adjective
grainier
grainiest
gram noun
grams
grammar noun
grammars
grammatical
adjective
grammatically

gramophone noun
gramophones
grand adjective
grander
grandest
grandly
grandad noun
grandads
grandchild noun
grandchildren
grandeur
grandfather noun
grandfathers
grandma noun
grandmas
grandmother noun
grandmothers
grandpa noun
grandpas
grandparent noun
grandparents
grandstand noun
grandstands
granite
granny noun
grannies
grant verb
grants
granting
granted
grant noun
grants
granulated
grape noun
grapes
grapefruit noun
grapefruit
grapevine noun
grapevines
graph noun
graphs

· ·

★ A **gorilla** is a large ape. ! guerrilla.

graphic *adjective*
graphically
graphics *plural noun*
graphite

-graphy
-graphy makes words for subjects of study, e.g. **geography** (= the study of the earth). A **bibliography** is a list of books on a subject, and the plural is **bibliographies**.

grapple *verb*
grapples
grappling
grappled
grasp *verb*
grasps
grasping
grasped
grasp *noun*
grasps
grass *noun*
grasses
grasshopper *noun*
grasshoppers
grassy *adjective*
grassier
grassiest
★ **grate** *verb*
grates
grating
grated
☆ **grate** *noun*
grates
grateful *adjective*
gratefully
grating *noun*
gratings

gratitude
grave *noun*
graves
grave *adjective*
graver
gravest
gravely
gravel
gravelled
gravestone *noun*
gravestones
graveyard *noun*
graveyards
gravitation
gravitational
gravity
gravy
graze *verb*
grazes
grazing
grazed
graze *noun*
grazes
grease
greasy *adjective*
greasier
greasiest
great *adjective*
greater
greatest
greatly
greatness
greed
greediness
greedy *adjective*
greedier
greediest
greedily

green *adjective* and *noun*
greener
greenest
greenery
greengage *noun*
greengages
greengrocer *noun*
greengrocers
greengrocery *noun*
greengroceries
greenhouse *noun*
greenhouses
greens *plural noun*
greet *verb*
greets
greeting
greeted
greeting *noun*
greetings
grenade *noun*
grenades
grew see grow
grey *adjective* and *noun*
greyer
greyest
greyhound *noun*
greyhounds
grid *noun*
grids
grief
grievance *noun*
grievances
grieve *verb*
grieves
grieving
grieved
✪ **grievous** *adjective*
grievously

★ To **grate** something is to shred it. ! great.
☆ A **grate** is a fireplace. ! great.
✪ Note that this word does not end *-ious*.

grill *verb*
  grills
  grilling
  grilled
grill *noun*
  grills
grim *adjective*
  grimmer
  grimmest
  grimly
grimace *noun*
  grimaces
grime
grimness
grimy *adjective*
  grimier
  grimiest
grin *noun*
  grins
grin *verb*
  grins
  grinning
  grinned
grind *verb*
  grinds
  grinding
  ground
grinder *noun*
  grinders
grindstone *noun*
  grindstones
grip *verb*
  grips
  gripping
  gripped
grip *noun*
  grips
★ **grisly** *adjective*
  grislier
  grisliest
gristle

gristly *adjective*
  gristlier
  gristliest
grit *verb*
  grits
  gritting
  gritted
grit *noun*
gritty *adjective*
  grittier
  grittiest
☆ **grizzly** *adjective*
groan *verb*
  groans
  groaning
  groaned
groan *noun*
  groans
grocer *noun*
  grocers
grocery *noun*
  groceries
groggy *adjective*
  groggier
  groggiest
groin *noun*
  groins
groom *verb*
  grooms
  grooming
  groomed
groom *noun*
  grooms
groove *noun*
  grooves
grope *verb*
  gropes
  groping
  groped
gross *adjective*
  grosser

  grossest
  grossly
gross *noun*
  gross
grossness
✪ **grotesque** *adjective*
  grotesquely
grotty *adjective*
  grottier
  grottiest
ground *noun*
  grounds
ground see grind
grounded
grounds *plural noun*
groundsheet *noun*
  groundsheets
groundsman *noun*
  groundsmen
group *noun*
  groups
group *verb*
  groups
  grouping
  grouped
grouse *verb*
  grouses
  grousing
  groused
grouse *noun*
  grouse
grove *noun*
  groves
grovel *verb*
  grovels
  grovelling
  grovelled
grow *verb*
  grows
  growing
  grew
  grown

* *

★ **Grisly** means 'revolting' or 'horrible'. **!** grizzly.
☆ You use **grizzly** in *grizzly bear*. **!** grisly.
✪ **Grotesque** means 'strange' and 'ugly'. It sounds like 'grotesk'.

grower *noun*
  growers
growl *verb*
  growls
  growling
  growled
growl *noun*
  growls
grown-up *noun*
  grown-ups
growth *noun*
  growths
grub *noun*
  grubs
grubby *adjective*
  grubbier
  grubbiest
grudge *verb*
  grudges
  grudging
  grudged
grudge *noun*
  grudges
grudgingly
gruelling
gruesome
gruff *adjective*
  gruffer
  gruffest
  gruffly
grumble *verb*
  grumbles
  grumbling
  grumbled
grumbler *noun*
  grumblers
grumpiness
grumpy *adjective*
  grumpier
  grumpiest
  grumpily

grunt *verb*
  grunts
  grunting
  grunted
grunt *noun*
  grunts
guarantee *noun*
  guarantees
guarantee *verb*
  guarantees
  guaranteeing
  guaranteed
guard *verb*
  guards
  guarding
  guarded
guard *noun*
  guards
guardian *noun*
  guardians
guardianship
★ **guerrilla** *noun*
  guerrillas
guess *verb*
  guesses
  guessing
  guessed
guess *noun*
  guesses
guesswork
guest *noun*
  guests
guidance
guide *verb*
  guides
  guiding
  guided
guide *noun*
  guides
guidelines *plural noun*

☆ **guild** *noun*
  guilds
guillotine *noun*
  guillotines
guilt
guilty *adjective*
  guiltier
  guiltiest
guinea *noun*
  guineas
guinea pig *noun*
  guinea pigs
guitar *noun*
  guitars
guitarist
gulf *noun*
  gulfs
gull *noun*
  gulls
gullet *noun*
  gullets
gullible
gully *noun*
  gullies
gulp *verb*
  gulps
  gulping
  gulped
gulp *noun*
  gulps
gum *noun*
  gums
gum *verb*
  gums
  gumming
  gummed
gummy *adjective*
  gummier
  gummiest
gun *noun*
  guns

★ A **guerrilla** is a member of a small army. ! gorilla.
☆ A **guild** is an organization of people. ! gild.

gun *verb*
  guns
  gunning
  gunned
gunboat *noun*
  gunboats
gunfire
gunman *noun*
  gunmen
gunner *noun*
  gunners
gunnery
gunpowder
gunshot *noun*
  gunshots
★ **gurdwara** *noun*
  gurdwaras
gurgle *verb*
  gurgles
  gurgling
  gurgled
guru *noun*
  gurus
☆ **Guru Granth Sahib**
gush *verb*
  gushes
  gushing
  gushed
gust *noun*
  gusts
gusty *adjective*
  gustier
  gustiest
gut *noun*
  guts
gut *verb*
  guts
  gutting
  gutted

gutter *noun*
  gutters
guy *noun*
  guys
guzzle *verb*
  guzzles
  guzzling
  guzzled
gym *noun*
  gyms
gymkhana *noun*
  gymkhanas
gymnasium *noun*
  gymnasiums
gymnast *noun*
  gymnasts
gymnastics *plural noun*
gypsy *noun*
  gypsies
○ **gyro** *noun*
  gyros
gyroscope *noun*
  gyroscopes

Hh

habit *noun*
  habits
habitat *noun*
  habitats
habitual *adjective*
  habitually
hack *verb*
  hacks
  hacking
  hacked

hacker *noun*
  hackers
hacksaw *noun*
  hacksaws
had see **has**
haddock *noun*
  haddock
hadn't *verb*
hag *noun*
  hags
haggard
haggis *noun*
  haggises
haggle *verb*
  haggles
  haggling
  haggled
✳ **haiku** *noun*
  haiku
hail *verb*
  hails
  hailing
  hailed
hail
hailstone *noun*
  hailstones
✴ **hair** *noun*
  hairs
hairbrush *noun*
  hairbrushes
haircut *noun*
  haircuts
hairdresser *noun*
  hairdressers
hairpin *noun*
  hairpins
hair-raising
hairstyle *noun*
  hairstyles

★ A Sikh place of worship.
☆ The holy book of Sikhs.
○ A **gyro** is type of compass. ! **giro**.
✳ A Japanese poem.
✴ **Hair** is the covering on the head. ! **hare**.

hairy adjective
hairier
hairiest
hake noun
hake
halal
half adjective and
noun
halves
half-baked
half-hearted
adjective
half-heartedly
half-life noun
half-lives
half-mast
★ **halfpenny** noun
halfpennies or
halfpence
half-term noun
half-terms
half-time noun
half-times
halfway
halibut noun
halibut
☆ **hall** noun
halls
hallo
○ **Halloween**
hallucination noun
hallucinations
halo noun
haloes
halt verb
halts
halting
halted

halt noun
halts
halter noun
halters
halting adjective
haltingly
halve verb
halves
halving
halved
halves see half
ham noun
hams
hamburger noun
hamburgers
hammer noun
hammers
hammer verb
hammers
hammering
hammered
hammock noun
hammocks
hamper verb
hampers
hampering
hampered
hamper noun
hampers
hamster noun
hamsters
hand noun
hands
hand verb
hands
handing
handed
handbag noun
handbags
handbook noun
handbooks

handcuffs plural
noun
handful noun
handfuls
handicap noun
handicaps
handicapped
handicraft noun
handicrafts
handiwork
handkerchief noun
handkerchiefs
handle noun
handles
handle verb
handles
handling
handled
handlebars plural
noun
handrail noun
handrails
handsome adjective
handsomer
handsomest
handsomely
hands-on
handstand noun
handstands
handwriting
handwritten
handy adjective
handier
handiest
handyman noun
handymen
hang verb
hangs
hanging
hung

- -

★ You use **halfpennies** when you mean several coins and **halfpence** for a sum of
money.
☆ A **hall** is a large space in a building. **! haul**.
○ You will also see this word spelt *Hallowe'en*.

★ **hangar** noun
hangars
☆ **hanger** noun
hangers
hang-glider noun
hang-gliders
hang-gliding
hangman noun
hangmen
hangover noun
hangovers
hank noun
hanks
hanker verb
hankers
hankering
hankered
hanky noun
hankies
✪ **Hanukkah**
haphazard adjective
haphazardly
happen verb
happens
happening
happened
happening noun
happenings
happiness
happy adjective
happier
happiest
happily
happy-go-lucky
❋ **harass** verb
harasses
harassing
harassed
harassment

harbour noun
harbours
harbour verb
harbours
harbouring
harboured
hard adjective
harder
hardest
hard adverb
harder
hardest
hardboard
hard-boiled
hard disk noun
hard disks
harden verb
hardens
hardening
hardened
hardly
hardness
hardship noun
hardships
hardware
hardwood noun
hardwoods
hardy adjective
hardier
hardiest
❋ **hare** noun
hares
hark verb
harks
harking
harked
harm verb
harms
harming
harmed
harm noun

harmful adjective
harmfully
harmless adjective
harmlessly
harmonic
harmonica noun
harmonicas
harmonious
adjective
harmoniously
harmonization
harmonize verb
harmonizes
harmonizing
harmonized
harmony noun
harmonies
harness verb
harnesses
harnessing
harnessed
harness noun
harnesses
harp noun
harps
harp verb
harps
harping
harped
harpist noun
harpists
harpoon noun
harpoons
harpsichord noun
harpsichords
harrow noun
harrows
harsh adjective
harsher
harshest
harshly

· ·

★ A **hangar** is a shed for aircraft. ! **hanger**.
☆ A **hanger** is a thing for hanging clothes on. ! **hangar**.
✪ A Jewish festival.
❋ Note that there is only one r in **harass** and **harassment**.
❋ A **hare** is an animal like a large rabbit. ! **hair**.

harshness
harvest noun
harvests
harvest verb
harvests
harvesting
harvested
hash noun
hashes
hasn't verb
hassle noun
hassles
haste
hasten verb
hastens
hastening
hastened
hastiness
hasty adjective
hastier
hastiest
hastily
hatch verb
hatches
hatching
hatched
hatch noun
hatches
hatchback noun
hatchbacks
hatchet noun
hatchets
hate verb
hates
hating
hated
hate noun
hates
hateful adjective
hatefully
hatred

hat trick noun
hat tricks
haughtiness
haughty adjective
haughtier
haughtiest
haughtily
★ **haul** verb
hauls
hauling
hauled
haul noun
hauls
haunt verb
haunts
haunting
haunted
have verb
has
having
had
haven noun
havens
haven't verb
haversack noun
haversacks
hawk noun
hawks
hawk verb
hawks
hawking
hawked
hawker noun
hawkers
hawthorn noun
hawthorns
hay fever
haymaking
haystack noun
haystacks

hazard noun
hazards
hazardous
haze noun
hazes
hazel noun
hazels
haziness
hazy adjective
hazier
haziest
hazily
H-bomb noun
H-bombs
head noun
heads
head verb
heads
heading
headed
headache noun
headaches
headdress noun
headdresses
header noun
headers
heading noun
headings
headland noun
headlands
headlight noun
headlights
headline noun
headlines
headlong
headmaster noun
headmasters
headmistress noun
headmistresses
head-on
headphones

· ·

★ To **haul** is to pull something heavy. **!** hall

headquarters *noun*
  headquarters
headteacher *noun*
  headteachers
headway
heal *verb*
  heals
  healing
  healed
healer *noun*
  healers
health
healthiness
healthy *adjective*
  healthier
  healthiest
  healthily
heap *verb*
  heaps
  heaping
  heaped
heap *noun*
  heaps
★ **hear** *verb*
  hears
  hearing
  heard
hearing *noun*
  hearings
hearse *noun*
  hearses
heart *noun*
  hearts
hearth *noun*
  hearths
heartiness
heartless
hearty *adjective*
  heartier
  heartiest
  heartily

heat *verb*
  heats
  heating
  heated
heat *noun*
  heats
heater *noun*
  heaters
heath *noun*
  heaths
heathen *noun*
  heathens
heather
heatwave *noun*
  heatwaves
☆ **heave** *verb*
  heaves
  heaving
  heaved *or* hove
heaven
heavenly
heaviness
heavy *adjective*
  heavier
  heaviest
  heavily
heavyweight *noun*
  heavyweights
Hebrew
hectare *noun*
  hectares
hectic *adjective*
  hectically
he'd *verb*
hedge *noun*
  hedges
hedge *verb*
  hedges
  hedging
  hedged

hedgehog *noun*
  hedgehogs
hedgerow *noun*
  hedgerows
heed *verb*
  heeds
  heeding
  heeded
heed *noun*
heedless
heel *noun*
  heels
heel *verb*
  heels
  heeling
  heeled
hefty *adjective*
  heftier
  heftiest
heifer *noun*
  heifers
height *noun*
  heights
heighten *verb*
  heightens
  heightening
  heightened
○ **heir** *noun*
  heirs
heiress *noun*
  heiresses
held see **hold**
helicopter *noun*
  helicopters
helium
helix *noun*
  helices
hell
he'll *verb*
hellish *adjective*
  hellishly

- -

★ You use **hear** in e.g. *I can't hear you.* ! **here.**
☆ You use **hove** in e.g. *the ship hove to.*
○ You do not pronounce the 'h' in **heir** (sounds like *air*).

hello
helm *noun*
  helms
helmsman *noun*
  helmsmen
helmet *noun*
  helmets
helmeted
help *verb*
  helps
  helping
  helped
help *noun*
  helps
helper *noun*
  helpers
helpful *adjective*
  helpfully
helping *noun*
  helpings
helpless *adjective*
  helplessly
helter-skelter *noun*
  helter-skelters
hem *noun*
  hems
hem *verb*
  hems
  hemming
  hemmed
hemisphere *noun*
  hemispheres
hemp
hence
henceforth
herald *noun*
  heralds
herald *verb*
  heralds
  heralding
  heralded

heraldic
heraldry
herb *noun*
  herbs
herbal
herbivore *noun*
  herbivores
herd *noun*
  herds
★ herd *verb*
  herds
  herding
  herded
☆ here
hereditary
heredity
heritage *noun*
  heritages
hermit *noun*
  hermits
hermitage
hero *noun*
  heroes
heroic *adjective*
  heroically
✪ heroin *noun*
✳ heroine *noun*
  heroines
heroism
heron *noun*
  herons
herring *noun*
  herring
  herrings
✳ hers
herself
he's *verb*

hesitant *adjective*
  hesitantly
hesitate *verb*
  hesitates
  hesitating
  hesitated
hesitation
hexagon *noun*
  hexagons
hexagonal
hibernate *verb*
  hibernates
  hibernating
  hibernated
hibernation
hiccup *noun*
  hiccups
hide *verb*
  hides
  hiding
  hidden
  hid
  hidden
hide-and-seek
hideous *adjective*
  hideously
hideout *noun*
  hideouts
hiding *noun*
  hidings
hieroglyphics *plural noun*
hi-fi *noun*
  hi-fis
higgledy-piggledy
high *adjective*
  higher
  highest
highland *adjective*
highlands *plural noun*

- -

★ A **herd** is a group of sheep. ! **heard**.
☆ You use **here** in e.g. *come here*. ! **hear**.
✪ **Heroin** is a drug. ! **heroine**.
✳ A **heroine** is a woman or girl in a story. ! **heroin**.
✳ You use **hers** in e.g. *the book is hers*. Note that there is no apostrophe in this word.

highlander noun
  highlanders
highlight noun
  highlights
highlighter noun
  highlighters
highly
Highness noun
  Highnesses
high-rise
highway noun
  highways
highwayman noun
  highwaymen
hijack verb
  hijacks
  hijacking
  hijacked
hijacker noun
  hijackers
hike verb
  hikes
  hiking
  hiked
hike noun
  hikes
hiker noun
  hikers
hilarious adjective
  hilariously
hilarity
hill noun
  hills
hillside noun
  hillsides
hilly adjective
  hillier
  hilliest
hilt noun
  hilts
himself

hind adjective
hind noun
  hinds
hinder verb
  hinders
  hindering
  hindered
Hindi
hindrance noun
  hindrances
Hindu noun
  Hindus
hinge noun
  hinges
hinge verb
  hinges
  hinging
  hinged
hint noun
  hints
hint verb
  hints
  hinting
  hinted
hip noun
  hips
hippo noun
  hippos
hippopotamus noun
  hippopotamuses
hire verb
  hires
  hiring
  hired
hiss verb
  hisses
  hissing
  hissed
histogram noun
  histograms

historian noun
  historians
historic
historical adjective
  historically
history noun
  histories
hit verb
  hits
  hitting
  hit
hit noun
  hits
hitch verb
  hitches
  hitching
  hitched
hitch noun
  hitches
hitch-hike verb
  hitch-hikes
  hitch-hiking
  hitch-hiked
hitch-hiker noun
  hitch-hikers
hi-tech
hither
hitherto
hive noun
  hives
hoard verb
  hoards
  hoarding
  hoarded
★ **hoard** noun
  hoards
hoarder noun
  hoarders
hoarding noun
  hoardings
hoar frost

· ·

★ A **hoard** is a secret store. ! horde.

★ **hoarse** adjective
  hoarser
  hoarsest
hoax verb
  hoaxes
  hoaxing
  hoaxed
hoax noun
  hoaxes
hobble verb
  hobbles
  hobbling
  hobbled
hobby noun
  hobbies
hockey
hoe noun
  hoes
hoe verb
  hoes
  hoeing
  hoed
hog noun
  hogs
hog verb
  hogs
  hogging
  hogged
Hogmanay
hoist verb
  hoists
  hoisting
  hoisted
hold verb
  holds
  holding
  held
hold noun
  holds
holdall noun
  holdalls

holder noun
  holders
hold-up noun
  hold-ups
☆ **hole** noun
  holes
✪ **holey** adjective
✳ **Holi**
holiday noun
  holidays
holiness
hollow adjective and
  adverb
hollow verb
  hollows
  hollowing
  hollowed
hollow noun
  hollows
holly
holocaust noun
  holocausts
hologram noun
  holograms
holster noun
  holsters
✴ **holy** adjective
  holier
  holiest
home noun
  homes
home verb
  homes
  homing
  homed
homeless
homely
home-made
homesick
homesickness

homestead noun
  homesteads
homeward adjective
homewards
  adjective and adverb
homework
homing
homosexual
  adjective and noun
  homosexuals
honest adjective
  honestly
honesty
honey noun
  honeys
honeycomb noun
  honeycombs
honeymoon noun
  honeymoons
honeysuckle
honk verb
  honks
  honking
  honked
honk noun
  honks
honour verb
  honours
  honouring
  honoured
honour noun
  honours
honourable adjective
  honourably
hood noun
  hoods

-hood
-hood makes nouns,
e.g. **childhood**. Other
noun suffixes are
-dom, **-ment**, **-ness**,
and **-ship**.

- -

★ A **hoarse** voice is rough or croaking. ! horse.
☆ A **hole** is a gap or opening. ! whole.
✪ **Holey** means 'full of holes'. ! holy.
✳ A Hindu festival.
✴ You use **holy** in e.g. *a holy man*. ! holey.

hooded
hoof noun
  hoofs
hook noun
  hooks
hook verb
  hooks
  hooking
  hooked
hooligan noun
  hooligans
hoop noun
  hoops
hoopla
hooray
hoot verb
  hoots
  hooting
  hooted
hoot noun
  hoots
hooter noun
  hooters
hop verb
  hops
  hopping
  hopped
hop noun
  hops
hope verb
  hopes
  hoping
  hoped
hope noun
  hopes
hopeful adjective
  hopefully
hopeless adjective
  hopelessly
hopscotch

★ **horde** noun
  hordes
horizon noun
  horizons
horizontal adjective
  horizontally
hormone noun
  hormones
horn noun
  horns
hornet noun
  hornets
horoscope noun
  horoscopes
horrible adjective
  horribly
horrid
horrific adjective
  horrifically
horrify verb
  horrifies
  horrifying
  horrified
horror noun
  horrors
horse noun
  horses
horseback
horseman noun
  horsemen
horsemanship
horsepower noun
  horsepower
horseshoe noun
  horseshoes
horsewoman noun
  horsewomen
horticulture
hose noun
  hoses

hospitable adjective
  hospitably
hospital noun
  hospitals
hospitality
host noun
  hosts
hostage noun
  hostages
hostel noun
  hostels
hostess noun
  hostesses
hostile
hostility noun
  hostilities
hot adjective
  hotter
  hottest
  hotly
hot verb
  hots
  hotting
  hotted
hotel noun
  hotels
hothouse noun
  hothouses
hotpot noun
  hotpots
hound noun
  hounds
hound verb
  hounds
  hounding
  hounded
☆ **hour** noun
  hours
hourglass noun
  hourglasses

. . . .

★ A **horde** is a large crowd. ! **hoard**.
☆ An **hour** is a measure of time. ! **our**.

hourly *adjective* and *adverb*
house *noun*
houses
house *verb*
houses
housing
housed
houseboat *noun*
houseboats
household *noun*
households
householder *noun*
householders
housekeeper *noun*
housekeepers
housekeeping
housewife *noun*
housewives
housework
housing *noun*
housings
hove see heave
hover *verb*
hovers
hovering
hovered
hovercraft *noun*
hovercraft
however
howl *verb*
howls
howling
howled
howl *noun*
howls
howler *noun*
howlers
hub *noun*
hubs

huddle *verb*
huddles
huddling
huddled
hue *noun*
hues
huff
hug *verb*
hugs
hugging
hugged
hug *noun*
hugs
huge *adjective*
huger
hugest
hugely
hugeness
hulk *noun*
hulks
hulking
hull *noun*
hulls
hullabaloo *noun*
hullabaloos
hullo
hum *verb*
hums
humming
hummed
hum *noun*
hums
human *adjective* and *noun*
humans
humane *adjective*
humanely
humanitarian
humanity *noun*
humanities

humble *adjective*
humbler
humblest
humbly
humid
humidity
humiliate *verb*
humiliates
humiliating
humiliated
humiliation
humility
hummingbird *noun*
hummingbirds
humorous *adjective*
humorously
humour *noun*
humour *verb*
humours
humouring
humoured
hump *noun*
humps
hump *verb*
humps
humping
humped
humpback
humus
hunch *verb*
hunches
hunching
hunched
hunch *noun*
hunches
hunchback *noun*
hunchbacks
hunchbacked
hundred *noun*
hundreds
hundredth

hundredweight noun
  hundredweights
hung see **hang**
hunger
hungry adjective
  hungrier
  hungriest
  hungrily
hunk noun
  hunks
hunt verb
  hunts
  hunting
  hunted
hunt noun
  hunts
hunter noun
  hunters
hurdle noun
  hurdles
hurdler noun
  hurdlers
hurdling
hurl verb
  hurls
  hurling
  hurled
hurrah or **hurray**
hurricane noun
  hurricanes
hurriedly
hurry verb
  hurries
  hurrying
  hurried
hurry noun
  hurries
hurt verb
  hurts
  hurting
  hurt
hurt noun

hurtle verb
  hurtles
  hurtling
  hurtled
husband noun
  husbands
hush verb
  hushes
  hushing
  hushed
hush noun
husk noun
  husks
huskiness
husky adjective
  huskier
  huskiest
  huskily
husky noun
  huskies
hustle verb
  hustles
  hustling
  hustled
hutch noun
  hutches
hyacinth noun
  hyacinths
hybrid noun
  hybrids
hydrangea noun
  hydrangeas
hydrant noun
  hydrants
hydraulic adjective
  hydraulically
hydroelectric
hydrofoil noun
  hydrofoils
hydrogen
hydrophobia

hyena noun
  hyenas
hygiene
hygienic adjective
  hygienically
hymn noun
  hymns
hyperactive
hypermarket noun
  hypermarkets
hyphen noun
  hyphens
hyphenated
hypnosis
hypnotism
hypnotist
hypnotize verb
  hypnotizes
  hypnotizing
  hypnotized
hypocrisy
hypocrite noun
  hypocrites
hypocritical
  adjective
  hypocritically
hypodermic
hypotenuse noun
  hypotenuses
hypothermia
hypothesis noun
  hypotheses
hypothetical
  adjective
  hypothetically
hysteria
hysterical adjective
  hysterically
hysterics plural noun

Ii

ice noun
  ices
ice verb
  ices
  icing
  iced
iceberg noun
  icebergs
ice cream noun
  ice creams
icicle noun
  icicles
icing
icon noun
  icons
icy adjective
  icier
  iciest
  icily

I'd verb
idea noun
  ideas
ideal adjective
  ideally
ideal noun
  ideals
identical adjective
  identically
identification
identify verb
  identifies
  identifying
  identified
identity noun
  identities
idiocy noun
  idiocies
idiom noun
  idioms
idiomatic
idiot noun
  idiots
idiotic adjective
  idiotically
★ **idle** adjective
  idler
  idlest
  idly
idle verb
  idles
  idling
  idled
☆ **idol** noun
  idols
idolatry
idolize verb
  idolizes
  idolizing
  idolized

igloo noun
  igloos
igneous
ignite verb
  ignites
  igniting
  ignited
ignition
ignorance
ignorant
ignore verb
  ignores
  ignoring
  ignored
I'll verb
ill
illegal adjective
  illegally
illegible adjective
  illegibly
illegitimate
illiteracy
illiterate
illness noun
  illnesses
illogical adjective
  illogically
illuminate verb
  illuminates
  illuminating
  illuminated
illumination noun
  illuminations
illusion noun
  illusions

★ **Idle** means 'lazy'. ! idol.
☆ An **idol** is someone people admire. ! idle.

illustrate verb
 illustrates
 illustrating
 illustrated
illustration noun
 illustrations
illustrious
I'm verb
image noun
 images
imagery
imaginable
imaginary
imagination noun
 imaginations
imaginative
 adjective
 imaginatively
imagine verb
 imagines
 imagining
 imagined
★ imam noun
 imams
imbecile noun
 imbeciles
imitate verb
 imitates
 imitating
 imitated
imitation noun
 imitations
imitator noun
 imitators
immature
immaturity
immediate adjective
 immediately
immense adjective
 immensely

immensity
immerse verb
 immerses
 immersing
 immersed
immersion
immigrant noun
 immigrants
immigrate verb
 immigrates
 immigrating
 immigrated
immigration
immobile
immobility
immobilize verb
 immobilizes
 immobilizing
 immobilized
immoral adjective
 immorally
immorality
immortal
immortality
immune
immunity noun
 immunities
immunization
immunize verb
 immunizes
 immunizing
 immunized
imp noun
 imps
impish
impact noun
 impacts
impair verb
 impairs
 impairing
 impaired

impale verb
 impales
 impaling
 impaled
impartial adjective
 impartially
impartiality
impassable
impatience
impatient adjective
 impatiently
impede verb
 impedes
 impeding
 impeded
imperative
imperceptible
 adjective
 imperceptibly
imperfect adjective
 imperfectly
imperfection noun
 imperfections
imperial
impersonal adjective
 impersonally
impersonate verb
 impersonates
 impersonating
 impersonated
impersonation
 noun
 impersonations
impersonator noun
 impersonators
impertinence
impertinent
 adjective
 impertinently

★ A Muslim religious leader.

implement verb
implements
implementing
implemented
implement noun
implements
implication noun
implications
implore verb
implores
imploring
implored
imply verb
implies
implying
implied
impolite adjective
impolitely
import verb
imports
importing
imported
import noun
imports
importance
important adjective
importantly
importer noun
importers
impose verb
imposes
imposing
imposed
imposition noun
impositions
impossibility
impossible adjective
impossibly
impostor noun
impostors
impracticable

impractical
impress verb
impresses
impressing
impressed
impression noun
impressions
impressive adjective
impressively
imprison verb
imprisons
imprisoning
imprisoned
imprisonment
improbability
improbable adjective
improbably
impromptu
improper adjective
improperly
impropriety noun
improprieties
improve verb
improves
improving
improved
improvement noun
improvements
improvisation noun
improvisations
improvise verb
improvises
improvising
improvised
impudence
impudent adjective
impudently
impulse noun
impulses
impulsive adjective
impulsively

impure
impurity adjective
impurities

in-
in- makes words with the meaning 'not', e.g. inedible, infertile. There is a fixed number of these, and you cannot freely add in- as you can with un-. in- changes to il- or im- before certain sounds, e.g. illogical, impossible.

inability
inaccessible
inaccuracy noun
inaccuracies
inaccurate adjective
inaccurately
inaction
inactive
inactivity
inadequacy
inadequate adjective
inadequately
inanimate
inappropriate adjective
inappropriately
inattention
inattentive
inaudible adjective
inaudibly
incapable
incapacity
incendiary
incense noun

incense *verb*
incenses
incensing
incensed
incentive *noun*
incentives
incessant *adjective*
incessantly
inch *noun*
inches
incident *noun*
incidents
incidental *adjective*
incidentally
incinerator *noun*
incinerators
inclination *noun*
inclinations
incline *verb*
inclines
inclining
inclined
incline *noun*
inclines
include *verb*
includes
including
included
inclusion
inclusive
income *noun*
incomes
incompatible
incompetence
incompetent
adjective
incompetently
incomplete *adjective*
incompletely
incomprehensible
adjective
incomprehensibly

incongruity
incongruous
adjective
incongruously
inconsiderate
adjective
inconsiderately
inconsistency *noun*
inconsistencies
inconsistent
adjective
inconsistently
inconspicuous
adjective
inconspicuously
inconvenience
inconvenient
adjective
inconveniently
incorporate *verb*
incorporates
incorporating
incorporated
incorporation
incorrect *adjective*
incorrectly
increase *verb*
increases
increasing
increased
increase *noun*
increases
increasingly
incredible *adjective*
incredibly
incredulity
incredulous
incubate *verb*
incubates
incubating
incubated

incubation
incubator *noun*
incubators
indebted
indecency
indecent *adjective*
indecently
indeed
indefinite *adjective*
indefinitely
indelible *adjective*
indelibly
indent *verb*
indents
indenting
indented
indentation
independence
independent
adjective
independently
index *noun*
indexes
Indian *adjective* and
noun
Indians
indicate *verb*
indicates
indicating
indicated
indication *noun*
indications
indicative
indicator *noun*
indicators
indifference
indifferent *adjective*
indifferently
indigestible
indigestion

indignant *adjective*
  indignantly
indignation
indigo
indirect *adjective*
  indirectly
indispensable
  adjective
  indispensably
indistinct *adjective*
  indistinctly
indistinguishable
individual *adjective*
  individually
individual *noun*
  individuals
individuality
indoctrinate *verb*
  indoctrinates
  indoctrinating
  indoctrinated
indoctrination
indoor *adjective*
indoors *adverb*
induce *verb*
  induces
  inducing
  induced
inducement *noun*
  inducements
indulge *verb*
  indulges
  indulging
  indulged
indulgence *noun*
  indulgences
indulgent
industrial
industrialist *noun*
  industrialists

industrialization
industrialize *verb*
  industrializes
  industrializing
  industrialized
industrious *adjective*
  industriously
industry *noun*
  industries
ineffective *adjective*
  ineffectively
ineffectual *adjective*
  ineffectually
inefficiency *noun*
  inefficiencies
inefficient *adjective*
  inefficiently
inequality *noun*
  inequalities
inert
inertia
inevitability
inevitable *adjective*
  inevitably
inexhaustible
inexpensive *adjective*
  inexpensively
inexperience
inexperienced
inexplicable *adjective*
  inexplicably
infallibility
infallible *adjective*
  infallibly
infamous *adjective*
  infamously
infamy
infancy
infant *noun*
  infants

infantile
infantry
infect *verb*
  infects
  infecting
  infected
infection *noun*
  infections
infectious *adjective*
  infectiously
infer *verb*
  infers
  inferring
  inferred
inference *noun*
  inferences
inferior *adjective* and
  noun
  inferiors
inferiority
infernal *adjective*
  infernally
inferno *noun*
  infernos
infested
infiltrate *verb*
  infiltrates
  infiltrating
  infiltrated
infiltration
infinite *adjective*
  infinitely
infinitive *noun*
  infinitives
infinity
infirm
infirmary *noun*
  infirmaries
infirmity

inflame *verb*
 inflames
 inflaming
 inflamed
inflammable
inflammation *noun*
 inflammations
inflammatory
inflatable
inflate *verb*
 inflates
 inflating
 inflated
inflation
inflect *verb*
 inflects
 inflecting
 inflected
inflection *noun*
 inflections
inflexibility
inflexible *adjective*
 inflexibly
inflict *verb*
 inflicts
 inflicting
 inflicted
influence *verb*
 influences
 influencing
 influenced
influence *noun*
 influences
influential *adjective*
 influentially
influenza
inform *verb*
 informs
 informing
 informed
informal *adjective*
 informally

informality
informant *noun*
 informants
information
informative
informed
informer *noun*
 informers
infrequency
infrequent *adjective*
 infrequently
infuriate *verb*
 infuriates
 infuriating
 infuriated

-ing
-*ing* makes present
participles and nouns,
e.g. **hunt - hunting.**
You normally drop an
e at the end, e.g.
change - changing,
smoke - smoking. An
exception is **ageing.**
Words ending in a
consonant following a
single vowel double
the consonant, e.g.
run - running.

ingenious *adjective*
 ingeniously
ingenuity
ingot *noun*
 ingots
ingrained
ingredient *noun*
 ingredients
inhabit *verb*
 inhabits
 inhabiting
 inhabited

inhabitant *noun*
 inhabitants
inhale *verb*
 inhales
 inhaling
 inhaled
inhaler *noun*
 inhalers
inherent *adjective*
 inherently
inherit *verb*
 inherits
 inheriting
 inherited
inheritance
inhibited
inhospitable
 adjective
 inhospitably
inhuman
inhumanity
initial *adjective*
 initially
initial *noun*
 initials
initiate *verb*
 initiates
 initiating
 initiated
initiation
initiative *noun*
 initiatives
inject *verb*
 injects
 injecting
 injected
injection *noun*
 injections
injure *verb*
 injures
 injuring
 injured

injurious *adjective*
injuriously
injury *noun*
injuries
injustice *noun*
injustices
ink *noun*
inks
inkling *noun*
inklings
inky *adjective*
inkier
inkiest
inland
inlet *noun*
inlets
inn *noun*
inns
innkeeper *noun*
innkeepers
inner
innermost
innings *noun*
innings
innocence
innocent *adjective*
innocently
innocuous *adjective*
innocuously
innovation *noun*
innovations
innovative
innovator *noun*
innovators
innumerable
inoculate *verb*
inoculates
inoculating
inoculated
inoculation

input *verb*
inputs
inputting
input
input *noun*
inputs
inquest *noun*
inquests
inquire *verb*
inquires
inquiring
inquired
★ **inquiry** *noun*
inquiries
inquisitive *adjective*
inquisitively
insane *adjective*
insanely
insanitary
insanity
inscribe *verb*
inscribes
inscribing
inscribed
inscription *noun*
inscriptions
insect *noun*
insects
insecticide *noun*
insecticides
insecure *adjective*
insecurely
insecurity
insensitive *adjective*
insensitively
insensitivity
inseparable
adjective
inseparably

insert *verb*
inserts
inserting
inserted
insertion *noun*
insertions
inshore *adjective* and
adverb
inside *noun*
insides
inside *adverb,
adjective,* and
preposition
insight *noun*
insights
insignificance
insignificant
adjective
insignificantly
insincere *adjective*
insincerely
insincerity
insist *verb*
insists
insisting
insisted
insistence
insistent *adjective*
insistently
insolence
insolent *adjective*
insolently
insolubility
insoluble *adjective*
insolubly
insomnia
inspect *verb*
inspects
inspecting
inspected

- -

★ An **inquiry** is an official investigation. ! ~~enquiry~~.

inspection noun
inspections
inspector noun
inspectors
inspiration
inspire verb
inspires
inspiring
inspired
install verb
installs
installing
installed
installation noun
installations
instalment noun
instalments
instance noun
instances
instant adjective
instantly
instant noun
instants
instantaneous
adjective
instantaneously
instead
instep noun
insteps
instinct noun
instincts
instinctive adjective
instinctively
institute verb
institutes
instituting
instituted
institute noun
institutes
institution noun
institutions

instruct verb
instructs
instructing
instructed
instruction noun
instructions
instrument noun
instruments
instrumental
insufficient adjective
insufficiently
insulate verb
insulates
insulating
insulated
insulation
insulin
insult verb
insults
insulting
insulted
insult noun
insults
insurance
insure verb
insures
insuring
insured
intact
intake noun
intakes
integer noun
integers
integral adjective
integrally
integrate verb
integrates
integrating
integrated
integration
integrity

intellect noun
intellects
intellectual adjective
intellectually
intellectual noun
intellectuals
intelligence
intelligent adjective
intelligently
intelligibility
intelligible adjective
intelligibly
intend verb
intends
intending
intended
intense adjective
intensely
intensification
intensify verb
intensifies
intensifying
intensified
intensity noun
intensities
intensive adjective
intensively
intent adjective
intently
intent noun
intents
intention noun
intentions
intentional adjective
intentionally
interact verb
interacts
interacting
interacted
interaction

interactive
intercept *verb*
  intercepts
  intercepting
  intercepted
interception
interchange *noun*
  interchanges
interchangeable
  adjective
  interchangeably
intercom *noun*
  intercoms
intercourse
interest *verb*
  interests
  interesting
  interested
interest *noun*
  interests
interface *noun*
  interfaces
interfere *verb*
  interferes
  interfering
  interfered
interference
interior *noun*
  interiors
interjection *noun*
  interjections
interlock *verb*
  interlocks
  interlocking
  interlocked
interlude *noun*
  interludes
intermediate
interminable
  adjective
  interminably

intermission *noun*
  intermissions
intermittent
  adjective
  intermittently
intern *verb*
  interns
  interning
  interned
internal *adjective*
  internally
international
  adjective
  internationally
internee
internment
internet
interplanetary
interpret *verb*
  interprets
  interpreting
  interpreted
interpretation *noun*
  interpretations
interpreter *noun*
  interpreters
interrogate *verb*
  interrogates
  interrogating
  interrogated
interrogation
interrogative
interrogator *noun*
  interrogators
interrupt *verb*
  interrupts
  interrupting
  interrupted
interruption *noun*
  interruptions

intersect *verb*
  intersects
  intersecting
  intersected
intersection *noun*
  intersections
interval *noun*
  intervals
intervene *verb*
  intervenes
  intervening
  intervened
intervention *noun*
  interventions
interview *noun*
  interviews
interview *verb*
  interviews
  interviewing
  interviewed
interviewer *noun*
  interviewers
intestinal
intestine
intimacy
intimate *adjective*
  intimately
intimate *verb*
  intimates
  intimating
  intimated
intimation *noun*
  intimations
intimidate *verb*
  intimidates
  intimidating
  intimidated
intimidation
into *preposition*
intolerable *adjective*
  intolerably

intolerance
intolerant *adjective*
　intolerantly
intonation *noun*
　intonations
intoxicate *verb*
　intoxicates
　intoxicating
　intoxicated
intoxication
intransitive
intrepid *adjective*
　intrepidly
intricacy *noun*
　intricacies
intricate *adjective*
　intricately
intrigue *verb*
　intrigues
　intriguing
　intrigued
introduce *verb*
　introduces
　introducing
　introduced
introduction *noun*
　introductions
introductory
intrude *verb*
　intrudes
　intruding
　intruded
intruder *noun*
　intruders
intrusion *noun*
　intrusions
intrusive *adjective*
　intrusively
intuition
intuitive *adjective*
　intuitively

Inuit *noun*
　Inuit *or* Inuits
inundate *verb*
　inundates
　inundating
　inundated
inundation *noun*
　inundations
invade *verb*
　invades
　invading
　invaded
invader *noun*
　invaders
invalid *noun*
　invalids
invalid *adjective*
　invalidly
invaluable
invariable *adjective*
　invariably
invasion *noun*
　invasions
invent *verb*
　invents
　inventing
　invented
invention *noun*
　inventions
inventive *adjective*
　inventively
inventor *noun*
　inventors
inverse *noun* and
　adjective
　inversely
inversion *noun*
　inversions
invert *verb*
　inverts
　inverting
　inverted

invertebrate *noun*
　invertebrates
invest *verb*
　invests
　investing
　invested
investigate *verb*
　investigates
　investigating
　investigated
investigation *noun*
　investigations
investigator *noun*
　investigators
investiture *noun*
　investitures
investment *noun*
　investments
investor *noun*
　investors
invigilate *verb*
　invigilates
　invigilating
　invigilated
invigilation
invigilator *noun*
　invigilators
invigorate *verb*
　invigorates
　invigorating
　invigorated
invincible
invisibility
invisible *adjective*
　invisibly
invitation *noun*
　invitations
invite *verb*
　invites
　inviting
　invited

invoice noun
invoices
involuntary
involve verb
involves
involving
involved
involvement
inward adjective
inwardly
inwards adverb
iodine
ion noun
ions
iris noun
irises
iron noun
irons
iron verb
irons
ironing
ironed
ironic adjective
ironically
ironmonger noun
ironmongers
ironmongery
irony noun
ironies
irrational adjective
irrationally
irregular adjective
irregularly
irregularity noun
irregularities
irrelevance
irrelevant adjective
irrelevantly
irresistible adjective
irresistibly

irresponsible adjective
irresponsibly
irresponsibility
irreverence
irreverent adjective
irreverently
irrigate verb
irrigates
irrigating
irrigated
irrigation
irritability
irritable adjective
irritably
irritant
irritate verb
irritates
irritating
irritated
irritation noun
irritations

-ish
-ish makes words meaning 'rather' or 'fairly', e.g. soft - softish. You normally drop an e at the end, e.g. blue - bluish. Words ending in a consonant following a single vowel double the consonant, e.g. fat - fattish.

Islam
Islamic
island noun
islands
islander noun
islanders

★ isle noun
isles
isn't verb
isobar noun
isobars
isolate verb
isolates
isolating
isolated
isolation
isosceles adjective
isotope noun
isotopes
issue verb
issues
issuing
issued
issue noun
issues
isthmus noun
isthmuses
italics
itch verb
itches
itching
itched
itch noun
itches
itchy adjective
itchier
itchiest
item noun
items
itinerary noun
itineraries
it'll verb
☆ its
✪ it's verb
itself

- -

★ An isle is a small island. ! aisle.
☆ You use its in e.g. the cat licked its paw. ! it's.
✪ You use it's in it's (= it is) raining and it's (= it has) been raining. ! its.

I've verb
ivory adjective and
  noun
  ivories
ivy

> **-ize** and **-ise**
> You can use -ize or
> -ise at the end of
> many verbs, e.g.
> **realize** or **realise**,
> **privatize** or **privatise**.
> This book prefers
> -ize, but some words
> have to be spelt -ise,
> e.g. **advertise**,
> **exercise**, **supervise**.
> Check each spelling if
> you are not sure.

Jj

jab verb
  jabs
  jabbing
  jabbed
jab noun
  jabs
jabber verb
  jabbers
  jabbering
  jabbered
jack noun
  jacks
jack verb
  jacks
  jacking
  jacked

jackal noun
  jackals
jackass noun
  jackasses
jackdaw noun
  jackdaws
jacket noun
  jackets
jack-in-the-box
  noun
  jack-in-the-boxes
jackknife verb
  jackknifes
  jackknifing
  jackknifed
jackpot noun
  jackpots
jacuzzi noun
  jacuzzis
jade
jaded
jagged
jaguar noun
  jaguars
jail noun
  jails
jail verb
  jails
  jailing
  jailed
jailer noun
  jailers
★ **Jain** noun
  Jains
jam noun
  jams
jam verb
  jams
  jamming
  jammed

jamboree noun
  jamborees
jammy adjective
  jammier
  jammiest
jangle verb
  jangles
  jangling
  jangled
January noun
  Januaries
jar noun
  jars
jar verb
  jars
  jarring
  jarred
jaundice
jaunt noun
  jaunts
jauntiness
jaunty adjective
  jauntier
  jauntiest
  jauntily
javelin noun
  javelins
jaw noun
  jaws
jay noun
  jays
jazz
jazzy adjective
  jazzier
  jazziest
jealous adjective
  jealously
jealousy
jeans
Jeep noun
  Jeeps

★ A member of an Indian religion.

jeer verb
  jeers
  jeering
  jeered
jellied
jelly noun
  jellies
jellyfish noun
  jellyfish
jerk verb
  jerks
  jerking
  jerked
jerk noun
  jerks
jerky adjective
  jerkier
  jerkiest
  jerkily
jersey noun
  jerseys
jest verb
  jests
  jesting
  jested
jest noun
  jests
jester noun
  jesters
jet noun
  jets
jet verb
  jets
  jetting
  jetted
jet-propelled
jetty noun
  jetties
Jew noun
  Jews

jewel noun
  jewels
jewelled
jeweller noun
  jewellers
jewellery
Jewish
jib noun
  jibs
jiffy noun
  jiffies
jig noun
  jigs
jig verb
  jigs
  jigging
  jigged
jigsaw noun
  jigsaws
jingle verb
  jingles
  jingling
  jingled
jingle noun
  jingles
job noun
  jobs
jobcentre noun
  jobcentres
jockey noun
  jockeys
jodhpurs plural noun
jog verb
  jogs
  jogging
  jogged
jogger noun
  joggers
jogtrot noun
  jogtrots

join verb
  joins
  joining
  joined
join noun
  joins
joiner noun
  joiners
joinery
joint noun
  joints
joint adjective
  jointly
joist noun
  joists
jojoba
joke verb
  jokes
  joking
  joked
joke noun
  jokes
joker noun
  jokers
jollity
jolly adjective
  jollier
  jolliest
jolly adverb
jolly verb
  jollies
  jollying
  jollied
jolt verb
  jolts
  jolting
  jolted
jolt noun
  jolts

jostle verb
  jostles
  jostling
  jostled
jot verb
  jots
  jotting
  jotted
jot noun
  jots
jotter noun
  jotters
joule noun
  joules
journal noun
  journals
journalism
journalist noun
  journalists
journey noun
  journeys
journey verb
  journeys
  journeying
  journeyed
joust verb
  jousts
  jousting
  jousted
jovial adjective
  jovially
joviality
joy noun
  joys
joyful adjective
  joyfully
joyous adjective
  joyously
joyride noun
  joyrides

joystick noun
  joysticks
jubilant adjective
  jubilantly
jubilation
jubilee noun
  jubilees
Judaism
judge verb
  judges
  judging
  judged
judge noun
  judges
judgement noun
  judgements
judicial adjective
  judicially
judicious adjective
  judiciously
judo
jug noun
  jugs
juggernaut noun
  juggernauts
juggle verb
  juggles
  juggling
  juggled
juggler noun
  jugglers
★ **juice** noun
  juices
juicy adjective
  juicier
  juiciest
jukebox noun
  jukeboxes
July noun
  Julys

jumble verb
  jumbles
  jumbling
  jumbled
jumble noun
jumbo jet noun
  jumbo jets
jump verb
  jumps
  jumping
  jumped
jump noun
  jumps
jumper noun
  jumpers
jumpy adjective
  jumpier
  jumpiest
junction noun
  junctions
June noun
  Junes
jungle noun
  jungles
jungly adjective
  junglier
  jungliest
junior adjective and
  noun
  juniors
junk noun
  junks
junket noun
  junkets
juror noun
  jurors
jury noun
  juries
just adjective
  justly

★ **Juice** is the liquid from fruit. **!** deuce.

just *adverb*
justice *noun*
  justices
justifiable *adjective*
  justifiably
justification
justify *verb*
  justifies
  justifying
  justified
jut *verb*
  juts
  jutting
  jutted
juvenile

Kk

kaleidoscope *noun*
  kaleidoscopes
kangaroo *noun*
  kangaroos
karaoke
karate
kayak *noun*
  kayaks
kebab *noun*
  kebabs
keel *noun*
  keels
keel *verb*
  keels
  keeling
  keeled
keen *adjective*
  keener
  keenest
  keenly

keenness
keep *verb*
  keeps
  keeping
  kept
keep *noun*
  keeps
keeper *noun*
  keepers
keg *noun*
  kegs
kennel *noun*
  kennels
kept see **keep**
★ **kerb** *noun*
  kerbs
kerbstone *noun*
  kerbstones
☆ **kernel** *noun*
  kernels
kestrel *noun*
  kestrels
ketchup
kettle *noun*
  kettles
kettledrum *noun*
  kettledrums
✪ **key** *noun*
  keys
keyboard *noun*
  keyboards
keyhole *noun*
  keyholes
keynote *noun*
  keynotes
khaki
kibbutz *noun*
  kibbutzim

kick *verb*
  kicks
  kicking
  kicked
kick *noun*
  kicks
kick-off *noun*
  kick-offs
kid *noun*
  kids
kid *verb*
  kids
  kidding
  kidded
kidnap *verb*
  kidnaps
  kidnapping
  kidnapped
kidnapper *noun*
  kidnappers
kidney *noun*
  kidneys
kill *verb*
  kills
  killing
  killed
killer *noun*
  killers
kiln *noun*
  kilns
kilo *noun*
  kilos
kilogram *noun*
  kilograms
kilometre *noun*
  kilometres
kilowatt *noun*
  kilowatts
kilt *noun*
  kilts
kin

- -

★ A **kerb** is the edge of a pavement. ! **curb**.
☆ **Kernel** is part of a nut. ! **colonel**.
✪ A **key** is a device for opening a lock. ! **quay**.

kind adjective
kinder
kindest
kindly
kind noun
kinds
kindergarten noun
kindergartens
kind-hearted
kindle verb
kindles
kindling
kindled
kindliness
kindling
kindly adjective
kindlier
kindliest
kindness
kinetic
king noun
kings
kingdom noun
kingdoms
kingfisher noun
kingfishers
kingly
kink noun
kinks
kinky adjective
kinkier
kinkiest
kiosk noun
kiosks
kipper noun
kippers
kiss verb
kisses
kissing
kissed

kiss noun
kisses
kit noun
kits
kitchen noun
kitchens
kite noun
kites
kitten noun
kittens
kitty noun
kitties
kiwi noun
kiwis
knack
knapsack noun
knapsacks
knave noun
knaves
★ **knead** verb
kneads
kneading
kneaded
knee noun
knees
kneecap noun
kneecaps
kneel verb
kneels
kneeling
knelt
☆ **knew** see know
knickers plural noun
knife noun
knives
knife verb
knifes
knifing
knifed

○ **knight** noun
knights
knight verb
knights
knighting
knighted
knighthood noun
knighthoods
knit verb
knits
knitting
knitted
knives see knife
knob noun
knobs
knobbly adjective
knobblier
knobbliest
knock verb
knocks
knocking
knocked
knock noun
knocks
knocker noun
knockers
knockout noun
knockouts
knot noun
knots
knot verb
knots
knotting
knotted
knotty adjective
knottier
knottiest
know verb
knows
knowing
knew
known

· ·

★ To **knead** is to work a mixture into a dough. ! need.
☆ **Knew** is the past tense of know. ! new.
○ A **knight** is a soldier in old times. ! night.

know-all *noun*
know-alls
know-how
knowing *adjective*
knowingly
knowledge
knowledgeable
adjective
knowledgeably
knuckle *noun*
knuckles
koala *noun*
koalas
kookaburra *noun*
kookaburras
Koran
kosher
kung fu

Ll

label *noun*
labels
label *verb*
labels
labelling
labelled
laboratory *noun*
laboratories
laborious *adjective*
laboriously
labour *noun*
labours
labourer *noun*
labourers
Labrador *noun*
Labradors

laburnum *noun*
laburnums
labyrinth *noun*
labyrinths
lace *noun*
laces
lace *verb*
laces
lacing
laced
lack *verb*
lacks
lacking
lacked
lack *noun*
lacquer
lacrosse
lad *noun*
lads
ladder *noun*
ladders
laden
ladle *noun*
ladles
lady *noun*
ladies
ladybird *noun*
ladybirds
ladylike
ladyship *noun*
ladyships
lag *verb*
lags
lagging
lagged
lager *noun*
lagers
lagoon *noun*
lagoons
laid see **lay**

lain see **lie**
lair *noun*
lairs
lake *noun*
lakes
lama *noun*
lamas
lamb *noun*
lambs
lame *adjective*
lamer
lamest
lamely
lameness
lament *verb*
laments
lamenting
lamented
lament *noun*
laments
lamentation *noun*
lamentations
laminated
lamp *noun*
lamps
lamp-post *noun*
lamp-posts
lampshade *noun*
lampshades
lance *noun*
lances
lance corporal
noun
lance corporals
land *noun*
lands
land *verb*
lands
landing
landed

landing *noun*
 landings
landlady *noun*
 landladies
landlord *noun*
 landlords
landmark *noun*
 landmarks
landowner *noun*
 landowners
landscape *noun*
 landscapes
landslide *noun*
 landslides
lane *noun*
 lanes
language *noun*
 languages
lankiness
lanky *adjective*
 lankier
 lankiest
lantern *noun*
 lanterns
lap *verb*
 laps
 lapping
 lapped
lap *noun*
 laps
lapel *noun*
 lapels
lapse *verb*
 lapses
 lapsing
 lapsed
lapse *noun*
 lapses
laptop *noun*
 laptops

lapwing *noun*
 lapwings
larch *noun*
 larches
lard
larder *noun*
 larders
large *adjective*
 larger
 largest
 largely
largeness
lark *noun*
 larks
lark *verb*
 larks
 larking
 larked
larva *noun*
 larvae
lasagne *noun*
 lasagnes
laser *noun*
 lasers
lash *verb*
 lashes
 lashing
 lashed
lash *noun*
 lashes
lass *noun*
 lasses
lasso *noun*
 lassos
lasso *verb*
 lassoes
 lassoing
 lassoed
last *adjective* and
 adverb
 lastly

last *verb*
 lasts
 lasting
 lasted
last *noun*
latch *noun*
 latches
late *adjective* and
 adverb
 later
 latest
lately
lateness
latent
lateral *adjective*
 laterally
lathe *noun*
 lathes
lather *noun*
 lathers
Latin
latitude *noun*
 latitudes
latter *adjective*
 latterly
lattice *noun*
 lattices
laugh *verb*
 laughs
 laughing
 laughed
laugh *noun*
 laughs
laughable *adjective*
 laughably
laughter
launch *verb*
 launches
 launching
 launched

launch noun
launches
launder verb
launders
laundering
laundered
launderette noun
launderettes
laundry noun
laundries
laurel noun
laurels
lava
lavatory noun
lavatories
lavender
lavish adjective
lavishly
law noun
laws
lawcourt noun
lawcourts
lawful adjective
lawfully
lawless adjective
lawlessly
lawn noun
lawns
lawnmower noun
lawnmowers
lawsuit noun
lawsuits
lawyer noun
lawyers
lax adjective
laxly
laxative noun
laxatives
lay verb
lays

laying
laid
lay see lie
layabout noun
layabouts
layer noun
layers
layman noun
laymen
layout noun
layouts
laze verb
lazes
lazing
lazed
laziness
lazy adjective
lazier
laziest
lazily
lead verb
leads
leading
led
★ **lead** noun
leads
leader noun
leaders
leadership
leaf noun
leaves
leaflet noun
leaflets
leafy adjective
leafier
leafiest
league noun
leagues
leak verb
leaks
leaking

leaked
☆ **leak** noun
leaks
leakage noun
leakages
leaky adjective
leakier
leakiest
lean verb
leans
leaning
leaned or leant
lean adjective
leaner
leanest
leap verb
leaps
leaping
leapt
leaped
leap noun
leaps
leapfrog
leap year noun
leap years
learn verb
learns
learning
learnt or learned
❂ **learned** adjective
learner noun
learners
lease noun
leases
leash noun
leashes
least adjective and
noun
leather noun
leathers

- -

★ A **lead** (pronounced *leed*) is a cord for leading a dog. **Lead** (pronounced *led*) is a metal.

☆ A **leak** is a hole or crack that liquid or gas can get through. ! **leek**

❂ Pronounced *ler-nid*.

leathery
leave *verb*
  leaves
  leaving
  left
leave *noun*
leaves see **leaf**
lectern *noun*
  lecterns
lecture *verb*
  lectures
  lecturing
  lectured
lecture *noun*
  lectures
lecturer *noun*
  lecturers
led see **lead**
ledge *noun*
  ledges
lee
★ leek *noun*
  leeks
leer *verb*
  leers
  leering
  leered
leeward
left *adjective* and
  noun
left see **leave**
left-handed
leftovers *plural noun*
leg *noun*
  legs
legacy *noun*
  legacies

legal *adjective*
  legally
legality
legalize *verb*
  legalizes
  legalizing
  legalized
legend *noun*
  legends
legendary
legibility
legible *adjective*
  legibly
legion *noun*
  legions
legislate *verb*
  legislates
  legislating
  legislated
legislation
legislator *noun*
  legislators
legitimacy
legitimate *adjective*
  legitimately
leisure
leisurely
lemon *noun*
  lemons
lemonade *noun*
  lemonades
lend *verb*
  lends
  lending
  lent
length *noun*
  lengths

lengthen *verb*
  lengthens
  lengthening
  lengthened
lengthways *adverb*
lengthwise *adverb*
lengthy *adjective*
  lengthier
  lengthiest
  lengthily
lenience
lenient *adjective*
  leniently
lens *noun*
  lenses
☆ Lent
lent see **lend**
lentil *noun*
  lentils
leopard *noun*
  leopards
leotard *noun*
  leotards
leper *noun*
  lepers
leprosy
less
✿ lessen *verb*
  lessens
  lessening
  lessened
lesser
✲ lesson *noun*
  lessons
lest *conjunction*
let *verb*
  lets
  letting
  let

★ A **leek** is a vegetable. ! **leak.**
☆ **Lent** is the Christian time of fasting. ! **lent.**
✿ To **lessen** something is to make it less. **lesson.**
✲ A **lesson** is a period of learning. ! **lessen.**

-let

-let makes nouns meaning 'a small version of', e.g. **booklet**, **piglet**. It also makes words for pieces of jewellery, e.g. **anklet** (worn on the ankle), **bracelet** (from a French word *bras* meaning 'arm')

lethal *adjective*
lethally
let's *verb*
letter *noun*
letters
letter box *noun*
letter boxes
lettering
lettuce *noun*
lettuces
leukaemia
level *verb*
levels
levelling
levelled
level *adjective* and *noun*
levels
lever *noun*
levers
leverage
liability *noun*
liabilities
liable
liar *noun*
liars
liberal *adjective*
liberally

liberate *verb*
liberates
liberating
liberated
liberation
liberty *noun*
liberties
librarian *noun*
librarians
librarianship
library *noun*
libraries
licence *noun*
licences
license *verb*
licenses
licensing
licensed
lichen *noun*
lichens
lick *verb*
licks
licking
licked
lick *noun*
licks
lid *noun*
lids
★ **lie** *verb*
lies
lying
lay
lain
☆ **lie** *verb*
lies
lying
lied
lie *noun*
lies
lieutenant *noun*
lieutenants

life *noun*
lives
lifebelt *noun*
lifebelts
lifeboat *noun*
lifeboats
life cycle *noun*
life cycles
lifeguard *noun*
lifeguards
lifeless *adjective*
lifelessly
lifelike
lifelong
lifestyle *noun*
lifestyles
lifetime *noun*
lifetimes
lift *verb*
lifts
lifting
lifted
lift *noun*
lifts
lift-off *noun*
lift-offs
light *adjective*
lighter
lightest
lightly
light *verb*
lights
lighting
lit *or* lighted
light *noun*
lights
lighten *verb*
lightens
lightening
lightened

★ As in *to lie on the bed.*
☆ Meaning 'to say something untrue'.

lighter *noun*
  lighters
lighthouse *noun*
  lighthouses
lighting
lightning
lightweight
like *verb*
  likes
  liking
  liked
like *preposition*
likeable
likely *adjective*
  likelier
  likeliest
liken *verb*
  likens
  likening
  likened
likeness *noun*
  likenesses
likewise
liking *noun*
  likings
lilac *noun*
  lilacs
lily *noun*
  lilies
limb *noun*
  limbs
limber *verb*
  limbers
  limbering
  limbered
lime *noun*
  limes
limelight

limerick *noun*
  limericks
limestone
limit *noun*
  limits
limit *verb*
  limits
  limiting
  limited
limitation *noun*
  limitations
limited
limitless
limp *adjective*
  limper
  limpest
  limply
limp *verb*
  limps
  limping
  limped
limp *noun*
  limps
limpet *noun*
  limpets
line *noun*
  lines
line *verb*
  lines
  lining
  lined
linen
liner *noun*
  liners
linesman *noun*
  linesmen

-ling
-ling makes words for
small things, e.g.
duckling.

linger *verb*
  lingers
  lingering
  lingered
lingerie
linguist *noun*
  linguists
linguistic
linguistics
lining *noun*
  linings
link *verb*
  links
  linking
  linked
link *noun*
  links
lino
linoleum
lint
lion *noun*
  lions
lioness *noun*
  lionesses
lip *noun*
  lips
lip-read *verb*
  lip-reads
  lip-reading
  lip-read
lipstick *noun*
  lipsticks
liquid *adjective* and
  noun
  liquids
liquidizer *noun*
  liquidizers
liquor *noun*
  liquors

liquorice
lisp *noun*
 lisps
lisp *verb*
 lisps
 lisping
 lisped
list *noun*
 lists
list *verb*
 lists
 listing
 listed
listen *verb*
 listens
 listening
 listened
listener *noun*
 listeners
listless *adjective*
 listlessly
lit see **light**
literacy
literal *adjective*
 literally
literary
literate
literature
litmus
litre *noun*
 litres
litter *noun*
 litters
litter *verb*
 litters
 littering
 littered
★ **little** *adjective* and
 adverb
 less
 least

live *verb*
 lives
 living
 lived
live *adjective*
livelihood *noun*
 livelihoods
liveliness
lively *adjective*
 livelier
 liveliest
liver *noun*
 livers
livery *noun*
 liveries
lives see **life**
livestock
livid
living *noun*
 livings
lizard *noun*
 lizards
llama *noun*
 llamas
load *verb*
 loads
 loading
 loaded
load *noun*
 loads
loaf *noun*
 loaves
loaf *verb*
 loafs
 loafing
 loafed
loafer *noun*
 loafers
loam

loamy *adjective*
 loamier
 loamiest
☆ **loan** *noun*
 loans
loan *verb*
 loans
 loaning
 loaned
✪ **loath** *adjective*
✱ **loathe** *verb*
 loathes
 loathing
 loathed
loathsome
loaves see **loaf**
lob *verb*
 lobs
 lobbing
 lobbed
lobby *noun*
 lobbies
lobby *verb*
 lobbies
 lobbying
 lobbied
lobe *noun*
 lobes
lobster *noun*
 lobsters
local *adjective*
 locally
local *noun*
 locals
locality *noun*
 localities
locate *verb*
 locates
 locating
 located

. . . .

★ You can also use **littler** and **littlest** when you are talking about size.
☆ A **loan** is a thing that is lent to someone. **! lone.**
✪ **Loath** means 'unwilling'. **! loathe.**
✱ To **loathe** is to dislike very much. **! loath.**

location *noun*
locations

★ loch *noun*
lochs

☆ lock *noun*
locks

lock *verb*
locks
locking
locked

locker *noun*
lockers

locket *noun*
lockets

locomotive *noun*
locomotives

locust *noun*
locusts

lodge *noun*
lodges

lodge *verb*
lodges
lodging
lodged

lodger *noun*
lodgers

lodgings *plural noun*

loft *noun*
lofts

lofty *adjective*
loftier
loftiest
loftily

log *noun*
logs

log *verb*
logs
logging
logged

logarithm *noun*
logarithms

logbook *noun*
logbooks

logic

logical *adjective*
logically

logo *noun*
logos

-logy
-logy makes words for subjects of study, e.g. **archaeology** (= the study of ancient remains). Most of these words end in *-ology*, but an important exception is **genealogy**. Some words have plurals, e.g. **genealogies**.

loiter *verb*
loiters
loitering
loitered

loiterer *noun*
loiterers

loll *verb*
lolls
lolling
lolled

lollipop *noun*
lollipops

lolly *noun*
lollies

○ lone

loneliness

lonely *adjective*
lonelier
loneliest

long *adjective* and *adverb*
longer
longest

long *verb*
longs
longing
longed

longitude *noun*
longitudes

longitudinal *adjective*
longitudinally

loo *noun*
loos

look *verb*
looks
looking
looked

look *noun*
looks

lookout *noun*
lookouts

loom *noun*
looms

loom *verb*
looms
looming
loomed

loop *noun*
loops

loop *verb*
loops
looping
looped

loophole *noun*
loopholes

loose *adjective*
looser
loosest
loosely

loose *verb*
looses
loosing
loosed

. . . .

★ A **loch** is a lake in Scotland. **! lock.**
☆ A **lock** is a mechanism for keeping something closed. **! loch.**
○ **Lone** means 'alone'. **! loan.**

loosen verb
loosens
loosening
loosened
looseness
loot verb
loots
looting
looted
loot noun
looter noun
looters
lopsided
lord noun
lords
lordly
lordship
lorry noun
lorries
lose verb
loses
losing
lost
loser noun
losers
loss noun
losses
lot noun
lots
lotion noun
lotions
lottery noun
lotteries
lotto
loud adjective
louder
loudest
loudly

loudness
loudspeaker noun
loudspeakers
lounge noun
lounges
lounge verb
lounges
lounging
lounged
louse noun
lice
lousy adjective
lousier
lousiest
lousily
lout noun
louts
lovable adjective
lovably
love verb
loves
loving
loved
love noun
loves
loveliness
lovely adjective
lovelier
loveliest
lover noun
lovers
loving adjective
lovingly
low adjective
lower
lowest
low verb
lows
lowing
lowed

lower verb
lowers
lowering
lowered
lowland adjective
lowlands plural
nouns
lowlander noun
lowlanders
lowliness
lowly adjective
lowlier
lowliest
lowness
loyal adjective
loyally
loyalty noun
loyalties
lozenge noun
lozenges
lubricant noun
lubricants
lubricate verb
lubricates
lubricating
lubricated
lubrication
lucid adjective
lucidly
lucidity
luck
lucky adjective
luckier
luckiest
luckily
ludicrous adjective
ludicrously
ludo

lug *verb*
 lugs
 lugging
 lugged
luggage
lukewarm
lull *verb*
 lulls
 lulling
 lulled
lull *noun*
 lulls
lullaby *noun*
 lullabies
lumber *verb*
 lumbers
 lumbering
 lumbered
lumber *noun*
lumberjack *noun*
 lumberjacks
luminosity
luminous
lump *noun*
 lumps
lump *verb*
 lumps
 lumping
 lumped
lumpy *adjective*
 lumpier
 lumpiest
lunacy *noun*
 lunacies
lunar
lunatic *noun*
 lunatics
lunch *noun*
 lunches
lung *noun*
 lungs

lunge *verb*
 lunges
 lunging *or* lungeing
 lunged
lupin *noun*
 lupins
lurch *verb*
 lurches
 lurching
 lurched
lurch *noun*
 lurches
lure *verb*
 lures
 luring
 lured
lurk *verb*
 lurks
 lurking
 lurked
luscious *adjective*
 lusciously
lush *adjective*
 lusher
 lushest
 lushly
lushness
lust *noun*
 lusts
lustful *adjective*
 lustfully
lustre *noun*
 lustres
lustrous
lute *noun*
 lutes
luxury *noun*
 luxuries
luxurious *adjective*
 luxuriously
Lycra

-ly
-*ly* makes adverbs from adjectives, e.g. **slow - slowly**. When the adjective ends in -*y* following a consonant, you change the *y* to *i*, e.g. **happy - happily**. -*ly* is also used to make some adjectives, e.g. **lovely**, and some words that are adjectives and adverbs, e.g. **kindly**, **hourly**.

lying *see* lie
lynch *verb*
 lynches
 lynching
 lynched
lyre *noun*
 lyres
lyric *noun*
 lyrics
lyrical *adjective*
 lyrically
lyrics *plural noun*

Mm

ma *noun*
 mas
mac *noun*
 macs
macabre
macaroni
machine *noun*
 machines

machinery
mackerel noun
  mackerel
mackintosh noun
  mackintoshes
mad adjective
  madder
  maddest
  madly
madam
madden verb
  maddens
  maddening
  maddened
★ **made** see make
madman noun
  madmen
madness
magazine noun
  magazines
maggot noun
  maggots
magic noun
  and adjective
magical adjective
  magically
magician noun
  magicians
magistrate noun
  magistrates
magma
magnesium
magnet noun
  magnets
magnetism
magnetic adjective
  magnetically
magnetize verb
  magnetizes
  magnetizing
  magnetized

magnificent
  adjective
  magnificently
magnificence
magnification
magnifier
magnify verb
  magnifies
  magnifying
  magnified
magnitude noun
  magnitudes
magnolia noun
  magnolias
magpie noun
  magpies
mahogany
☆ **maid** noun
  maids
maiden noun
  maidens
◐ **mail** noun
mail verb
  mails
  mailing
  mailed
maim verb
  maims
  maiming
  maimed
✱ **main** adjective
  mainly
mainland
mainly
mains plural noun
maintain verb
  maintains
  maintaining
  maintained
maintenance

maisonette noun
  maisonettes
maize
majestic adjective
  majestically
majesty noun
  majesties
major adjective
major noun
  majors
majority noun
  majorities
make verb
  makes
  making
  made
make noun
  makes
make-believe
maker noun
  makers
make-up
maladjusted
malaria
✳ **male** adjective and
  noun
  males
malevolence
malevolent adjective
  malevolently
malice
malicious adjective
  maliciously
mallet noun
  mallets
malnourished
malnutrition
malt
malted

- -

★ You use **made** in e.g. *I made a cake.* **! maid.**
☆ A **maid** is a female servant. **! made.**
◐ **Mail** is letters and parcels sent by post. **! male.**
✱ **Main** means 'most important'. **! mane.**
✳ A **male** is a man or an animal of the same gender as a man. **! mail.**

mammal noun
mammals
mammoth adjective
and noun
mammoths
man noun
men
man verb
mans
manning
manned
manage verb
manages
managing
managed
manageable
management
manager noun
managers
manageress noun
manageresses
★ **mane** noun
manes
manger noun
mangers
mangle verb
mangles
mangling
mangled
mango noun
mangoes
manhandle verb
manhandles
manhandling
manhandled
manhole noun
manholes
mania noun
manias

maniac noun
maniacs
manic adjective
manically
manifesto noun
manifestos
manipulate verb
manipulates
manipulating
manipulated
manipulation
manipulator
mankind
manliness
manly adjective
manlier
manliest
☆ **manner** noun
manners
manoeuvrable
manoeuvre verb
manoeuvres
manoeuvring
manoeuvred
manoeuvre noun
manoeuvres
man-of-war noun
men-of-war
✪ **manor** noun
manors
mansion noun
mansions
manslaughter
mantelpiece noun
mantelpieces
mantle noun
mantles
manual adjective
manually

manual noun
manuals
manufacture verb
manufactures
manufacturing
manufactured
manufacture noun
manufacturer noun
manufacturers
manure
manuscript noun
manuscripts
Manx
many adjective and
noun
more
most
Maori noun
Maoris
map noun
maps
map verb
maps
mapping
mapped
maple noun
maples
mar verb
mars
marring
marred
marathon noun
marathons
marauder noun
marauders
marauding
marble noun
marbles
March noun
Marches

- -

★ A **mane** is the long piece of hair on a horse or lion. ! **main**.
☆ You use **manner** in e.g. *a friendly manner.* ! **manor**.
✪ A **manor** is a big house in the country. ! **manner**.

march *verb*
marches
marching
marched
march *noun*
marches
marcher *noun*
marchers
★ **mare** *noun*
mares
margarine
margin *noun*
margins
marginal *adjective*
marginally
marigold *noun*
marigolds
marijuana
marina *noun*
marinas
marine *adjective* and *noun*
marines
mariner *noun*
mariners
marionette *noun*
marionettes
mark *verb*
marks
marking
marked
mark *noun*
marks
market *noun*
markets
market *verb*
markets
marketing
marketed
marksman *noun*
marksmen

marksmanship
marmalade
maroon *verb*
maroons
marooning
marooned
maroon *adjective* and *noun*
marquee *noun*
marquees
marriage *noun*
marriages
marrow *noun*
marrows
marry *verb*
marries
marrying
married
marsh *noun*
marshes
marshal *noun*
marshals
marshmallow *noun*
marshmallows
marshy *adjective*
marshier
marshiest
marsupial *noun*
marsupials
martial
Martian *noun*
Martians
martin *noun*
martins
martyr *noun*
martyrs
martyrdom
marvel *verb*
marvels
marvelling
marvelled

marvel *noun*
marvels
marvellous *adjective*
marvellously
Marxism
Marxist
marzipan
mascot *noun*
mascots
masculine
masculinity
mash *verb*
mashes
mashing
mashed
mash *noun*
mask *noun*
masks
mask *verb*
masks
masking
masked
☆ **Mason** *noun*
Masons
○ **mason** *noun*
masons
masonry
✳ **Mass** *noun*
Masses
mass *noun*
masses
mass *verb*
masses
massing
massed
massacre *verb*
massacres
massacring
massacred

- -

★ A mare is a female horse. ! mayor.
☆ You use a capital M when you mean a member of the Freemasons.
○ Use a small m when you mean someone who builds with stone.
✳ Use a capital M when you mean the Roman Catholic service.

massacre noun
massacres
massage verb
massages
massaging
massaged
massage noun
massive adjective
massively
mast noun
masts
master noun
masters
master verb
masters
mastering
mastered
masterly
mastermind noun
masterminds
masterpiece noun
masterpieces
mastery
★ **mat** noun
mats
matador noun
matadors
match verb
matches
matching
matched
match noun
matches
mate noun
mates
mate verb
mates
mating
mated
material noun
materials

materialistic
maternal adjective
maternally
maternity
mathematical
adjective
mathematically
mathematician
noun
mathematicians
mathematics
maths
matinée noun
matinées
matrimonial
matrimony
matrix noun
matrices
matron noun
matrons
☆ **matt**
matted
matter verb
matters
mattering
mattered
matter noun
matters
matting
mattress noun
mattresses
mature
maturity
mauve
maximum adjective
and noun
maxima or
maximums
May noun
Mays

may verb
might
may
maybe
May Day
✪ **mayday** noun
maydays
mayonnaise
✳ **mayor** noun
mayors
mayoress noun
mayoresses
maypole noun
maypoles
maze noun
mazes
meadow noun
meadows
meagre
meal noun
meals
mean adjective
meaner
meanest
meanly
mean verb
means
meaning
meant
meander verb
meanders
meandering
meandered
meaning noun
meanings
meaningful adjective
meaningfully
meaningless
adjective
meaninglessly

. . . .

★ A **mat** is a covering for a floor. ! matt.
☆ **Matt** means 'not shiny'. ! mat.
✪ An international radio signal.
✳ You use **mayor** in e.g. *the Mayor of London*. ! mare.

meanness
means *plural noun*
meantime
meanwhile
measles *plural noun*
measly *adjective*
  measlier
  measliest
measure *verb*
  measures
  measuring
  measured
measure *noun*
  measures
measurement *noun*
  measurements
★ **meat** *noun*
  meats
meaty *adjective*
  meatier
  meatiest
mechanic *noun*
  mechanics
mechanical
  adjective
  mechanically
mechanics
mechanism *noun*
  mechanisms
medal *noun*
  medals
medallist *noun*
  medallists
meddle *verb*
  meddles
  meddling
  meddled
meddler *noun*
  meddlers
meddlesome

media *plural noun*
median *noun*
  medians
medical *adjective*
  medically
medicine *noun*
  medicines
medicinal
medieval
mediocre
mediocrity
meditate *verb*
  meditates
  meditating
  meditated
meditation
Mediterranean
medium *adjective*
medium *noun*
  media *or* mediums
meek *adjective*
  meeker
  meekest
  meekly
meekness
☆ **meet** *verb*
  meets
  meeting
  met
meeting *noun*
  meetings
megaphone *noun*
  megaphones
melancholy
mellow *adjective*
  mellower
  mellowest
melodious *adjective*
  melodiously

melodrama *noun*
  melodramas
melodramatic
  adjective
  melodramatically
melody *noun*
  melodies
melodic
melon *noun*
  melons
melt *verb*
  melts
  melting
  melted
member *noun*
  members
membership
Member of
Parliament *noun*
  Members of
  Parliament
membrane *noun*
  membranes
memoirs *plural noun*
memorable
  adjective
  memorably
memorial *noun*
  memorials
memorize *verb*
  memorizes
  memorizing
  memorized
memory *noun*
  memories
men see **man**
menace *verb*
  menaces
  menacing
  menaced

- -

★ **Meat** is the flesh of an animal. **! meet**.
☆ People **meet** when they come together. **! meat**.

menace *noun*
menaces
menagerie *noun*
menageries
mend *verb*
mends
mending
mended
mender *noun*
menders
menstrual
menstruation

-ment
-ment makes nouns
from adjectives e.g.
contentment. There
is a fixed number of
these, and you cannot
freely add -ment as
you can with -ness.
When the adjective
ends in -y following a
consonant, you
change the y to i, e.g.
merry - merriment.

mental *adjective*
mentally
mention *verb*
mentions
mentioning
mentioned
mention *noun*
mentions
menu *noun*
menus
mercenary *adjective*
and *noun*
mercenaries
merchandise
merchant *noun*
merchants

merciful *adjective*
mercifully
merciless *adjective*
mercilessly
mercury
mercy *noun*
mercies
mere *adjective*
mere *noun*
meres
merely *adverb*
merge *verb*
merges
merging
merged
merger *noun*
mergers
meridian *noun*
meridians
meringue *noun*
meringues
merit *noun*
merits
merit *verb*
merits
meriting
merited
mermaid *noun*
mermaids
merriment
merry *adjective*
merrier
merriest
merrily
merry-go-round
noun
merry-go-rounds
mesh *noun*
meshes
mess *noun*
messes

mess *verb*
messes
messing
messed
message *noun*
messages
messenger *noun*
messengers
Messiah
messiness
messy *adjective*
messier
messiest
messily
met see meet
★ metal *noun*
metals
metallic
metallurgical
metallurgist
metallurgy
metamorphosis
noun
metamorphoses
metaphor *noun*
metaphors
metaphorical
adjective
metaphorically
meteor *noun*
meteors
meteoric
meteorite *noun*
meteorites
meteorological
meteorologist
meteorology
☆ meter *noun*
meters
methane

★ **Metal** is a hard substance used to make things. ! **mettle**.
☆ A **meter** is a device that shows how much of something has been used. ! **metre**.

method *noun*
  methods
methodical *adjective*
  methodically
Methodist *noun*
  Methodists
meths
methylated spirit
meticulous *adjective*
  meticulously
★ **metre** *noun*
  metres
metric *adjective*
metrical *adjective*
  metrically
metronome *noun*
  metronomes
☆ **mettle**
mew *verb*
  mews
  mewing
  mewed
miaow *verb*
  miaows
  miaowing
  miaowed
mice see *mouse*

micro-
micro- makes words meaning 'small', e.g. *microwave*. When the word begins with a vowel you add a hyphen, e.g. *micro-organism*.

microbe *noun*
  microbes
microchip *noun*
  microchips

microcomputer *noun*
  microcomputers
microfilm *noun*
  microfilms
microphone *noun*
  microphones
microprocessor *noun*
  microprocessors
microscope *noun*
  microscopes
microscopic *adjective*
  microscopically
microwave *noun*
  microwaves
microwave *verb*
  microwaves
  microwaving
  microwaved
○ **mid**
midday
middle *noun*
  middles
Middle Ages
Middle East
midge *noun*
  midges
midget *noun*
  midgets
midland *adjective*
midnight
midst
midsummer
midway
midwife *noun*
  midwives
midwifery
✳ **might** *noun*

might see *may*
mightiness
mighty *adjective*
  mightier
  mightiest
  mightily
migraine *noun*
  migraines
migrant *noun*
  migrants
migrate *verb*
  migrates
  migrating
  migrated
migration *noun*
  migrations
migratory
mike *noun*
  mikes
mild *adjective*
  milder
  mildest
  mildly
mildness
mile *noun*
  miles
mileage *noun*
  mileages
milestone *noun*
  milestones
militancy
militant
militarism
militaristic
military
milk *noun*
milk *verb*
  milks
  milking
  milked

- -

★ A **metre** is a unit of length. ! meter.
☆ As in *to be on your mettle*. ! metal.
○ You use a hyphen, e.g. *mid-August*.
✳ **Might** means 'force' or 'strength'. ! mite.

milkman noun
milkmen
milky adjective
milkier
milkiest
Milky Way
mill noun
mills
mill verb
mills
milling
milled
millennium noun
millenniums
miller noun
millers
millet
milligram noun
milligrams
millilitre noun
millilitres
millimetre noun
millimetres
million noun
millions
millionth
millionaire noun
millionaires
millstone noun
millstones
milometer noun
milometers
mime verb
mimes
miming
mimed
mime noun
mimes
mimic verb
mimics
mimicking
mimicked

mimic noun
mimics
mimicry
minaret noun
minarets
mince verb
minces
mincing
minced
mince noun
mincemeat
mincer noun
mincers
mind noun
minds
mind verb
minds
minding
minded
mindless adjective
mindlessly
mine adjective
mine verb
mines
mining
mined
mine noun
mines
minefield noun
minefields
miner noun
miners
mineral noun
minerals
mingle verb
mingles
mingling
mingled

mini-
mini- makes words
meaning 'small', e.g.
miniskirt. You do not
normally need a
hyphen.

mingy adjective
mingier
mingiest
miniature adjective
and noun
miniatures
minibus noun
minibuses
minim noun
minims
minimal adjective
minimally
minimize verb
minimizes
minimizing
minimized
minimum adjective
and noun
minima or minimums
minister noun
ministers
ministry noun
ministries
mink noun
minks
minnow noun
minnows
minor adjective and
noun
minors
minority noun
minorities
minstrel noun
minstrels

mint noun
  mints
mint verb
  mints
  minting
  minted
minus preposition
minute adjective
  minutely
minute noun
  minutes
miracle noun
  miracles
miraculous adjective
  miraculously
mirage noun
  mirages
mirror noun
  mirrors
mirth
misbehave verb
  misbehaves
  misbehaving
  misbehaved
misbehaviour
miscarriage noun
  miscarriages
miscellaneous
miscellany noun
  miscellanies
mischief
mischievous
  adjective
  mischievously
miser noun
  misers
miserable adjective
  miserably
miserly
misery noun
  miseries

misfire verb
  misfires
  misfiring
  misfired
misfit noun
  misfits
misfortune noun
  misfortunes
mishap noun
  mishaps
misjudge verb
  misjudges
  misjudging
  misjudged
mislay verb
  mislays
  mislaying
  mislaid
mislead verb
  misleads
  misleading
  misled
misprint noun
  misprints
miss verb
  misses
  missing
  missed
miss noun
  misses
missile noun
  missiles
missing
mission noun
  missions
missionary noun
  missionaries
misspell verb
  misspells
  misspelling
  misspelt or
  misspelled

★ **mist** noun
  mists
mistake noun
  mistakes
mistake verb
  mistakes
  mistaking
  mistook
  mistaken
mister
mistiness
mistletoe
mistreat verb
  mistreats
  mistreating
  mistreated
mistreatment
mistress noun
  mistresses
mistrust verb
  mistrusts
  mistrusting
  mistrusted
misty adjective
  mistier
  mistiest
  mistily
misunderstand verb
  misunderstands
  misunderstanding
  misunderstood
misunderstanding
  noun
  misunderstandings
misuse verb
  misuses
  misusing
  misused
misuse noun
  misuses

- -

★ **Mist** is damp air that is difficult to see through. ! missed.

* **mite** *noun*
  mites
mitre *noun*
  mitres
mitten *noun*
  mittens
mix *verb*
  mixes
  mixing
  mixed
mixer *noun*
  mixers
mixture *noun*
  mixtures
mix-up *noun*
  mix-ups
moan *verb*
  moans
  moaning
  moaned
moan *noun*
  moans
moat *noun*
  moats
mob *noun*
  mobs
mob *verb*
  mobs
  mobbing
  mobbed
mobile *adjective* and
  noun
  mobiles
mobility
mobilization
mobilize *verb*
  mobilizes
  mobilizing
  mobilized
moccasin *noun*
  moccasins
mock *adjective*

mock *verb*
  mocks
  mocking
  mocked
mockery *noun*
  mockeries
mock-up *noun*
  mock-ups
mode *noun*
  modes
model *noun*
  models
model *verb*
  models
  modelling
  modelled
modem *noun*
  modems
moderate *adjective*
  moderately
moderate *verb*
  moderates
  moderating
  moderated
moderation
modern
modernity
modernization
modernize *verb*
  modernizes
  modernizing
  modernized
modest *adjective*
  modestly
modesty
modification *noun*
  modifications
modify *verb*
  modifies
  modifying
  modified

module *noun*
  modules
moist *adjective*
  moister
  moistest
moisture
moisten *verb*
  moistens
  moistening
  moistened
molar *noun*
  molars
mole *noun*
  moles
molecular
molecule *noun*
  molecules
molehill *noun*
  molehills
molest *verb*
  molests
  molesting
  molested
mollusc *noun*
  molluscs
molten
moment *noun*
  moments
momentary
  adjective
  momentarily
momentous
  adjective
  momentously
momentum
monarch *noun*
  monarchs
monarchy *noun*
  monarchies

• •

* A mite is a tiny insect. ! might.

monastery *noun*
monasteries
monastic
Monday *noun*
Mondays
money
mongoose *noun*
mongooses
mongrel *noun*
mongrels
monitor *verb*
monitors
monitoring
monitored
monitor *noun*
monitors
monk *noun*
monks
monkey *noun*
monkeys
monogram *noun*
monograms
monologue *noun*
monologues
monopolize *verb*
monopolizes
monopolizing
monopolized
monopoly *noun*
monopolies
monorail *noun*
monorails
monotonous
adjective
monotonously
monotony
monsoon *noun*
monsoons
monster *noun*
monsters

monstrosity *noun*
monstrosities
monstrous *adjective*
monstrously
month *noun*
months
monthly *adjective*
and *adverb*
monument *noun*
monuments
monumental
adjective
monumentally
moo *verb*
moos
mooing
mooed
mood *noun*
moods
moodiness
moody *adjective*
moodier
moodiest
moodily
moon *noun*
moons
moonlight
moonlit
★ **moor** *verb*
moors
mooring
moored
☆ **moor** *noun*
moors
moorhen *noun*
moorhens
mooring *noun*
moorings
✪ **moose** *noun*
moose

mop *noun*
mops
mop *verb*
mops
mopping
mopped
mope *verb*
mopes
moping
moped
moped *noun*
mopeds
moraine *noun*
moraines
moral *adjective*
morally
moral *noun*
morals
morale
morality
morals *plural noun*
morbid *adjective*
morbidly
✳ **more** *adjective,*
adverb, and *noun*
moreover
Mormon *noun*
Mormons
morning *noun*
mornings
moron *noun*
morons
moronic *adjective*
moronically
morose *adjective*
morosely
morphine
morris dance *noun*
morris dances
Morse code

. . . .

★ To **moor** a boat is to tie it up. ! more.
☆ A **moor** is an area of rough land. ! more.
✪ A **moose** is an American elk. ! mouse, mousse.
✳ You use **more** in e.g. *I'd like more to eat.* ! moor.

morsel noun
  morsels
mortal adjective
  mortally
mortality
mortar
mortgage noun
  mortgages
mortuary noun
  mortuaries
mosaic noun
  mosaics
mosque noun
  mosques
mosquito noun
  mosquitoes
moss noun
  mosses
mossy adjective
  mossier
  mossiest
most adjective,
  adverb, and noun
mostly adverb
motel noun
  motels
moth noun
  moths
mother noun
  mothers
motherhood
mother-in-law noun
  mothers-in-law
motherly
motion noun
  motions
motionless
motivate verb
  motivates
  motivating
  motivated

motive noun
  motives
motor noun
  motors
motorbike noun
  motorbikes
motor boat noun
  motor boats
motor car noun
  motor cars
motorcycle noun
  motorcycles
motorcyclist noun
  motorcyclists
motorist noun
  motorists
motorway noun
  motorways
mottled
motto noun
  mottoes
mould verb
  moulds
  moulding
  moulded
mould noun
  moulds
mouldy adjective
  mouldier
  mouldiest
moult verb
  moults
  moulting
  moulted
mound noun
  mounds
mount verb
  mounts
  mounting
  mounted

mount noun
  mounts
mountain noun
  mountains
mountaineer noun
  mountaineers
mountaineering
mountainous
mourn verb
  mourns
  mourning
  mourned
mourner noun
  mourners
mournful adjective
  mournfully
★ **mouse** noun
  mice
mousetrap noun
  mousetraps
☆ **mousse** noun
  mousses
moustache noun
  moustaches
mousy adjective
  mousier
  mousiest
mouth noun
  mouths
mouthful noun
  mouthfuls
mouthpiece noun
  mouthpieces
movable
move verb
  moves
  moving
  moved
move noun
  moves

★ A mouse is a small animal. ! moose, mousse.
☆ A mousse is a creamy pudding. ! moose, mouse.

movement *noun*
movements
movie *noun*
movies
mow *verb*
mows
mowing
mowed
mown
mower *noun*
mowers
much *adjective,*
adverb, and *noun*
muck *noun*
muck *verb*
mucks
mucking
mucked
mucky *adjective*
muckier
muckiest
mud
muddle *verb*
muddles
muddling
muddled
muddle *noun*
muddles
muddler *noun*
muddlers
muddy *adjective*
muddier
muddiest
mudguard *noun*
mudguards
muesli
★ **muezzin** *noun*
muezzins
muffle *verb*
muffles
muffling

muffled
mug *noun*
mugs
mug *verb*
mugs
mugging
mugged
mugger *noun*
muggers
muggy *adjective*
muggier
muggiest
mule *noun*
mules

multi-
multi- makes words
with the meaning
'many', e.g.
multicultural. You do
not normally need a
hyphen.

multiple *adjective*
and *noun*
multiples
multiplication
multiply *verb*
multiplies
multiplying
multiplied
multiracial
multitude *noun*
multitudes
mumble *verb*
mumbles
mumbling
mumbled
mummify *verb*
mummifies
mummifying
mummified

mummy *noun*
mummies
mumps
munch *verb*
munches
munching
munched
mundane
municipal
mural *noun*
murals
murder *verb*
murders
murdering
murdered
murder *noun*
murders
murderer *noun*
murderers
murderous *adjective*
murderously
murky *adjective*
murkier
murkiest
murmur *verb*
murmurs
murmuring
murmured
murmur *noun*
murmurs
☆ **muscle** *noun*
muscles
muscle *verb*
muscles
muscling
muscled
muscular
museum *noun*
museums
mushroom *noun*
mushrooms

- -

★ A man who calls Muslims to prayer.
☆ A **muscle** is a part of the body. **! mussel.**

mushroom verb
mushrooms
mushrooming
mushroomed
music
musical adjective
musically
musical noun
musicals
musician noun
musicians
musket noun
muskets
musketeer noun
musketeers
Muslim noun
Muslims
muslin
★ **mussel** noun
mussels
must
mustard
muster verb
musters
mustering
mustered
mustiness
musty adjective
mustier
mustiest
mutation noun
mutations
mute adjective
mutely
mute noun
mutes
muted
mutilate verb
mutilates
mutilating
mutilated

mutilation
mutineer noun
mutineers
mutiny noun
mutinies
mutinous adjective
mutinously
mutiny verb
mutinies
mutinying
mutinied
mutter verb
mutters
muttering
muttered
mutton
mutual adjective
mutually
muzzle verb
muzzles
muzzling
muzzled
muzzle noun
muzzles
myself
mysterious adjective
mysteriously
mystery noun
mysteries
mystification
mystify verb
mystifies
mystifying
mystified
myth noun
myths
mythical
mythological
  adjective
mythology

Nn

nab verb
nabs
nabbing
nabbed
nag verb
nags
nagging
nagged
nag noun
nags
nail noun
nails
nail verb
nails
nailing
nailed
naive adjective
naively
naivety
naked
nakedness
name noun
names
name verb
names
naming
named
nameless
namely
nanny noun
nannies
nap noun
naps
napkin noun
napkins

★ A **mussel** is a shellfish. **! muscle.**

nappy *noun*
  nappies
narcissus *noun*
  narcissi
narcotic *noun*
  narcotics
narrate *verb*
  narrates
  narrating
  narrated
narration *noun*
  narrations
narrative *noun*
  narratives
narrator *noun*
  narrators
narrow *adjective*
  narrower
  narrowest
  narrowly
nasal *adjective*
  nasally
nastiness
nasturtium *noun*
  nasturtiums
nasty *adjective*
  nastier
  nastiest
  nastily
nation *noun*
  nations
national *adjective*
  nationally
nationalism
nationalist
nationality *noun*
  nationalities
nationalization
nationalize *verb*
  nationalizes
  nationalizing
  nationalized

nationwide *adjective*
native *adjective* and
  noun
  natives
Native American
  noun
  Native Americans
nativity *noun*
  nativities
natural *adjective*
  naturally
natural *noun*
  naturals
naturalist *noun*
  naturalists
naturalization
naturalize *verb*
  naturalizes
  naturalizing
  naturalized
nature *noun*
  natures
naughtiness
naughty *adjective*
  naughtier
  naughtiest
  naughtily
nausea
nautical
★ **naval** *adjective*
nave *noun*
  naves
☆ **navel** *noun*
  navels
navigable
navigate *verb*
  navigates
  navigating
  navigated
navigation

navigator *noun*
  navigators
navy *noun*
  navies
Nazi *noun*
  Nazis
Nazism
near *adjective* and
  adverb
  nearer
  nearest
near *preposition*
near *verb*
  nears
  nearing
  neared
nearby
nearly
neat *adjective*
  neater
  neatest
  neatly
neatness
necessarily
necessary
necessity *noun*
  necessities
neck *noun*
  necks
neckerchief *noun*
  neckerchiefs
necklace *noun*
  necklaces
nectar
nectarine *noun*
  nectarines
need *verb*
  needs
  needing
  needed

· ·

★ **Naval** means 'to do with a navy'. ! navel.
☆ A **navel** is a small hollow in your stomach. ! naval.

★ **need** *noun*
　needs
needle *noun*
　needles
needless *adjective*
　needlessly
needlework
needy *adjective*
　needier
　neediest
negative *adjective*
　negatively
negative *noun*
　negatives
neglect *verb*
　neglects
　neglecting
　neglected
neglect *noun*
neglectful *adjective*
　neglectfully
negligence
negligent *adjective*
　negligently
negligible *adjective*
　negligibly
negotiate *verb*
　negotiates
　negotiating
　negotiated
negotiation *noun*
　negotiations
negotiator *noun*
　negotiators
neigh *verb*
　neighs
　neighing
　neighed
neigh *noun*
　neighs

neighbour *noun*
　neighbours
neighbouring
neighbourhood
　noun
　neighbourhoods
neighbourly
neither *adjective* and
　conjunction
neon
nephew *noun*
　nephews
nerve *noun*
　nerves
nerve-racking
nervous *adjective*
　nervously
nervousness

-ness
-*ness* makes nouns
from adjectives, e.g.
soft - softness. When
the adjective ends in
-*y* following a
consonant, you
change the *y* to *i*, e.g.
lively - liveliness.

nest *noun*
　nests
nest *verb*
　nests
　nesting
　nested
nestle *verb*
　nestles
　nestling
　nestled
nestling *noun*
　nestlings

net *noun*
　nets
net *adjective*
netball
nettle *noun*
　nettles
network *noun*
　networks
neuter *adjective*
neuter *verb*
　neuters
　neutering
　neutered
neutral *adjective*
　neutrally
neutrality
neutralize *verb*
　neutralizes
　neutralizing
　neutralized
neutron *noun*
　neutrons
never
nevertheless
　conjunction
☆ **new** *adjective*
　newer
　newest
　newly
newcomer *noun*
　newcomers
newness
news
newsagent *noun*
　newsagents
newsletter *noun*
　newsletters
newspaper *noun*
　newspapers

★ To **need** is to require something. ! knead.
☆ You use **new** in e.g *She has a new bike.* ! knew.

newt noun
newts
New Testament
newton noun
newtons
next adjective and
adverb
next door
nib noun
nibs
nibble verb
nibbles
nibbling
nibbled
nice adjective
nicer
nicest
nicely
niceness
nicety noun
niceties
nick verb
nicks
nicking
nicked
nick noun
nicks
nickel noun
nickels
nickname noun
nicknames
nicotine
niece noun
nieces
★ **night** noun
nights
nightclub noun
nightclubs
nightdress noun
nightdresses

nightfall
nightingale noun
nightingales
nightly
nightmare noun
nightmares
nightmarish
nil
nimble adjective
nimbler
nimblest
nimbly
nine noun
nines
nineteen noun
nineteens
nineteenth
ninetieth
ninety noun
nineties
ninth adjective
ninthly
nip verb
nips
nipping
nipped
nip noun
nips
nipple noun
nipples
nippy adjective
nippier
nippiest
nit noun
nits
nitrate noun
nitrates
nitric acid
nitrogen
nitty-gritty

nitwit noun
nitwits
nobility
noble adjective
nobler
noblest
nobly
noble noun
nobles
nobleman noun
noblemen
noblewoman noun
noblewomen
nobody noun
nobodies
nocturnal adjective
nocturnally
nod verb
nods
nodding
nodded
noise noun
noises
noiseless adjective
noiselessly
noisiness
noisy adjective
noisier
noisiest
noisily
nomad noun
nomads
nomadic
no man's land
nominate verb
nominates
nominating
nominated
nomination noun
nominations

· ·

★ **Night** is the opposite of day. ! knight.

-nomy
-nomy makes words for subjects of study, e.g. **astronomy** (= the study of the stars). Most of these words end in -onomy.

★ **none**

non-
non- makes words meaning 'not', e.g. **non-existent**, **non-smoker**. You use a hyphen to make these words. When an un- word has a special meaning, e.g. **unprofessional**, you can use non- to make a word without the special meaning, e.g. **non-professional**.

non-existent
non-fiction
non-flammable
nonsense
nonsensical adjective
  nonsensically
non-stop
noodle
noon
no one
noose noun
  nooses
normal adjective
  normally
normality
north adjective and
  adverb

☆ **north** noun
north-east noun and
  adjective
northerly adjective
  and noun
  northerlies
northern
northerner noun
  northerners
northward adjective
  and adverb
northwards adverb
north-west
nose noun
  noses
nose verb
  noses
  nosing
  nosed
nosedive verb
  nosedives
  nosediving
  nosedived
nosedive noun
  nosedives
nosiness
nostalgia
nostalgic adjective
  nostalgically
nostril noun
  nostrils
nosy adjective
  nosier
  nosiest
  nosily
notable adjective
  notably
notch noun
  notches
note noun
  notes

note verb
  notes
  noting
  noted
notebook noun
  notebooks
notepaper
nothing
notice verb
  notices
  noticing
  noticed
notice noun
  notices
noticeable adjective
  noticeably
noticeboard noun
  noticeboards
notion noun
  notions
notoriety
notorious adjective
  notoriously
nougat
nought noun
  noughts
noun noun
  nouns
nourish verb
  nourishes
  nourishing
  nourished
nourishment
novel adjective
novel noun
  novels
novelist noun
  novelists
novelty noun
  novelties

★ You use **none** in e.g. none of us went. ! **nun**.
☆ You use a capital N in **the North**, when you mean a particular region.

November *noun*
 Novembers
novice *noun*
 novices
nowadays
nowhere
nozzle *noun*
 nozzles
nuclear
nucleus *noun*
 nuclei
nude *adjective* and
 noun
 nudes
nudge *verb*
 nudges
 nudging
 nudged
nudist *noun*
 nudists
nudity
nugget *noun*
 nuggets
nuisance *noun*
 nuisances
numb *adjective*
 numbly
number *noun*
 numbers
number *verb*
 numbers
 numbering
 numbered
numbness
numeracy
numeral *noun*
 numerals
numerate
numerator *noun*
 numerators

numerical *adjective*
 numerically
numerous
★ nun *noun*
 nuns
nunnery *noun*
 nunneries
nurse *noun*
 nurses
nurse *verb*
 nurses
 nursing
 nursed
nursery *noun*
 nurseries
nurture *verb*
 nurtures
 nurturing
 nurtured
nut *noun*
 nuts
nutcrackers *plural*
 noun
nutmeg *noun*
 nutmegs
nutrient *noun*
 nutrients
nutrition
nutritional *adjective*
 nutritionally
nutritious
nutshell *noun*
 nutshells
nutty *adjective*
 nuttier
 nuttiest
nuzzle *verb*
 nuzzles
 nuzzling
 nuzzled

nylon *adjective* and
 noun
 nylons
nymph *noun*
 nymphs

-o
Most nouns ending in
-o, e.g. hero, potato,
have plurals ending in
-oes, e.g. heroes,
potatoes, but a few
end in -os. The most
important are kilos,
photos, pianos,
radios, ratios, solos,
videos, zeros. Verbs
ending in -o usually
have the forms -oes
and -oed, e.g. video -
videoes - videoed.

oak *noun*
 oaks
☆ oar *noun*
 oars
oarsman *noun*
 oarsmen
oarswoman *noun*
 oarswomen
oasis *noun*
 oases
oath *noun*
 oaths
oatmeal
oats *plural noun*

★ A **nun** is a member of a convent. ! none.
☆ An **oar** is used for rowing a boat. ! or, ore.

obedience
obedient *adjective*
 obediently
obey *verb*
 obeys
 obeying
 obeyed
obituary *noun*
 obituaries
object *noun*
 objects
object *verb*
 objects
 objecting
 objected
objection *noun*
 objections
objectionable
objective *adjective*
 objectively
objective *noun*
 objectives
objector *noun*
 objectors
obligation *noun*
 obligations
obligatory
oblige *verb*
 obliges
 obliging
 obliged
oblique *adjective*
 obliquely
oblong *adjective* and
 noun
 oblongs
oboe *noun*
 oboes
oboist *noun*
 oboists

obscene *adjective*
 obscenely
obscenity *noun*
 obscenities
obscure *adjective*
 obscurer
 obscurest
 obscurely
obscurity
observance *noun*
 observances
observant *adjective*
 observantly
observation *noun*
 observations
observatory *noun*
 observatories
observe *verb*
 observes
 observing
 observed
observer *noun*
 observers
obsessed
obsession *noun*
 obsessions
obsolete
obstacle *noun*
 obstacles
obstinacy
obstinate *adjective*
 obstinately
obstruct *verb*
 obstructs
 obstructing
 obstructed
obstruction *noun*
 obstructions
obstructive *adjective*
 obstructively

obtain *verb*
 obtains
 obtaining
 obtained
obtainable
obtuse *adjective*
 obtuser
 obtusest
 obtusely
obvious *adjective*
 obviously
occasion *noun*
 occasions
occasional *adjective*
 occasionally
occupant *noun*
 occupants
occupation *noun*
 occupations
occupy *verb*
 occupies
 occupying
 occupied
occur *verb*
 occurs
 occurring
 occurred
occurrence *noun*
 occurrences
ocean *noun*
 oceans
o'clock
octagon *noun*
 octagons
octagonal *adjective*
 octagonally
octave *noun*
 octaves
October *noun*
 Octobers

octopus noun
  octopuses
odd adjective
  odder
  oddest
  oddly
oddity noun
  oddities
oddments plural noun
oddness
odds plural noun
odour noun
  odours
odorous
oesophagus noun
  oesophagi or
  oesophaguses
★ **of**
☆ **off**
offence noun
  offences
offend verb
  offends
  offending
  offended
offender noun
  offenders
offensive adjective
  offensively
offer verb
  offers
  offering
  offered
offer noun
  offers
offhand
office noun
  offices
officer noun
  officers

official adjective
  officially
official noun
  officials
officious adjective
  officiously
off-licence noun
  off-licences
offset verb
  offsets
  offsetting
  offset
offshore adjective
  and adverb
offside
offspring noun
  offspring
often
ogre noun
  ogres
ohm noun
  ohms
oil noun
  oils
oil verb
  oils
  oiling
  oiled
oilfield noun
  oilfields
oilskin noun
  oilskins
oil well noun
  oil wells
oily adjective
  oilier
  oiliest
ointment noun
  ointments

old adjective
  older
  oldest
Old Testament
olive noun
  olives
Olympic Games plural noun
Olympics plural noun
ombudsman noun
  ombudsmen
omelette noun
  omelettes
omen noun
  omens
ominous adjective
  ominously
✪ **omission** noun
  omissions
omit verb
  omits
  omitting
  omitted
omnivorous
once
✳ **one** adjective and noun
  ones
oneself
one-sided
one-way
ongoing
onion noun
  onions
onlooker noun
  onlookers
only
onshore adjective and adverb

· ·

★ You use **of** in e.g. *a box of matches*. **! off**.
☆ You use **off** in e.g. *turn off the light*. **! of**.
✪ An **omission** is something left out. **! emission**.
✳ You use **one** in e.g. *one more time*. **! won**.

onto *preposition*
onward *adjective* and *adverb*
onwards *adverb*
ooze *verb*
oozes
oozing
oozed
opaque
open *adjective*
openly
open *verb*
opens
opening
opened
opener *noun*
openers
opening *noun*
openings
opera *noun*
operas
operate *verb*
operates
operating
operated
operatic
operation *noun*
operations
operator *noun*
operators
opinion *noun*
opinions
opium
opponent *noun*
opponents
opportunity *noun*
opportunities
oppose *verb*
opposes
opposing
opposed

opposite *adjective*
opposite *noun*
opposites
opposition
oppress *verb*
oppresses
oppressing
oppressed
oppression
oppressive *adjective*
oppressively
oppressor *noun*
oppressors
opt *verb*
opts
opting
opted
optical *adjective*
optically
optician *noun*
opticians
optimism
optimist *noun*
optimists
optimistic *adjective*
optimistically
option *noun*
options
optional *adjective*
optionally
opulence
opulent *adjective*
opulently
★ **or** *conjunction*
☆ **oral** *adjective*
orally
orange *adjective* and *noun*
oranges
orangeade *noun*
orangeades

orang-utan *noun*
orang-utans
oration *noun*
orations
orator *noun*
orators
oratorical
oratorio *noun*
oratorios
oratory
orbit *noun*
orbits
orbit *verb*
orbits
orbiting
orbited
orbital
orchard *noun*
orchards
orchestra *noun*
orchestras
orchestral
orchid *noun*
orchids
ordeal *noun*
ordeals
order *noun*
orders
order *verb*
orders
ordering
ordered
orderliness
orderly
ordinal number *noun*
ordinal numbers
ordinary *adjective*
ordinarily
✿ **ore** *noun*
ores

. . . .

★ You use **or** in e.g. *Do you want a cake or a biscuit?* ! **oar, ore.**
☆ **Oral** means spoken aloud. ! **aural.**
✿ **Ore** is rock with metal in it. ! **oar, or.**

organ noun
organs
organic adjective
organically
organism noun
organisms
organist noun
organists
organization noun
organizations
organize verb
organizes
organizing
organized
organizer noun
organizers
oriental
orienteering
origami
origin noun
origins
original adjective
originally
originality
originate verb
originates
originating
originated
origination
originator noun
originators
ornament noun
ornaments
ornamental
adjective
ornamentally
ornamentation
ornithological
ornithologist
ornithology

orphan noun
orphans
orphanage noun
orphanages
orthodox
Orthodox Church
orthodoxy
oscillate verb
oscillates
oscillating
oscillated
oscillation noun
oscillations
ostrich noun
ostriches
other adjective and
noun
others
otherwise
otter noun
otters
ought
ounce noun
ounces
ours
ourselves
outback
outboard motor
noun
outboard motors
outbreak noun
outbreaks
outburst noun
outbursts
outcast noun
outcasts
outcome noun
outcomes
outcry noun
outcries

outdated
outdo verb
outdoes
outdoing
outdid
outdone
outdoor adjective
outdoors adverb
outer
outfit noun
outfits
outgrow verb
outgrows
outgrowing
outgrew
outgrown
outhouse noun
outhouses
outing noun
outings
outlast verb
outlasts
outlasting
outlasted
outlaw noun
outlaws
outlaw verb
outlaws
outlawing
outlawed
outlet noun
outlets
outline noun
outlines
outline verb
outlines
outlining
outlined
outlook noun
outlooks
outlying

outnumber verb
  outnumbers
  outnumbering
  outnumbered
outpatient noun
  outpatients
outpost noun
  outposts
output verb
  outputs
  outputting
  output
output noun
  outputs
outrage noun
  outrages
outrage verb
  outrages
  outraging
  outraged
outrageous adjective
  outrageously
outright
outset
outside adverb and
preposition
outside noun
  outsides
outsider noun
  outsiders
outskirts plural noun
outspoken
outstanding
adjective
  outstandingly
outward adjective
  outwardly
outwards adverb
outweigh verb
  outweighs
  outweighing
  outweighed

outwit verb
  outwits
  outwitting
  outwitted
oval adjective and
noun
  ovals
ovary noun
  ovaries
oven noun
  ovens
over adverb and
preposition
over noun
  overs

over-
over- makes words
meaning 'too' or 'too
much', e.g. overactive
and overcook. You do
not need a hyphen,
except in some words
beginning with e, e.g.
over-eager.

overall adjective
overalls plural noun
overarm adjective
overboard
overcast
overcoat noun
  overcoats
overcome verb
  overcomes
  overcoming
  overcame
  overcome
overdo verb
  overdoes
  overdoing
  overdid
  overdone

overdose noun
  overdoses
overdue
overflow verb
  overflows
  overflowing
  overflowed
overgrown
overhang verb
  overhangs
  overhanging
  overhung
overhaul verb
  overhauls
  overhauling
  overhauled
overhead adjective
overheads plural
noun
overhear verb
  overhears
  overhearing
  overheard
overland adjective
overlap verb
  overlaps
  overlapping
  overlapped
overlook verb
  overlooks
  overlooking
  overlooked
overnight
overpower verb
  overpowers
  overpowering
  overpowered
overrun verb
  overruns
  overrunning
  overran
  overrun

overseas *adjective*
and *adverb*
oversight *noun*
oversights
oversleep *verb*
oversleeps
oversleeping
overslept
overtake *verb*
overtakes
overtaking
overtook
overtaken
overthrow *verb*
overthrows
overthrowing
overthrew
overthrown
overthrow *noun*
overthrows
overtime
overture *noun*
overtures
overturn *verb*
overturns
overturning
overturned
overwhelm *verb*
overwhelms
overwhelming
overwhelmed
overwork *verb*
overworks
overworking
overworked
overwork *noun*
ovum *noun*
ova
owe *verb*
owes
owing
owed

owl *noun*
owls
own *adjective*
own *verb*
owns
owning
owned
owner *noun*
owners
ownership
ox *noun*
oxen
oxidation
oxide *noun*
oxides
oxidize *verb*
oxidizes
oxidizing
oxidized
oxygen
oyster *noun*
oysters
oz. *abbreviation*
ozone

Pp

pa *noun*
pas
pace *noun*
paces
pace *verb*
paces
pacing
paced
pacemaker *noun*
pacemakers

pacification
pacifism
pacifist *noun*
pacifists
pacify *verb*
pacifies
pacifying
pacified
pack *verb*
packs
packing
packed
pack *noun*
packs
package *noun*
packages
packet *noun*
packets
pad *noun*
pads
pad *verb*
pads
padding
padded
padding
paddle *verb*
paddles
paddling
paddled
paddle *noun*
paddles
paddock *noun*
paddocks
paddy *noun*
paddies
padlock *noun*
padlocks
pagan *adjective* and
noun
pagans

page noun
pages

pageant noun
pageants

pageantry

pagoda noun
pagodas

paid see **pay**

★ **pail** noun
pails

☆ **pain** noun
pains

pain verb
pains
paining
pained

painful adjective
painfully

painkiller noun
painkillers

painless adjective
painlessly

painstaking

paint noun
paints

paint verb
paints
painting
painted

paintbox noun
paintboxes

paintbrush noun
paintbrushes

painter noun
painters

painting noun
paintings

○ **pair** noun
pairs

pair verb
pairs
pairing
paired

pal noun
pals

palace noun
palaces

palate noun
palates

✳ **pale** adjective
paler
palest

paleness

palette noun
palettes

paling noun
palings

palisade noun
palisades

pall verb
palls
palling
palled

pallid

pallor

palm noun
palms

palm verb
palms
palming
palmed

palmistry

Palm Sunday

paltry adjective
paltrier
paltriest

pampas plural noun

pamper verb
pampers
pampering
pampered

pamphlet noun
pamphlets

pan noun
pans

pancake noun
pancakes

panda noun
pandas

pandemonium

pander verb
panders
pandering
pandered

✴ **pane** noun
panes

panel noun
panels

pang noun
pangs

panic

panic verb
panics
panicking
panicked

panicky

pannier noun
panniers

panorama noun
panoramas

panoramic adjective
panoramically

pansy noun
pansies

pant verb
pants
panting
panted

★ A **pail** is a bucket. ! **pale**.
☆ A **pain** is an unpleasant feeling caused by injury or disease. ! **pane**.
○ A **pair** is a set of two. ! **pear**.
✳ **Pale** means 'almost white'. ! **pail**
✴ A **pane** is a piece of glass in a window. ! **pain**.

panther noun
panthers
panties plural noun
pantomime noun
pantomimes
pantry noun
pantries
pants plural noun
paper noun
papers
paper verb
papers
papering
papered
paperback noun
paperbacks
papier mâché
papyrus noun
papyri
parable noun
parables
parachute noun
parachutes
parachutist
parade noun
parades
parade verb
parades
parading
paraded
paradise
paradox noun
paradoxes
paradoxical
adjective
paradoxically
paraffin
paragraph noun
paragraphs
parallel

parallelogram noun
parallelograms
paralyse verb
paralyses
paralysing
paralysed
paralysis noun
paralyses
paralytic adjective
paralytically
parapet noun
parapets
paraphernalia
paraphrase verb
paraphrases
paraphrasing
paraphrased
parasite noun
parasites
parasitic adjective
parasitically
parasol noun
parasols
paratrooper
paratroops plural
noun
parcel noun
parcels
parched
parchment
pardon verb
pardons
pardoning
pardoned
pardon noun
pardons
pardonable
parent noun
parents
parentage

parental
parenthood
parenthesis noun
parentheses
parish noun
parishes
parishioner noun
parishioners
park noun
parks
park verb
parks
parking
parked
parka noun
parkas
parliament noun
parliaments
parliamentary
parody noun
parodies
parole
parrot noun
parrots
parsley
parsnip noun
parsnips
parson noun
parsons
parsonage noun
parsonages
part noun
parts
part verb
parts
parting
parted
partial adjective
partially
partiality

participant *noun*
participants
participate *verb*
participates
participating
participated
participation
participle *noun*
participles
particle *noun*
particles
particular *adjective*
particularly
particulars *plural noun*
parting *noun*
partings
partition *noun*
partitions
partly
partner *noun*
partners
partnership
partridge *noun*
partridges
part-time *adjective*
party *noun*
parties
pass *verb*
passes
passing
passed
pass *noun*
passes
passable
passage *noun*
passages
passageway *noun*
passageways
★ **passed** see pass

passenger *noun*
passengers
passer-by *noun*
passers-by
passion *noun*
passions
passionate *adjective*
passionately
passive *adjective*
passively
Passover
passport *noun*
passports
password *noun*
passwords
☆ **past** *noun, adjective, and preposition*
pasta *noun*
pastas
paste *noun*
pastes
paste *verb*
pastes
pasting
pasted
pastel *noun*
pastels
pasteurization
pasteurize *verb*
pasteurizes
pasteurizing
pasteurized
pastille *noun*
pastilles
pastime *noun*
pastimes
pastoral
pastry *noun*
pastries

pasture *noun*
pastures
pasty *noun*
pasties
pasty *adjective*
pastier
pastiest
pat *verb*
pats
patting
patted
pat *noun*
pats
patch *noun*
patches
patch *verb*
patches
patching
patched
patchwork
patchy *adjective*
patchier
patchiest
patent *adjective*
patently
patent *verb*
patents
patenting
patented
patent *noun*
patents
paternal *adjective*
paternally
path *noun*
paths
pathetic *adjective*
pathetically
patience
patient *adjective*
patiently

★ You use passed in e.g. We *passed the house.* ! past.
☆ You use past in e.g. We *went past the house.* ! passed.

patient noun
patients
patio noun
patios
patriot noun
patriots
patriotic adjective
patriotically
patriotism
patrol verb
patrols
patrolling
patrolled
patrol noun
patrols
patron noun
patrons
patronage
patronize verb
patronizes
patronizing
patronized
patter verb
patters
pattering
pattered
patter noun
patters
pattern noun
patterns
pause verb
pauses
pausing
paused
pause noun
pauses
pave verb
paves
paving
paved
pavement noun
pavements

pavilion noun
pavilions
paw noun
paws
paw verb
paws
pawing
pawed
pawn noun
pawns
pawn verb
pawns
pawning
pawned
pawnbroker noun
pawnbrokers
pay verb
pays
paying
paid
pay noun
payment noun
payments
pea noun
peas
★ **peace**
peaceful adjective
peacefully
peach noun
peaches
peacock noun
peacocks
☆ **peak** noun
peaks
⊙ **peak** verb
peaks
peaking
peaked
peaked

✳ **peal** verb
peals
pealing
pealed
✴ **peal** noun
peals
peanut noun
peanuts
✳ **pear** noun
pears
pearl noun
pearls
pearly adjective
pearlier
pearliest
peasant noun
peasants
peasantry
peat
pebble noun
pebbles
pebbly adjective
pebblier
pebbliest
peck verb
pecks
pecking
pecked
peck noun
pecks
peckish
peculiar adjective
peculiarly
peculiarity noun
peculiarities
pedal noun
pedals
pedal verb
pedals
pedalling
pedalled

. . . .

★ **Peace** is a time when there is no war. ! **piece**.
☆ A **peak** is the top of something. ! **peek**.
⊙ To **peak** is to reach the highest point. ! **peek**.
✳ To **peal** is to make a ringing sound of bells. ! **peel**.
✴ A **peal** is a ringing of bells. ! **peel**.
✳ A **pear** is a fruit. ! **pair**.

★ **peddle** verb
peddles
peddling
peddled
pedestal noun
pedestals
pedestrian noun
pedestrians
pedestrian adjective
pedigree noun
pedigrees
pedlar noun
pedlars
☆ **peek** verb
peeks
peeking
peeked
○ **peel** noun
peels
✳ **peel** verb
peels
peeling
peeled
peep verb
peeps
peeping
peeped
peep noun
peeps
✳ **peer** verb
peers
peering
peered
peer noun
peers
peerless
peewit noun
peewits
peg noun
pegs

peg verb
pegs
pegging
pegged
Pekinese noun
Pekinese
pelican noun
pelicans
pellet noun
pellets
pelt verb
pelts
pelting
pelted
pelt noun
pelts
pen noun
pens
penalize verb
penalizes
penalizing
penalized
penalty noun
penalties
pence see **penny**
pencil noun
pencils
pencil verb
pencils
pencilling
pencilled
pendant noun
pendants
pendulum noun
pendulums
penetrate verb
penetrates
penetrating
penetrated
penetration
penfriend noun
penfriends

penguin noun
penguins
penicillin
peninsula noun
peninsulas
peninsular
penis noun
penises
penitence
penitent
penknife noun
penknives
pennant noun
pennants
penniless
penny noun
pennies or pence
pension noun
pensions
pensioner noun
pensioners
pentagon noun
pentagons
pentathlon noun
pentathlons
peony noun
peonies
people plural noun
people noun
peoples
pepper noun
peppers
peppermint noun
peppermints
peppery
perceive verb
perceives
perceiving
perceived
per cent

· ·

★ To **peddle** is to sell things on the street. ! **pedal**
☆ To **peek** is to look secretly at something. ! **peak**
○ **Peel** is the skin of fruit and vegetables. ! **peal**
✳ To **peel** something is to take the skin off it. ! **peal**
✳ To **peer** is to look closely at something. ! **pier**.

percentage *noun*
  percentages
perceptible *adjective*
  perceptibly
perception *noun*
  perceptions
perceptive *adjective*
  perceptively
perch *verb*
  perches
  perching
  perched
perch *noun*
  perch
percolator *noun*
  percolators
percussion
percussive
perennial *adjective*
  perennially
perennial *noun*
  perennials
perfect *adjective*
  perfectly
perfect *verb*
  perfects
  perfecting
  perfected
perfection
perforate *verb*
  perforates
  perforating
  perforated
perforation *noun*
  perforations
perform *verb*
  performs
  performing
  performed
performance *noun*
  performances

performer *noun*
  performers
perfume *noun*
  perfumes
perhaps
peril *noun*
  perils
perilous *adjective*
  perilously
perimeter *noun*
  perimeters
period *noun*
  periods
periodic *adjective*
  periodically
periodical *noun*
  periodicals
periscope *noun*
  periscopes
perish *verb*
  perishes
  perishing
  perished
perishable
perm *noun*
  perms
perm *verb*
  perms
  perming
  permed
permanence
permanent *adjective*
  permanently
permissible
permission
permissive *adjective*
  permissively
permissiveness
permit *verb*
  permits
  permitting
  permitted

permit *noun*
  permits
perpendicular
perpetual
  adjective
  perpetually
perpetuate *verb*
  perpetuates
  perpetuating
  perpetuated
perplex *verb*
  perplexes
  perplexing
  perplexed
perplexity
persecute *verb*
  persecutes
  persecuting
  persecuted
persecution *noun*
  persecutions
persecutor *noun*
  persecutors
perseverance
persevere *verb*
  perseveres
  persevering
  persevered
persist *verb*
  persists
  persisting
  persisted
persistence
persistent *adjective*
  persistently
★ person *noun*
  persons *or* people
personal *adjective*
  personally
personality *noun*
  personalities

★ The normal plural is **people**: *three people came.* **Persons** is formal, e.g. in official reports.

personnel *plural noun*

perspective *noun*
perspectives

perspiration

perspire *verb*
perspires
perspiring
perspired

persuade *verb*
persuades
persuading
persuaded

persuasion

persuasive *adjective*
persuasively

perverse *adjective*
perversely

perversion *noun*
perversions

perversity

pervert *verb*
perverts
perverting
perverted

pervert *noun*
perverts

★ **Pesach**

pessimism

pessimist *noun*
pessimists

pessimistic *adjective*
pessimistically

pest *noun*
pests

pester *verb*
pesters
pestering
pestered

pesticide *noun*
pesticides

pestle *noun*
pestles

pet *noun*
pets

petal *noun*
petals

petition *noun*
petitions

petrify *verb*
petrifies
petrifying
petrified

petrochemical *noun*
petrochemicals

petrol

petroleum

petticoat *noun*
petticoats

pettiness

petty *adjective*
pettier
pettiest
pettily

pew *noun*
pews

pewter

pharmacy *noun*
pharmacies

phase *noun*
phases

phase *verb*
phases
phasing
phased

pheasant *noun*
pheasants

phenomenal *adjective*
phenomenally

phenomenon *noun*
phenomena

philatelist *noun*
philatelists

philately

philosopher *noun*
philosophers

philosophical *adjective*
philosophically

philosophy *noun*
philosophies

phobia *noun*
phobias

-phobia
-phobia makes words meaning 'a strong fear or dislike', e.g. xenophobia (= a dislike of strangers'). It comes from a Greek word and is only used with other Greek or Latin words.

phoenix *noun*
phoenixes

phone *noun*
phones

phone *verb*
phones
phoning
phoned

-phone
-phone makes words to do with sound, e.g. telephone, saxophone. You can sometimes make adjectives by using *-phonic*, e.g. telephonic, and nouns by using *-phony*, e.g. telephony.

★ The Hebrew name for Passover.

phonecard noun
  phonecards
phone-in noun
  phone-ins
phosphorescence
phosphorescent
phosphoric
phosphorus
photo noun
  photos

> **photo-**
>
> *photo-* makes words to do with light, e.g. **photograph**, **photocopy**. It is also used in more technical words such as **photochemistry** (= the chemistry of light) and as a separate word in **photo** (= photograph) and **photo finish** (= close finish to a race).

photocopier noun
  photocopiers
photocopy noun
  photocopies
photocopy verb
  photocopies
  photocopying
  photocopied
photoelectric
photograph noun
  photographs
photograph verb
  photographs
  photographing
  photographed
photographer noun
  photographers

photographic adjective
  photographically
photography
phrase noun
  phrases
phrase verb
  phrases
  phrasing
  phrased
physical adjective
  physically
physician noun
  physicians
physicist noun
  physicists
physics
physiological adjective
  physiologically
physiologist noun
  physiologists
physiology
★ **pi**
pianist noun
  pianists
piano noun
  pianos
piccolo noun
  piccolos
pick verb
  picks
  picking
  picked
pick noun
  picks
pickaxe noun
  pickaxes
picket noun
  pickets

picket verb
  pickets
  picketing
  picketed
pickle noun
  pickles
pickle verb
  pickles
  pickling
  pickled
pickpocket noun
  pickpockets
pick-up noun
  pick-ups
picnic noun
  picnics
picnic verb
  picnics
  picnicking
  picnicked
picnicker noun
  picnickers
pictogram noun
  pictograms
pictorial adjective
  pictorially
picture noun
  pictures
picture verb
  pictures
  picturing
  pictured
picturesque
☆ **pie** noun
  pies
✪ **piece** noun
  pieces
piece verb
  pieces
  piecing
  pieced

- -

★ **Pi** is a Greek letter, used in mathematics. ! **pie.**
☆ A **pie** is a food with pastry. ! **pi.**
✪ You use **piece** in e.g. *a piece of cake.* ! **peace.**

piecemeal
pie chart *noun*
  pie charts
★ **pier** *noun*
  piers
pierce *verb*
  pierces
  piercing
  pierced
pig *noun*
  pigs
pigeon *noun*
  pigeons
pigeon-hole *noun*
  pigeon-holes
piggy *noun*
  piggies
piggyback *noun*
  piggybacks
piglet *noun*
  piglets
pigment *noun*
  pigments
pigmy *noun*
  use **pygmy**
pigsty *noun*
  pigsties
pigtail *noun*
  pigtails
pike *noun*
  pikes
pilchard *noun*
  pilchards
pile *noun*
  piles
pile *verb*
  piles
  piling
  piled

pilfer *verb*
  pilfers
  pilfering
  pilfered
pilgrim *noun*
  pilgrims
pilgrimage *noun*
  pilgrimages
pill *noun*
  pills
pillage *verb*
  pillages
  pillaging
  pillaged
pillar *noun*
  pillars
pillion *noun*
  pillions
pillow *noun*
  pillows
pillowcase *noun*
  pillowcases
pilot *noun*
  pilots
pilot *verb*
  pilots
  piloting
  piloted
pimple *noun*
  pimples
pimply *adjective*
  pimplier
  pimpliest
pin *noun*
  pins
pin *verb*
  pins
  pinning
  pinned
pinafore *noun*
  pinafores

pincer *noun*
  pincers
pinch *verb*
  pinches
  pinching
  pinched
pinch *noun*
  pinches
pincushion *noun*
  pincushions
pine *noun*
  pines
pine *verb*
  pines
  pining
  pined
pineapple *noun*
  pineapples
ping-pong
pink *adjective*
  pinker
  pinkest
pink *noun*
  pinks
pint *noun*
  pints
pioneer *noun*
  pioneers
pious *adjective*
  piously
pip *noun*
  pips
pipe *noun*
  pipes
pipe *verb*
  pipes
  piping
  piped
pipeline *noun*
  pipelines

★ A **pier** is a long building on stilts going into the sea. **! peer.**

piper noun
pipers
piracy
pirate noun
pirates
★ **pistil** noun
pistils
★ **pistol** noun
pistols
piston noun
pistons
pit noun
pits
pit verb
pits
pitting
pitted
pitch noun
pitches
pitch verb
pitches
pitching
pitched
pitch-black
pitcher noun
pitchers
pitchfork noun
pitchforks
pitfall noun
pitfalls
pitiful adjective
pitifully
pitiless adjective
pitilessly
pity verb
pities
pitying
pitied
pity noun

pivot noun
pivots
pivot verb
pivots
pivoting
pivoted
pixie noun
pixies
pizza noun
pizzas
pizzicato
placard noun
placards
☆ **place** noun
places
place verb
places
placing
placed
placid adjective
placidly
plague noun
plagues
plague verb
plagues
plaguing
plagued
○ **plaice** noun
plaice
plaid noun
plaids
✳ **plain** adjective
plainer
plainest
plainly
plain noun
plains
plain clothes
plainness

plaintiff noun
plaintiffs
plaintive
plaintively
plait noun
plaits
plait verb
plaits
plaiting
plaited
plan noun
plans
plan verb
plans
planning
planned
✳ **plane** noun
planes
✳ **plane** verb
planes
planing
planed
planet noun
planets
planetary
plank noun
planks
plankton
planner noun
planners
plant noun
plants
plant verb
plants
planting
planted
plantation noun
plantations
planter noun
planters

- -

★ A **pistil** is a part of a flower and a **pistol** is a gun.
☆ You use **place** in e.g. *a place in the country*. ! **plaice**.
○ A **plaice** is a fish. ! **place**.
✳ **Plain** means 'not pretty or decorated'. ! **plane**.
✳ A **plane** is an aeroplane, a level surface, a tool, or a tree. ! **plain**.
✳ To **plane** wood is to make it smooth with a tool. ! **plain**.

plaque noun
  plaques
plasma
plaster noun
  plasters
plaster verb
  plasters
  plastering
  plastered
plasterer noun
  plasterers
plaster of Paris
plastic adjective and
  noun
  plastics
Plasticine
plate noun
  plates
plate verb
  plates
  plating
  plated
plateau noun
  plateaux
plateful noun
  platefuls
platform noun
  platforms
platinum
platoon noun
  platoons
platypus noun
  platypuses
play verb
  plays
  playing
  played
play noun
  plays
playback noun
  playbacks

player noun
  players
playful adjective
  playfully
playfulness
playground noun
  playgrounds
playgroup noun
  playgroups
playmate noun
  playmates
play-off noun
  play-offs
playtime noun
  playtimes
playwright noun
  playwrights
plea noun
  pleas
plead verb
  pleads
  pleading
  pleaded
pleasant adjective
  pleasanter
  pleasantest
  pleasantly
please verb
  pleases
  pleasing
  pleased
pleasurable
  adjective
  pleasurably
pleasure noun
  pleasures
pleat noun
  pleats
pleated

pledge verb
  pledges
  pledging
  pledged
pledge noun
  pledges
plentiful adjective
  plentifully
plenty
pliable
pliers plural noun
plight noun
  plights
plod verb
  plods
  plodding
  plodded
plodder noun
  plodders
plop verb
  plops
  plopping
  plopped
plop noun
  plops
plot noun
  plots
plot verb
  plots
  plotting
  plotted
plotter noun
  plotters
plough noun
  ploughs
plough verb
  ploughs
  ploughing
  ploughed
ploughman noun
  ploughmen

plover noun
  plovers
pluck verb
  plucks
  plucking
  plucked
pluck noun
plucky adjective
  pluckier
  pluckiest
  pluckily
plug noun
  plugs
plug verb
  plugs
  plugging
  plugged
★ **plum** noun
  plums
plumage
☆ **plumb** verb
  plumbs
  plumbing
  plumbed
plumber noun
  plumbers
plumbing
plume noun
  plumes
plumed
plump adjective
  plumper
  plumpest
plump verb
  plumps
  plumping
  plumped
plunder verb
  plunders
  plundering
  plundered

plunder noun
plunderer noun
  plunderers
plunge verb
  plunges
  plunging
  plunged
plunge noun
  plunges
plural adjective and
  noun
  plurals
plus preposition
plus noun
  pluses
plutonium
plywood
pneumatic
pneumonia
poach verb
  poaches
  poaching
  poached
poacher noun
  poachers
pocket noun
  pockets
pocket verb
  pockets
  pocketing
  pocketed
pocketful noun
  pocketfuls
pod noun
  pods
podgy adjective
  podgier
  podgiest
poem noun
  poems

poet noun
  poets
poetic adjective
  poetically
poetry
point noun
  points
point verb
  points
  pointing
  pointed
point-blank adjective
pointed adjective
  pointedly
pointer noun
  pointers
pointless adjective
  pointlessly
poise noun
poise verb
  poises
  poising
  poised
poison noun
  poisons
poison verb
  poisons
  poisoning
  poisoned
poisoner noun
  poisoners
poisonous adjective
  poisonously
poke verb
  pokes
  poking
  poked
poke noun
  pokes
poker noun
  pokers

- -

★ A **plum** is a fruit. **! plumb**.
☆ To **plumb** water is to see how deep it is. **! plum**.

polar
Polaroid
★ pole noun
   poles
police plural noun
policeman noun
   policemen
police officer noun
   police officers
policewoman noun
   policewomen
policy noun
   policies
polio
poliomyelitis
polish verb
   polishes
   polishing
   polished
polish noun
   polishes
polished
polite adjective
   politer
   politest
   politely
politeness
political adjective
   politically
politician noun
   politicians
politics
polka noun
   polkas
☆ poll noun
   polls
pollen
pollute verb
   pollutes
   polluting
   polluted

pollution
polo
polo neck noun
   polo necks
poltergeist noun
   poltergeists
polygon noun
   polygons
polystyrene
polythene
pomp
pomposity
pompous adjective
   pompously
pond noun
   ponds
ponder verb
   ponders
   pondering
   pondered
ponderous adjective
   ponderously
pony noun
   ponies
ponytail noun
   ponytails
pony-trekking
poodle noun
   poodles
pool noun
   pools
pool verb
   pools
   pooling
   pooled
poor adjective
   poorer
   poorest
   poorly

poorly adjective and
   adverb
pop verb
   pops
   popping
   popped
pop noun
   pops
popcorn
Pope noun
   Popes
poplar noun
   poplars
poppadom noun
   poppadoms
poppy noun
   poppies
popular adjective
   popularly
popularity
popularize verb
   popularizes
   popularizing
   popularized
populated
population noun
   populations
populous
porcelain
porch noun
   porches
porcupine noun
   porcupines
pore noun
   pores
○ pore verb
   pores
   poring
   pored
pork

. . . .

★ A **pole** is a long thin stick. ! **poll**.
☆ A **poll** is a vote in an election. ! **pole**.
○ To **pore** over something is to study it closely. ! **pour**.

pornographic
pornography
porosity
porous
porpoise *noun*
  porpoises
porridge
port *noun*
  ports
portable
portcullis *noun*
  portcullises
porter *noun*
  porters
porthole *noun*
  portholes
portion *noun*
  portions
portliness
portly *adjective*
  portlier
  portliest
portrait *noun*
  portraits
portray *verb*
  portrays
  portraying
  portrayed
portrayal *noun*
  portrayals
pose *verb*
  poses
  posing
  posed
pose *noun*
  poses
poser *noun*
  posers
posh *adjective*
  posher
  poshest

position *noun*
  positions
positive *adjective*
  positively
positive *noun*
  positives
posse *noun*
  posses
possess *verb*
  possesses
  possessing
  possessed
possession *noun*
  possessions
possessive *adjective*
  possessively
possessor *noun*
  possessors
possibility *noun*
  possibilities
possible *adjective*
  possibly
post *verb*
  posts
  posting
  posted
post *noun*
  posts
postage
postal
postbox *noun*
  postboxes
postcard *noun*
  postcards
postcode *noun*
  postcodes
poster *noun*
  posters
postman *noun*
  postmen

postmark *noun*
  postmarks
post-mortem *noun*
  post-mortems
postpone *verb*
  postpones
  postponing
  postponed
postponement *noun*
  postponements
postscript *noun*
  postscripts
posture *noun*
  postures
posy *noun*
  posies
pot *noun*
  pots
pot *verb*
  pots
  potting
  potted
potassium
potato *noun*
  potatoes
potency
potent *adjective*
  potently
potential *adjective*
  potentially
potential *noun*
  potentials
pothole *noun*
  potholes
potholer *noun*
  potholer
potholing
potion *noun*
  potions
potter *noun*
  potters

potter verb
  potters
  pottering
  pottered
pottery noun
  potteries
potty adjective
  pottier
  pottiest
  pottily
potty noun
  potties
pouch noun
  pouches
poultry
pounce verb
  pounces
  pouncing
  pounced
pound noun
  pounds
pound verb
  pounds
  pounding
  pounded
★ **pour** verb
  pours
  pouring
  poured
pout verb
  pouts
  pouting
  pouted
poverty
powder noun
  powders
powder verb
  powders
  powdering
  powdered
powdery

power noun
  powers
powered
powerful adjective
  powerfully
powerhouse noun
  powerhouses
powerless
practicable
practical adjective
  practically
practice noun
  practices
practise verb
  practises
  practising
  practised
prairie noun
  prairies
praise verb
  praises
  praising
  praised
praise noun
  praises
pram noun
  prams
prance verb
  prances
  prancing
  pranced
prank noun
  pranks
prawn noun
  prawns
☆ **pray** verb
  prays
  praying
  prayed
prayer noun
  prayers

pre-
pre- makes words meaning 'before', e.g. pre-date (= to exist before something else), prefabricated (= made in advance). Many are spelt joined up, but not all.

preach verb
  preaches
  preaching
  preached
preacher noun
  preachers
precarious adjective
  precariously
precaution noun
  precautions
precede verb
  precedes
  preceding
  preceded
precedence
precedent noun
  precedents
precinct noun
  precincts
precious adjective
  preciously
precipice noun
  precipices
précis noun
  précis
precise adjective
  precisely
precision
predator noun
  predators
predatory

★ To pour a liquid is to tip it from a jug etc. ! pore.
☆ To pray is to say prayers. ! prey.

predecessor noun
predecessors
predict verb
predicts
predicting
predicted
predictable adjective
predictably
prediction noun
predictions
predominance
predominant
adjective
predominantly
predominate verb
predominates
predominating
predominated
preface noun
prefaces
prefect noun
prefects
prefer verb
prefers
preferring
preferred
preferable adjective
preferably
preference noun
preferences
prefix noun
prefixes
pregnancy noun
pregnancies
pregnant
prehistoric
prehistory
prejudice noun
prejudices
prejudiced

preliminary
adjective and noun
preliminaries
prelude noun
preludes
premier noun
premiers
première noun
premières
premises plural noun
premium noun
premiums
Premium Bond noun
Premium Bonds
preoccupation noun
preoccupations
preoccupied
prep
preparation noun
preparations
preparatory
prepare verb
prepares
preparing
prepared
preposition noun
prepositions
prescribe verb
prescribes
prescribing
prescribed
prescription noun
prescriptions
presence
present adjective
presently
present noun
presents
present verb
presents
presenting
presented

presentation noun
presentations
presenter noun
presenters
preservation
preservative noun
preservatives
preserve verb
preserves
preserving
preserved
preside verb
presides
presiding
presided
presidency noun
presidencies
president noun
presidents
presidential
adjective
presidentially
press verb
presses
pressing
pressed
press noun
presses
press-up noun
press-ups
pressure noun
pressures
pressurize verb
pressurizes
pressurizing
pressurized
prestige
prestigious adjective
prestigiously
presumably

presume verb
presumes
presuming
presumed
presumption noun
presumptions
presumptuous adjective
presumptuously
pretence noun
pretences
pretend verb
pretends
pretending
pretended
pretender noun
pretenders
prettiness
pretty adjective and adverb
prettier
prettiest
prettily
prevail verb
prevails
prevailing
prevailed
prevalent
prevent verb
prevents
preventing
prevented
prevention
preventive
preview noun
previews
previous adjective
previously
★ **prey** verb
preys
preying
preyed
prey noun
price noun
prices
price verb
prices
pricing
priced
priceless
prick verb
pricks
pricking
pricked
prick noun
pricks
prickle noun
prickles
prickly adjective
pricklier
prickliest
pride noun
prides
priest noun
priests
priestess noun
priestesses
priesthood
prig noun
prigs
priggish adjective
priggishly
prim adjective
primmer
primmest
primly
primness
primary adjective
primarily
primate noun
primates
prime adjective

prime verb
primes
priming
primed
prime noun
primes
prime minister noun
prime ministers
primer noun
primers
primeval
primitive adjective
primitively
primrose noun
primroses
prince noun
princes
princely
princess noun
princesses
☆ **principal** adjective
principally
❍ **principal** noun
principals
✻ **principle** noun
principles
print verb
prints
printing
printed
print noun
prints
printer noun
printers
printout noun
printouts
priority noun
priorities

★ To **prey** on animals is to hunt and kill them. ! **pray**.
☆ **Principal** means 'chief' or 'main'. ! **principle**.
❍ A **principal** is a head of a college. ! **principle**.
✻ A **principle** is a rule or belief. ! **principal**.

★ **prise** verb
prises
prising
prised
prism noun
prisms
prison noun
prisons
prisoner noun
prisoners
privacy
private adjective
privately
private noun
privates
privatization
privatize verb
privatizes
privatizing
privatized
privet
privilege noun
privileges
privileged
prize noun
prizes
☆ **prize** verb
prizes
prizing
prized
pro noun
pros

pro-
pro- makes words meaning 'in favour of', e.g. *pro-choice*. In this type of word you use a hyphen.

probability noun
probabilities

probable adjective
probably
probation
probationary
probe verb
probes
probing
probed
probe noun
probes
problem noun
problems
procedure noun
procedures
proceed verb
proceeds
proceeding
proceeded
proceedings plural noun
proceeds plural noun
process noun
processes
process verb
processes
processing
processed
procession noun
processions
proclaim verb
proclaims
proclaiming
proclaimed
proclamation noun
proclamations
prod verb
prods
prodding
prodded
prodigal adjective
prodigally

produce verb
produces
producing
produced
produce noun
producer noun
producers
product noun
products
production noun
productions
productive adjective
productively
productivity
profession noun
professions
professional adjective
professionally
professional noun
professionals
professor noun
professors
proficiency
proficient adjective
proficiently
profile noun
profiles
○ **profit** noun
profits
profit verb
profits
profiting
profited
profitable adjective
profitably
profound adjective
profoundly
profundity
profuse adjective
profusely

★ To **prise** something is to open it. ! **prize**.
☆ To **prize** something is to value it highly. ! **prise**.
○ A **profit** is extra money made by selling something. ! **prophet**.

profusion
* **program** noun
  programs
program verb
  programs
  programming
  programmed
* **programme** noun
  programmes
progress noun
progress verb
  progresses
  progressing
  progressed
progression
progressive adjective
  progressively
prohibit verb
  prohibits
  prohibiting
  prohibited
prohibition noun
  prohibitions
project noun
  projects
project verb
  projects
  projecting
  projected
projection noun
  projections
projectionist noun
  projectionists
projector noun
  projectors
prologue noun
  prologues
prolong verb
  prolongs
  prolonging
  prolonged

promenade noun
  promenades
prominence
prominent adjective
  prominently
promise verb
  promises
  promising
  promised
promise noun
  promises
promontory noun
  promontories
promote verb
  promotes
  promoting
  promoted
promoter noun
  promoter
promotion noun
  promotions
prompt adjective
  prompter
  promptest
  promptly
prompt verb
  prompts
  prompting
  prompted
prompter noun
  prompters
promptness
prone
prong noun
  prongs
pronoun noun
  pronouns
pronounce verb
  pronounces
  pronouncing
  pronounced

pronouncement
  noun
  pronouncements
pronunciation noun
  pronunciations
proof adjective and
  noun
  proofs
prop verb
  props
  propping
  propped
prop noun
  props
propaganda
propel verb
  propels
  propelling
  propelled
propellant noun
  propellants
propeller noun
  propellers
proper adjective
  properly
property noun
  properties
prophecy noun
  prophecies
prophesy verb
  prophesies
  prophesying
  prophesied
☆ **prophet** noun
  prophets
prophetic adjective
  prophetically
proportion noun
  proportions

* You use **program** when you are talking about computers. In other meanings
    you use **programme**.
☆ A **prophet** is someone who makes predictions about the future. ! **profit**.

proportional
adjective
proportionally
proportionate
adjective
proportionately
propose verb
proposes
proposing
proposed
proposal noun
proposals
proprietor noun
proprietors
propulsion
prose
prosecute verb
prosecutes
prosecuting
prosecuted
prosecution noun
prosecutions
prosecutor noun
prosecutors
prospect noun
prospects
prospect verb
prospects
prospecting
prospected
prospector noun
prospectors
prosper verb
prospers
prospering
prospered
prosperity
prosperous adjective
prosperously
prostitute noun
prostitutes

protect verb
protects
protecting
protected
protection
protective adjective
protectively
protector noun
protectors
protein noun
proteins
protest verb
protests
protesting
protested
protest noun
protests
protester noun
protesters
Protestant noun
Protestants
proton noun
protons
protoplasm
prototype noun
prototypes
protractor noun
protractors
protrude verb
protrudes
protruding
protruded
protrusion noun
protrusions
proud adjective
prouder
proudest
proudly
prove verb
proves
proving
proved

proverb noun
proverbs
proverbial adjective
proverbially
provide verb
provides
providing
provided
province noun
provinces
provincial
provision noun
provisions
provisional adjective
provisionally
provocative
adjective
provocatively
provoke verb
provokes
provoking
provoked
provocation noun
provocations
prow noun
prows
prowl verb
prowls
prowling
prowled
prowler noun
prowlers
prudence
prudent adjective
prudently
prune noun
prunes
prune verb
prunes
pruning
pruned

pry *verb*
pries
prying
pried
psalm *noun*
psalms
pseudonym *noun*
pseudonyms
psychiatric
psychiatrist *noun*
psychiatrists
psychiatry
psychic
psychological
adjective
psychologically
psychologist *noun*
psychologists
psychology
pub *noun*
pubs
puberty
public *adjective* and
noun
publicly
publication *noun*
publications
publicity
publicize *verb*
publicizes
publicizing
publicized
publish *verb*
publishes
publishing
published
publisher *noun*
publishers
puck *noun*
pucks

pucker *verb*
puckers
puckering
puckered
pudding *noun*
puddings
puddle *noun*
puddles
puff *verb*
puffs
puffing
puffed
puff *noun*
puffs
puffin *noun*
puffins
pull *verb*
pulls
pulling
pulled
pull *noun*
pulls
pulley *noun*
pulleys
pullover *noun*
pullovers
pulp *noun*
pulps
pulp *verb*
pulps
pulping
pulped
pulpit *noun*
pulpits
pulse *noun*
pulses
pulverize *verb*
pulverizes
pulverizing
pulverized
puma *noun*
pumas

pumice
pump *verb*
pumps
pumping
pumped
pump *noun*
pumps
pumpkin *noun*
pumpkins
pun *noun*
puns
pun *verb*
puns
punning
punned
punch *verb*
punches
punching
punched
punch *noun*
punches
punch *noun*
punches
punchline *noun*
punchlines
punch-up *noun*
punch-ups
punctual *adjective*
punctually
punctuality
punctuate *verb*
punctuates
punctuating
punctuated
punctuation
puncture *noun*
punctures
punish *verb*
punishes
punishing
punished

punishment noun
 punishments
punk noun
 punks
punt noun
 punts
punt verb
 punts
 punting
 punted
puny adjective
 punier
 puniest
pup noun
 pups
pupa noun
 pupae
pupil noun
 pupils
puppet noun
 puppets
puppy noun
 puppies
purchase verb
 purchases
 purchasing
 purchased
purchase noun
 purchases
purchaser noun
 purchasers
purdah
pure adjective
 purer
 purest
 purely
purge verb
 purges
 purging
 purged
purge noun
 purges

purification
purifier noun
 purifiers
purify verb
 purifies
 purifying
 purified
★ **Puritan** noun
 Puritans
puritan noun
 puritans
puritanical adjective
 puritanically
purity
purple noun
purpose noun
 purposes
purposely
purr verb
 purrs
 purring
 purred
purse noun
 purses
pursue verb
 pursues
 pursuing
 pursued
pursuer noun
 pursuers
pursuit noun
 pursuits
☆ **pus** noun
push verb
 pushes
 pushing
 pushed
push noun
 pushes
pushchair noun
 pushchairs

○ **puss** or **pussy** noun
 pusses or pussies
✻ **put** verb
 puts
 putting
 put
✹ **putt** verb
 putts
 putting
 putted
putter noun
 putters
putty
puzzle verb
 puzzles
 puzzling
 puzzled
puzzle noun
 puzzles
pygmy noun
 pygmies
pyjamas
pylon noun
 pylons
pyramid noun
 pyramids
pyramidal
python noun
 pythons

Qq

quack verb
 quacks
 quacking
 quacked
quack noun
 quacks

★ You use a capital P when you are talking about people in history, and a small p when you mean anyone who is morally strict.
☆ **Pus** is yellow stuff produced in sore places on the body. ! puss.
○ **Puss** is a word for a cat. ! pus.
✻ To **put** something somewhere is to place it there. ! putt.
✹ To **putt** a ball is to tap it gently. ! put.

quad noun
  quads
quadrangle noun
  quadrangles
quadrant noun
  quadrants
quadrilateral noun
  quadrilaterals
quadruple adjective
  and noun
quadruple verb
  quadruples
  quadrupling
  quadrupled
quadruplet noun
  quadruplets
quail verb
  quails
  quailing
  quailed
quail noun
  quail or quails
quaint adjective
  quainter
  quaintest
  quaintly
quaintness noun
quake verb
  quakes
  quaking
  quaked
Quaker noun
  Quakers
qualification noun
  qualifications
qualify verb
  qualifies
  qualifying
  qualified
quality noun
  qualities

quantity noun
  quantities
quarantine
quarrel noun
  quarrels
quarrel verb
  quarrels
  quarrelling
  quarrelled
quarrelsome
quarry noun
  quarries
quart noun
  quarts
quarter noun
  quarters
quartet noun
  quartets
quartz
quaver verb
  quavers
  quavering
  quavered
quaver noun
  quavers
★ **quay** noun
  quays
queasy adjective
  queasier
  queasiest
queen noun
  queens
queer adjective
  queerer
  queerest
quench verb
  quenches
  quenching
  quenched
query verb
  queries
  querying

  queried
query noun
  queries
quest noun
  quests
question noun
  questions
question verb
  questions
  questioning
  questioned
questionable
  adjective
  questionably
questioner noun
  questioner
questionnaire noun
  questionnaires
☆ **queue** noun
  queues
queue verb
  queues
  queueing
  queued
quibble verb
  quibbles
  quibbling
  quibbled
quibble noun
  quibbles
quiche noun
  quiches
quick adjective
  quicker
  quickest
  quickly
quicken verb
  quickens
  quickening
  quickened

★ A **quay** is a place where ships tie up. ! key.
☆ A **queue** is a line of people waiting for something. ! cue.

quicksand noun
quicksands
quid noun
quid
quiet adjective
quieter
quietest
quietly
quieten verb
quietens
quietening
quietened
quill noun
quills
quilt noun
quilts
quintet noun
quintets
quit verb
quits
quitting
quitted
quit
quitter noun
quitters
quite
quiver verb
quivers
quivering
quivered
quiver noun
quivers
quiz noun
quizzes
quiz verb
quizzes
quizzing
quizzed
quoit noun
quoits
quota noun
quotas

quotation noun
quotations
quote verb
quotes
quoting
quoted
quotient noun
quotients

Rr

rabbi noun
rabbis
rabbit noun
rabbits
rabid
rabies
raccoon noun
raccoons
race noun
races
race verb
races
racing
raced
race noun
races
racecourse noun
racecourses
racer noun
racers
racial adjective
racially
racism
racist noun
racists
rack noun
racks

rack verb
racks
racking
racked
racket noun
rackets
radar
radial adjective
radially
radiance
radiant adjective
radiantly
radiate verb
radiates
radiating
radiated
radiation
radiator noun
radiators
radical adjective
radically
radical noun
radicals
radii see **radius**
radio noun
radios
radioactive
radioactivity
radish noun
radishes
radium
radius noun
radii
raffle noun
raffles
raffle verb
raffles
raffling
raffled

raft noun
  rafts
rafter noun
  rafters
rag noun
  rags
rage noun
  rages
rage verb
  rages
  raging
  raged
ragged
ragtime
raid noun
  raids
raid verb
  raids
  raiding
  raided
raider noun
  raiders
rail noun
  rails
railings plural noun
railway noun
  railways
rain verb
  rains
  raining
  rained
rain noun
  rains
rainbow noun
  rainbows
raincoat noun
  raincoats
raindrop noun
  raindrops
rainfall

rainforest noun
  rainforests
raise verb
  raises
  raising
  raised
raisin noun
  raisins
rake verb
  rakes
  raking
  raked
rake noun
  rakes
rally verb
  rallies
  rallying
  rallied
rally noun
  rallies
ram verb
  rams
  ramming
  rammed
ram noun
  rams
Ramadan
ramble noun
  rambles
ramble verb
  rambles
  rambling
  rambled
rambler noun
  ramblers
ramp noun
  ramps
rampage verb
  rampages
  rampaging
  rampaged

rampage noun
ran see **run**
ranch noun
  ranches
random
rang see **ring**
range noun
  ranges
range verb
  ranges
  ranging
  ranged
★ **ranger** noun
  rangers
rank noun
  ranks
rank verb
  ranks
  ranking
  ranked
ransack verb
  ransacks
  ransacking
  ransacked
ransom verb
  ransoms
  ransoming
  ransomed
ransom noun
  ransoms
☆ **rap** verb
  raps
  rapping
  rapped
rap noun
  raps
rapid adjective
  rapidly
rapidity
rapids plural noun

· ·

★ You use a capital R when you mean a senior Guide.
☆ To **rap** is to knock loudly. ! **wrap**.

rare *adjective*
rarer
rarest
rarely
rarity *noun*
rarities
rascal *noun*
rascals
rash *adjective*
rasher
rashest
rashly
rash *noun*
rashes
rasher *noun*
rashers
raspberry *noun*
raspberries
Rastafarian *noun*
Rastafarians
rat *noun*
rats
rate *noun*
rates
rate *verb*
rates
rating
rated
rather
ratio *noun*
ratios
ration *noun*
rations
ration *verb*
rations
rationing
rationed
rational *adjective*
rationally
rationalize *verb*
rationalizes
rationalizing
rationalized

rattle *verb*
rattles
rattling
rattled
rattle *noun*
rattles
rattlesnake *noun*
rattlesnakes
rave *verb*
raves
raving
raved
rave *noun*
raves
raven *noun*
ravens
ravenous *adjective*
ravenously
ravine *noun*
ravines
raw *adjective*
rawer
rawest
ray *noun*
rays
razor *noun*
razors

re-
re- makes words
meaning 'again', e.g.
reproduce. These
words are normally
spelt joined up, but a
few need a hyphen so
you don't confuse
them with other
words, e.g. **re-cover**
(= to put a new cover
on); **recover** has
another meaning. You
also need a hyphen in
words beginning with
e, e.g. **re-enter**.

reach *verb*
reaches
reaching
reached
reach *noun*
reaches
react *verb*
reacts
reacting
reacted
reaction *noun*
reactions
reactor *noun*
reactors
★ **read** *verb*
reads
reading
read
readable
reader *noun*
readers
readily
readiness
reading *noun*
readings
ready *adjective*
readier
readiest
☆ **real** *adjective*
realism
realist *noun*
realists
realistic *adjective*
realistically
reality *noun*
realities
realization
realize *verb*
realizes
realizing
realized

. . . .

★ To **read** is to look at something written or printed. **!** reed.
☆ **Real** means 'true' or 'existing'. **!** reel.

really
realm *noun*
 realms
reap *verb*
 reaps
 reaping
 reaped
reaper *noun*
 reapers
reappear *verb*
 reappears
 reappearing
 reappeared
reappearance *noun*
 reappearances
rear *adjective* and
 noun
 rears
rear *verb*
 rears
 rearing
 reared
rearrange *verb*
 rearranges
 rearranging
 rearranged
rearrangement
 noun
 rearrangements
reason *noun*
 reasons
reason *verb*
 reasons
 reasoning
 reasoned
reasonable *adjective*
 reasonably
reassurance *noun*
 reassurances
reassure *verb*
 reassures

 reassuring
 reassured
rebel *verb*
 rebels
 rebelling
 rebelled
rebel *noun*
 rebels
rebellion *noun*
 rebellions
rebellious *adjective*
 rebelliously
rebound *verb*
 rebounds
 rebounding
 rebounded
rebuild *verb*
 rebuilds
 rebuilding
 rebuilt
recall *verb*
 recalls
 recalling
 recalled
recap *verb*
 recaps
 recapping
 recapped
recapture *verb*
 recaptures
 recapturing
 recaptured
recede *verb*
 recedes
 receding
 receded
receipt *noun*
 receipts
receive *verb*
 receives
 receiving

 received
receiver *noun*
 receivers
recent *adjective*
 recently
receptacle *noun*
 receptacles
reception *noun*
 receptions
receptionist *noun*
 receptionists
recess *noun*
 recesses
recession *noun*
 recessions
recipe *noun*
 recipes
reciprocal *adjective*
 reciprocally
reciprocal *noun*
 reciprocals
recital *noun*
 recitals
recitation *noun*
 recitations
recite *verb*
 recites
 reciting
 recited
reckless *adjective*
 recklessly
recklessness
reckon *verb*
 reckons
 reckoning
 reckoned
reclaim *verb*
 reclaims
 reclaiming
 reclaimed

reclamation noun
reclamations
recline verb
reclines
reclining
reclined
recognition
recognizable
adjective
recognizably
recognize verb
recognizes
recognizing
recognized
recoil verb
recoils
recoiling
recoiled
recollect verb
recollects
recollecting
recollected
recollection noun
recollections
recommend verb
recommends
recommending
recommended
recommendation
noun
recommendations
reconcile verb
reconciles
reconciling
reconciled
reconciliation noun
reconciliations
reconstruction noun
reconstructions
record noun
records

record verb
records
recording
recorded
recorder noun
recorders
recover verb
recovers
recovering
recovered
recovery noun
recoveries
recreation noun
recreations
recreational
adjective
recreationally
recruit noun
recruits
recruit verb
recruits
recruiting
recruited
rectangle noun
rectangles
rectangular
recur verb
recurs
recurring
recurred
recurrence noun
recurrences
recycle verb
recycles
recycling
recycled
red adjective
redder
reddest
red noun
reds

redden verb
reddens
reddening
reddened
reddish
redeem verb
redeems
redeeming
redeemed
redeemer noun
redeemers
redemption noun
redemptions
redhead noun
redheads
reduce verb
reduces
reducing
reduced
reduction noun
reductions
redundancy noun
redundancies
redundant adjective
redundantly
★ **reed** noun
reeds
reedy
reef noun
reefs
reef knot noun
reef knots
reek verb
reeks
reeking
reeked
☆ **reel** noun
reels
reel verb
reels
reeling
reeled

- -

★ A **reed** is a plant or a thin strip. **! read.**
☆ A **reel** is a cylinder on which something is wound. **! real.**

refer verb
refers
referring
referred
referee noun
referees
referee verb
referees
refereeing
refereed
reference noun
references
referendum noun
referendums
refill verb
refills
refilling
refilled
refill noun
refills
refine verb
refines
refining
refined
refinement noun
refinements
refinery noun
refineries
reflect verb
reflects
reflecting
reflected
reflective adjective
reflectively
reflex noun
reflexes
reflexive adjective
reflexively
reform verb
reforms
reforming
reformed

reform noun
reforms
reformation noun
reformations
★ **Reformation**
reformer noun
reformers
refract verb
refracts
refracting
refracted
refraction
refrain verb
refrains
refraining
refrained
refrain noun
refrains
refresh verb
refreshes
refreshing
refreshed
refreshment noun
refreshments
refrigerate verb
refrigerates
refrigerating
refrigerated
refrigeration
refrigerator noun
refrigerators
refuel verb
refuels
refuelling
refuelled
refuge noun
refuges
refugee noun
refugees
refund verb
refunds

refunding
refunded
refund noun
refunds
refusal
refuse verb
refuses
refusing
refused
refuse
regain verb
regains
regaining
regained
regard verb
regards
regarding
regarded
regard noun
regards
regarding
preposition
regardless
regatta noun
regattas
reggae
regiment noun
regiments
regimental
region noun
regions
regional adjective
regionally
register noun
registers
register verb
registers
registering
registered
registration noun
registrations

★ You use a capital R when you mean the historical religious movement.

regret noun
  regrets
regret verb
  regrets
  regretting
  regretted
regretful adjective
  regretfully
regrettable adjective
  regrettably
regular adjective
  regularly
regularity
regulate verb
  regulates
  regulating
  regulated
regulation noun
  regulations
regulator noun
  regulators
rehearsal noun
  rehearsals
rehearse verb
  rehearses
  rehearsing
  rehearsed
★ **reign** verb
  reigns
  reigning
  reigned
reign noun
  reigns
☆ **rein** noun
  reins
reindeer noun
  reindeer
reinforce verb
  reinforces
  reinforcing
  reinforced

reinforcement noun
  reinforcements
reject verb
  rejects
  rejecting
  rejected
reject noun
  rejects
rejection noun
  rejections
rejoice verb
  rejoices
  rejoicing
  rejoiced
relate verb
  relates
  relating
  related
relation noun
  relations
relationship noun
  relationships
relative adjective
  relatively
relative noun
  relatives
relax verb
  relaxes
  relaxing
  relaxed
relaxation
relay verb
  relays
  relaying
  relayed
relay noun
  relays
release verb
  releases
  releasing
  released

release noun
  releases
relegate verb
  relegates
  relegating
  relegated
relegation
relent verb
  relents
  relenting
  relented
relentless adjective
  relentlessly
relevance
relevant adjective
  relevantly
reliability
reliable adjective
  reliably
reliance
reliant
relic noun
  relics
relief noun
  reliefs
relieve verb
  relieves
  relieving
  relieved
religion noun
  religions
religious adjective
  religiously
reluctance
reluctant adjective
  reluctantly
rely verb
  relies
  relying
  relied

. . . .

★ To **reign** is to rule as a king or queen. **! rein.**
☆ A **rein** is a strap used to guide a horse. **! reign.**

remain verb
  remains
  remaining
  remained
remainder noun
  remainders
remains
remark verb
  remarks
  remarking
  remarked
remark noun
  remarks
remarkable
  adjective
  remarkably
remedial adjective
  remedially
remedy noun
  remedies
remember verb
  remembers
  remembering
  remembered
remembrance
remind verb
  reminds
  reminding
  reminded
reminder noun
  reminders
reminisce verb
  reminisces
  reminiscing
  reminisced
reminiscence noun
  reminiscences
reminiscent
remnant noun
  remnants
remorse

remorseful adjective
  remorsefully
remorseless
  adjective
  remorselessly
remote adjective
  remoter
  remotest
  remotely
remoteness
removal noun
  removals
remove verb
  removes
  removing
  removed
★ **Renaissance**
render verb
  renders
  rendering
  rendered
rendezvous noun
  rendezvous
renew verb
  renews
  renewing
  renewed
renewable
renewal noun
  renewals
renown
renowned
rent noun
  rents
rent verb
  rents
  renting
  rented
repair verb
  repairs
  repairing
  repaired

repair noun
  repairs
repay verb
  repays
  repaying
  repaid
repayment noun
  repayments
repeat verb
  repeats
  repeating
  repeated
repeat noun
  repeats
repeatedly
repel verb
  repels
  repelling
  repelled
repellent
repent verb
  repents
  repenting
  repented
repentance
repentant
repetition noun
  repetitions
repetitive adjective
  repetitively
replace verb
  replaces
  replacing
  replaced
replacement noun
  replacements
replay noun
  replays
replica noun
  replicas

★ You use a capital R when you mean the historical period.

reply verb
replies
replying
replied
reply noun
replies
report verb
reports
reporting
reported
report noun
reports
reporter noun
reporters
repossess verb
repossesses
repossessing
repossessed
represent verb
represents
representing
represented
representation noun
representations
representative adjective and noun
representatives
repress verb
represses
repressing
repressed
repression noun
repressions
repressive adjective
repressively
reprieve verb
reprieves
reprieving
reprieved
reprieve noun
reprieves

reprimand verb
reprimands
reprimanding
reprimanded
reprisal noun
reprisals
reproach verb
reproaches
reproaching
reproached
reproduce verb
reproduces
reproducing
reproduced
reproduction noun
reproduction
reproductive adjective
reproductively
reptile noun
reptiles
republic noun
republics
republican adjective and noun
republicans
★ **Republican** adjective and noun
Republicans
repulsion
repulsive adjective
repulsively
reputation noun
reputations
request verb
requests
requesting
requested
request noun
requests

require verb
requires
requiring
required
requirement noun
requirements
reread verb
rereads
rereading
reread
rescue verb
rescues
rescuing
rescued
rescue noun
rescues
rescuer noun
rescuers
research noun
researches
researcher noun
researchers
resemblance noun
resemblances
resemble verb
resembles
resembling
resembled
resent verb
resents
resenting
resented
resentful adjective
resentfully
resentment
reservation noun
reservations
reserve verb
reserves
reserving
reserved

★ You use a capital R when you mean the political party in the USA.

reserve noun
reserves
reservoir noun
reservoirs
reshuffle noun
reshuffles
reside verb
resides
residing
resided
residence noun
residences
resident noun
residents
resign verb
resigns
resigning
resigned
resignation noun
resignations
resin noun
resins
resinous
resist verb
resists
resisting
resisted
resistance noun
resistances
resistant
resolute adjective
resolutely
resolution noun
resolutions
resolve verb
resolves
resolving
resolved
resort noun
resorts

resort verb
resorts
resorting
resorted
resound verb
resounds
resounding
resounded
resource noun
resources
respect verb
respects
respecting
respected
respect noun
respects
respectability
respectable
adjective
respectably
respectful adjective
respectfully
respective adjective
respectively
respiration
respirator noun
respirators
respiratory
respond verb
responds
responding
responded
response noun
responses
responsibility noun
responsibilities
responsible adjective
responsibly
rest verb
rests
resting
rested

rest noun
rests
restaurant noun
restaurants
restful adjective
restfully
restless adjective
restlessly
restlessness
restoration noun
restorations
restore verb
restores
restoring
restored
restrain verb
restrains
restraining
restrained
restraint noun
restraints
restrict verb
restricts
restricting
restricted
restriction noun
restrictions
restrictive adjective
restrictively
result verb
results
resulting
resulted
result noun
results
resume verb
resumes
resuming
resumed
resumption noun
resumptions

resuscitate *verb*
  resuscitates
  resuscitating
  resuscitated
retail *verb*
  retails
  retailing
  retailed
retail *noun*
retain *verb*
  retains
  retaining
  retained
retina *noun*
  retinas
retire *verb*
  retires
  retiring
  retired
retirement
retort *verb*
  retorts
  retorting
  retorted
retort *noun*
  retorts
retrace *verb*
  retraces
  retracing
  retraced
retreat *verb*
  retreats
  retreating
  retreated
retrievable
  adjective
  retrievably
retrieval *noun*
  retrievals

retrieve *verb*
  retrieves
  retrieving
  retrieved
retriever *noun*
  retrievers
return *verb*
  returns
  returning
  returned
return *noun*
  returns
reunion *noun*
  reunions
rev *verb*
  revs
  revving
  revved
rev *noun*
  revs
reveal *verb*
  reveals
  revealing
  revealed
revelation *noun*
  revelations
revenge
revenue *noun*
  revenues
revere *verb*
  reveres
  revering
  revered
reverence
★ **Reverend**
★ **reverent** *adjective*
  reverently
reversal *noun*
  reversals
reverse *verb*
  reverses

  reversing
  reversed
reverse *noun*
  reverses
reversible *adjective*
  reversibly
review *verb*
  reviews
  reviewing
  reviewed
☆ **review** *noun*
  reviews
reviewer *noun*
  reviewers
revise *verb*
  revises
  revising
  revised
revision *noun*
  revisions
revival *noun*
  revivals
revive *verb*
  revives
  reviving
  revived
revolt *verb*
  revolts
  revolting
  revolted
revolt *noun*
  revolts
revolution *noun*
  revolutions
revolutionary
  adjective and *noun*
  revolutionaries
revolutionize *verb*
  revolutionizes
  revolutionizing
  revolutionized

- -

★ You use **Reverend** as a title of a member of the clergy, and **reverent** as an
  ordinary word meaning 'showing respect'.
☆ A **review** is a piece of writing about a film, play, etc. ! **revue.**

revolve verb
  revolves
  revolving
  revolved
revolver noun
  revolvers
★ **revue** noun
  revues
reward verb
  rewards
  rewarding
  rewarded
reward noun
  rewards
rewind verb
  rewinds
  rewinding
  rewound
rewrite verb
  rewrites
  rewriting
  rewrote
  rewritten
rheumatic
rheumatism
rhinoceros noun
  rhinoceroses or
  rhinoceros
rhododendron noun
  rhododendrons
rhombus noun
  rhombuses
rhubarb
rhyme verb
  rhymes
  rhyming
  rhymed
rhyme noun
  rhymes
rhythm noun
  rhythms

rhythmic or
rhythmical adjective
  rhythmically
rib noun
  ribs
ribbon noun
  ribbons
rice
rich adjective
  richer
  richest
  richly
riches plural noun
richness
rick noun
  ricks
rickety
rickshaw noun
  rickshaws
ricochet verb
  ricochets
  ricocheting
  ricocheted
rid verb
  rids
  ridding
  rid
riddance
riddle noun
  riddles
ride verb
  rides
  riding
  rode
  ridden
ride noun
  rides
rider noun
  riders
ridge noun
  ridges

ridicule verb
  ridicules
  ridiculing
  ridiculed
ridiculous adjective
  ridiculously
rifle noun
  rifles
rift noun
  rifts
rig verb
  rigs
  rigging
  rigged
rigging
right adjective
  rightly
☆ **right** noun
  rights
❍ **right** verb
  rights
  righting
  righted
righteous adjective
  righteously
righteousness
rightful adjective
  rightfully
right-handed
rightness
rigid adjective
  rigidly
rigidity
rim noun
  rims
rind noun
  rinds
ring noun
  rings

. . . .

★ A revue is an entertainment of short sketches. ! review.
☆ A right is something you are entitled to. ! rite, write.
❍ To right something is to make it right. ! rite, write.

★ **ring** *verb*
rings
ringing
rang
rung

☆ **ring** *verb*
rings
ringing
ringed

ring *noun*
rings

ringleader *noun*
ringleaders

ringlet *noun*
ringlets

ringmaster *noun*
ringmasters

rink *noun*
rinks

rinse *verb*
rinses
rinsing
rinsed

rinse *noun*
rinses

riot *verb*
riots
rioting
rioted

riot *noun*
riots

riotous *adjective*
riotously

rip *verb*
rips
ripping
ripped

rip *noun*
rips

ripe *adjective*
riper
ripest

ripen *verb*
ripens
ripening
ripened

ripeness

rip-off *noun*
rip-offs

ripple *noun*
ripples

ripple *verb*
ripples
rippling
rippled

rise *verb*
rises
rising
rose
risen

rise *noun*
rises

risk *verb*
risks
risking
risked

risk *noun*
risks

risky *adjective*
riskier
riskiest
riskily

risotto *noun*
risottos

rissole *noun*
rissoles

○ **rite** *noun*
rites

ritual *noun*
rituals

rival *noun*
rivals

rival *verb*
rivals
rivalling
rivalled

rivalry *noun*
rivalries

river *noun*
rivers

rivet *noun*
rivets

rivet *verb*
rivets
riveting
riveted

✳ **road** *noun*
roads

roadroller *noun*
roadrollers

roadside *noun*
roadsides

roadway *noun*
roadways

roam *verb*
roams
roaming
roamed

roar *verb*
roars
roaring
roared

roar *noun*
roars

roast *verb*
roasts
roasting
roasted

rob *verb*
robs
robbing
robbed

- -

★ The past tense is **rang** and the past participle is **rung** when you mean 'to make a sound like a bell'. **! wring.**

☆ The past tense and past participle is **ringed** when you mean 'to put a ring round something'. **! wring.**

○ A **rite** is a ceremony or ritual. **! right, write.**

✳ A **road** is a hard surface for traffic to use. **! rode.**

robber *noun*
robbers
robbery *noun*
robberies
robe *noun*
robes
robin *noun*
robins
robot *noun*
robots
robust *adjective*
robustly
rock *verb*
rocks
rocking
rocked
rock *noun*
rocks
rocker *noun*
rockers
rockery *noun*
rockeries
rocket *noun*
rockets
rocky *adjective*
rockier
rockiest
rockily
rod *noun*
rods
★ **rode** see **ride**
rodent *noun*
rodents
rodeo *noun*
rodeos
rogue *noun*
rogues
roguish *adjective*
roguishly

☆ **role** *noun*
roles
roll *verb*
rolls
rolling
rolled
○ **roll** *noun*
rolls
roller *noun*
rollers
Roman *adjective* and
noun
Romans
Roman Catholic
noun
Roman Catholics
romance *noun*
romances
Roman numeral
romantic *adjective*
romantically
Romany
romp *verb*
romps
romping
romped
romp *noun*
romps
rompers *plural noun*
roof *noun*
roofs
rook *noun*
rooks
room *noun*
rooms
roomful *adjective*
roomfuls
roomy *adjective*
roomier
roomiest
roomily

roost *noun*
roosts
✳ **root** *noun*
roots
root *verb*
roots
rooting
rooted
rope *noun*
ropes
rose *noun*
roses
rose see **rise**
rosette *noun*
rosettes
rosy *adjective*
rosier
rosiest
rosily
rot *verb*
rots
rotting
rotted
rot *noun*
rota *noun*
rotas
rotary
rotate *verb*
rotates
rotating
rotated
rotation *noun*
rotations
rotor *noun*
rotors
rotten
rottenness
rottweiler *noun*
rottweilers

· ·

★ **Rode** is the past tense of **ride**. ! **road**.
☆ A **role** is a part in a play or film. ! **roll**.
○ A **roll** is a small loaf of bread or an act of rolling. ! **role**.
✳ A **root** is the part of a plant that grows underground. ! **route**.

rough *adjective*
 rougher
 roughest
 roughly
roughness
roughage
roughen *verb*
 roughens
 roughening
 roughened
round *adjective,*
 adverb, and
 preposition
 rounder
 roundest
 roundly
round *noun*
 rounds
round *verb*
 rounds
 rounding
 rounded
roundabout
 adjective and *noun*
 roundabouts
rounders *noun*
Roundhead *noun*
 Roundheads
rouse *verb*
 rouses
 rousing
 roused
rout *verb*
 routs
 routing
 routed
rout *noun*
 routs
★ **route** *noun*
 routes

routine *noun*
 routines
routine *adjective*
 routinely
rove *verb*
 roves
 roving
 roved
rover *noun*
 rovers
☆ **row** *noun*
 rows
❍ **row** *verb*
 rows
 rowing
 rowed
rowdiness
rowdy *adjective*
 rowdier
 rowdiest
 rowdily
rower *noun*
 rowers
rowlock *noun*
 rowlocks
royal *adjective*
 royally
royalty
rub *verb*
 rubs
 rubbing
 rubbed
rub *noun*
 rubs
rubber *noun*
 rubbers
rubbery
rubbish
rubble
ruby *noun*
 rubies

rucksack *noun*
 rucksacks
rudder *noun*
 rudders
ruddy *adjective*
 ruddier
 ruddiest
rude *adjective*
 ruder
 rudest
 rudely
rudeness
ruffian *noun*
 ruffians
ruffle *verb*
 ruffles
 ruffling
 ruffled
rug *noun*
 rugs
✳ **rugby**
rugged *adjective*
 ruggedly
rugger
ruin *verb*
 ruins
 ruining
 ruined
ruin *noun*
 ruins
ruinous *adjective*
 ruinously
rule *noun*
 rules
rule *verb*
 rules
 ruling
 ruled
ruler *noun*
 rulers
ruling *noun*
 rulings

. . . .

★ A **route** is the way you go to get to a place. **!** root.
☆ A **row** is a line of people or things and rhymes with 'go'
. A **row** is also a noise or argument and rhymes with 'cow'.
❍ To **row** means to use oars to make a boat move and rhymes with 'go'.
✳ You can use a small r when you mean the game.

rum *noun*
  rums
rumble *verb*
  rumbles
  rumbling
  rumbled
rumble *noun*
  rumbles
rummage *verb*
  rummages
  rummaging
  rummaged
rummy
rumour *noun*
  rumours
rump *noun*
  rumps
run *verb*
  runs
  running
  ran
  run
run *noun*
  runs
runaway *noun*
  runaways
rung *noun*
  rungs
rung see **ring**
runner *noun*
  runners
runner-up *noun*
  runners-up
runny *adjective*
  runnier
  runniest
  runnily
runway *noun*
  runways
rural

rush *verb*
  rushes
  rushing
  rushed
rush *noun*
  rushes
rusk *noun*
  rusks
rust *noun*
rust *verb*
  rusts
  rusting
  rusted
rustic
rustle *verb*
  rustles
  rustling
  rustled
rustler *noun*
  rustlers
rusty *adjective*
  rustier
  rustiest
  rustily
rut *noun*
  ruts
ruthless *adjective*
  ruthlessly
ruthlessness
rutted
★ **rye** *noun*

Ss

sabbath *noun*
  sabbaths
sabotage *noun*

sabotage *verb*
  sabotages
  sabotaging
  sabotaged
saboteur *noun*
  saboteurs
☆ **sac** *noun*
  sacs
saccharin
sachet *noun*
  sachets
✪ **sack** *noun*
  sacks
sack *verb*
  sacks
  sacking
  sacked
sacred
sacrifice *noun*
  sacrifices
sacrificial *adjective*
  sacrificially
sacrifice *verb*
  sacrifices
  sacrificing
  sacrificed
sad *adjective*
  sadder
  saddest
  sadly
sadness
sadden *verb*
  saddens
  saddening
  saddened
saddle *noun*
  saddles
saddle *verb*
  saddles
  saddling
  saddled

. . . .

★ **Rye** is a type of cereal or bread. ! **wry.**
☆ A **sac** is a bag-like part of an animal or plant. ! **sack.**
✪ A **sack** is a large bag. ! **sac.**

sadist noun
  sadists
sadism
sadistic adjective
  sadistically
safari noun
  safaris
safe adjective
  safer
  safest
  safely
safe noun
  safes
safeguard noun
  safeguards
safety
sag verb
  sags
  sagging
  sagged
saga noun
  sagas
sago
said see say
sail verb
  sails
  sailing
  sailed
★ **sail** noun
  sails
sailboard noun
  sailboards
sailor noun
  sailors
saint noun
  saints
saintly adjective
  saintlier
  saintliest
sake

salaam interjection
salad noun
  salads
salami noun
  salamis
salary noun
  salaries
☆ **sale** noun
  sales
salesman noun
  salesmen
salesperson noun
  salespersons
saleswoman noun
  saleswomen
saline
saliva
sally verb
  sallies
  sallying
  sallied
salmon noun
  salmon
salon noun
  salons
saloon noun
  saloons
salt noun
salt verb
  salts
  salting
  salted
salty adjective
  saltier
  saltiest
salute verb
  salutes
  saluting
  saluted

salute noun
  salutes
salvage verb
  salvages
  salvaging
  salvaged
salvation
same
samosa noun
  samosas
sample noun
  samples
sample verb
  samples
  sampling
  sampled
sanctuary noun
  sanctuaries
sand noun
  sands
sand verb
  sands
  sanding
  sanded
sander noun
  sanders
sandal noun
  sandals
sandbag noun
  sandbags
sandpaper
sands plural noun
sandstone
sandwich noun
  sandwiches
sandy adjective
  sandier
  sandiest
sane adjective
  saner
  sanest
  sanely

. . . .

★ A **sail** is a sheet that catches the wind to make a boat go. ! **sale**.
☆ You use **sale** in e.g. *The house is for sale.* ! **sail**.

sang see sing
sanitary
sanitation
sanity
sank see sink
Sanskrit
sap noun
sap verb
saps
sapping
sapped
sapling noun
saplings
sapphire noun
sapphires
sarcasm
sarcastic adjective
sarcastically
sardine noun
sardines
sari noun
saris
sash noun
sashes
sat see sit
satchel noun
satchels
satellite noun
satellites
satin
satire noun
satires
satirical adjective
satirically
satirist noun
satirists
satisfaction
satisfactory
adjective
satisfactorily

satisfy verb
satisfies
satisfying
satisfied
saturate verb
saturates
saturating
saturated
saturation
Saturday noun
Saturdays
★ sauce noun
sauces
saucepan noun
saucepans
saucer noun
saucers
saucy adjective
saucier
sauciest
saucily
sauna noun
saunas
saunter verb
saunters
sauntering
sauntered
sausage noun
sausages
savage adjective
savagely
savage noun
savages
savage verb
savages
savaging
savaged
savagery
savannah noun
savannahs

save verb
saves
saving
saved
saver noun
savers
savings plural noun
saviour noun
saviours
savoury
saw noun
saws
saw verb
saws
sawing
sawed
sawn
saw see see
sawdust
saxophone noun
saxophones
say verb
says
saying
said
say noun
saying noun
sayings
scab noun
scabs
scabbard noun
scabbards
scaffold noun
scaffolds
scaffolding
scald verb
scalds
scalding
scalded

★ A sauce is a liquid you put on food. ! source.

scale noun
 scales
scale verb
 scales
 scaling
 scaled
scales plural noun
scaly adjective
 scalier
 scaliest
scalp noun
 scalps
scalp verb
 scalps
 scalping
 scalped
scamper verb
 scampers
 scampering
 scampered
scampi plural noun
scan verb
 scans
 scanning
 scanned
scan noun
 scans
scandal noun
 scandals
scandalous adjective
 scandalous
scanner noun
 scanners
scanty adjective
 scantier
 scantiest
 scantily
scapegoat noun
 scapegoats
scar noun
 scars

scar verb
 scars
 scarring
 scarred
scarce adjective
 scarcer
 scarcest
 scarcely
scarcity noun
 scarcities
scare verb
 scares
 scaring
 scared
scare noun
 scares
scarecrow noun
 scarecrows
scarf noun
 scarves
scarlet
scary adjective
 scarier
 scariest
 scarily
scatter verb
 scatters
 scattering
 scattered
★ **scene** noun
 scenes
scenery
☆ **scent** noun
 scents
scent verb
 scents
 scenting
 scented
sceptic noun
 sceptics

sceptical adjective
 sceptically
scepticism
schedule noun
 schedules
scheme noun
 schemes
scheme verb
 schemes
 scheming
 schemed
schemer noun
 schemers
scholar noun
 scholars
scholarly
scholarship noun
 scholarships
school noun
 schools
schoolboy noun
 schoolboys
schoolchild noun
 schoolchildren
schoolgirl noun
 schoolgirls
schoolteacher noun
 schoolteachers
schooner noun
 schooners
science
scientific adjective
 scientifically
scientist noun
 scientists
scissors plural noun
scoff verb
 scoffs
 scoffing
 scoffed

★ A **scene** is a place or part of a play. ! **seen**.
☆ A **scent** is a smell or perfume. ! **cent**, **sent**.

scold verb
scolds
scolding
scolded
scone noun
scones
scoop noun
scoops
scoop verb
scoops
scooping
scooped
scooter noun
scooters
scope
scorch verb
scorches
scorching
scorched
score noun
scores
score verb
scores
scoring
scored
scorer noun
scorers
scorn noun
scorn verb
scorns
scorning
scorned
scorpion noun
scorpions
Scot noun
Scots
scoundrel noun
scoundrels
scour verb
scours
scouring
scoured

★ **Scout** noun
Scouts
scout noun
scouts
scowl verb
scowls
scowling
scowled
scramble verb
scrambles
scrambling
scrambled
scramble noun
scrambles
scrap verb
scraps
scrapping
scrapped
scrap noun
scraps
scrape verb
scrapes
scraping
scraped
scrape noun
scrapes
scraper noun
scrapers
scrappy adjective
scrappier
scrappiest
scrappily
scratch verb
scratches
scratching
scratched
scratch noun
scratches
scrawl verb
scrawls
scrawling
scrawled

scrawl noun
scrawls
scream verb
screams
screaming
screamed
scream noun
screams
screech verb
screeches
screeching
screeched
screech noun
screeches
screen noun
screens
screen verb
screens
screening
screened
screw noun
screws
screw verb
screws
screwing
screwed
screwdriver noun
screwdrivers
scribble verb
scribbles
scribbling
scribbled
scribble noun
scribbles
scribbler noun
scribblers
script noun
scripts
scripture noun
scriptures

★ You use a capital S when you mean a member of the Scout Association.

scroll noun
  scrolls
scrotum noun
  scrotums or scrota
scrounge verb
  scrounges
  scrounging
  scrounged
scrounger noun
  scroungers
scrub verb
  scrubs
  scrubbing
  scrubbed
scrub noun
scruffy adjective
  scruffier
  scruffiest
  scruffily
scrum noun
  scrums
scrummage noun
  scrummages
scrutinize verb
  scrutinizes
  scrutinizing
  scrutinized
scrutiny noun
  scrutinies
scuba diving
scuffle noun
  scuffles
scuffle verb
  scuffles
  scuffling
  scuffled
scullery noun
  sculleries
sculptor noun
  sculptors

sculpture noun
  sculptures
scum
scurry verb
  scurries
  scurrying
  scurried
scurvy
scuttle verb
  scuttles
  scuttling
  scuttled
scuttle noun
  scuttles
scythe noun
  scythes
★ **sea** noun
  seas
seabed
seafarer noun
  seafarers
seafaring
seafood
seagull noun
  seagulls
sea horse noun
  sea horses
seal verb
  seals
  sealing
  sealed
seal noun
  seals
sea lion noun
  sea lions
☆ **seam** noun
  seams
seaman noun
  seamen
seamanship

seaplane noun
  seaplanes
seaport noun
  seaports
search verb
  searches
  searching
  searched
search noun
  searches
searcher noun
  searchers
searchlight noun
  searchlights
seashore noun
  seashores
seasick
seasickness
seaside
season noun
  seasons
season verb
  seasons
  seasoning
  seasoned
seasonal adjective
  seasonally
seasoning noun
  seasonings
seat noun
  seats
seat verb
  seats
  seating
  seated
seat belt noun
  seat belts
seaward adjective
  and adverb

. . . .

★ A **sea** is an area of salt water. ! **see.**
☆ A **seam** is a line of stitching in cloth. ! **seem.**

seawards adverb
seaweed noun
  seaweeds
secateurs plural noun
secluded
seclusion
second adjective
  secondly
second noun
  seconds
second verb
  seconds
  seconding
  seconded
secondary
second-hand
  adjective
secrecy
secret adjective
  secretly
secret noun
  secrets
secretary noun
  secretaries
secrete verb
  secretes
  secreting
  secreted
secretion noun
  secretions
secretive adjective
  secretively
secretiveness
sect noun
  sects
section noun
  sections
sectional
sector noun
  sectors

secure adjective
  securer
  securest
  securely
secure verb
  secures
  securing
  secured
security
sedate adjective
  sedately
sedation
sedative noun
  sedatives
sediment
sedimentary
★ **see** verb
  sees
  seeing
  saw
  seen
seed noun
  seeds
seedling noun
  seedlings
seek verb
  seeks
  seeking
  sought
☆ **seem** verb
  seems
  seeming
  seemed
seemingly
✪ **seen** see see
seep verb
  seeps
  seeping
  seeped
seepage

see-saw noun
  see-saws
seethe verb
  seethes
  seething
  seethed
segment noun
  segments
segmented
segregate verb
  segregates
  segregating
  segregated
segregation
seismograph noun
  seismographs
seize verb
  seizes
  seizing
  seized
seizure noun
  seizures
seldom
select verb
  selects
  selecting
  selected
select adjective
self noun
  selves
self-confidence
self-confident
  adjective
  self-confidently
self-conscious
  adjective
  self-consciously
self-contained
selfish adjective
  selfishly

. . . .

★ You use see in e.g. I can't see anything. ! sea.
☆ You use seem in e.g. they seem tired. ! seam.
✪ Seen is the past participle of see. ! scene.

selfishness
selfless *adjective*
  selflessly
self-service
★ sell *verb*
  sells
  selling
  sold
semaphore
semen

semi-
semi- makes words
meaning 'half', e.g.
semi-automatic,
semi-skimmed.
A few words are spelt
joined up, e.g.
semicircle,
semicolon, but most
of them have hyphens.

semibreve *noun*
  semibreves
semicircle *noun*
  semicircles
semicircular
semicolon *noun*
  semicolons
semi-detached
semi-final *noun*
  semi-finals
semi-finalist *noun*
  semi-finalists
semitone *noun*
  semitones
semolina
senate
senator *noun*
  senators

send *verb*
  sends
  sending
  sent
senior *adjective* and
  noun
  seniors
seniority
sensation *noun*
  sensations
sensational *adjective*
  sensationally
sense *noun*
  senses
sense *verb*
  senses
  sensing
  sensed
senseless *adjective*
  senselessly
sensible *adjective*
  sensibly
sensitive *adjective*
  sensitively
sensitivity *noun*
  sensitivities
sensitize *verb*
  sensitizes
  sensitizing
  sensitized
sensor *noun*
  sensors
☆ sent see send
sentence *noun*
  sentences
sentence *verb*
  sentences
  sentencing
  sentenced
sentiment *noun*
  sentiments

sentimental
  adjective
  sentimentally
sentimentality
sentinel *noun*
  sentinels
sentry *noun*
  sentries
separable
separate *adjective*
  separately
separate *verb*
  separates
  separating
  separated
separation *noun*
  separations
September *noun*
  Septembers
septic
sequel *noun*
  sequels
sequence *noun*
  sequences
sequin *noun*
  sequins
serene *adjective*
  serenely
serenity
sergeant *noun*
  sergeants
sergeant major
  noun
  sergeant majors
✪ serial *noun*
  serials
series *noun*
  series
serious *adjective*
  seriously

★ To **sell** something means 'to exchange it for money'. **!** cell.
☆ You use **sent** in e.g. *he was sent home.* **!** cent, scent.
✪ A **serial** is a story or programme in separate parts. **!** cereal.

seriousness
sermon *noun*
  sermons
serpent *noun*
  serpents
servant *noun*
  servants
serve *verb*
  serves
  serving
  served
server *noun*
  servers
serve *noun*
  serves
service *noun*
  services
service *verb*
  services
  servicing
  serviced
serviette *noun*
  serviettes
session *noun*
  sessions
set *verb*
  sets
  setting
  set
set *noun*
  sets
set square *noun*
  set squares
★ **sett** *noun*
  setts
settee *noun*
  settees
setting *noun*
  settings
settle *verb*
  settles

  settling
  settled
settlement *noun*
  settlements
settler *noun*
  settlers
set-up *noun*
  set-ups
seven
seventeen
seventeenth
seventh *adjective* and
  noun
  seventhly
seventieth
seventy *adjective* and
  noun
  seventies
sever *verb*
  severs
  severing
  severed
several *adjective*
  severally
severe *adjective*
  severer
  severest
  severely
severity
☆ **sew** *verb*
  sews
  sewing
  sewed
  sewn
sewage
sewer *noun*
  sewers
sex *noun*
  sexes
sexism

sexist *adjective* and
  noun
  sexists
sextet *noun*
  sextets
sexual *adjective*
  sexually
sexuality
sexy *adjective*
  sexier
  sexiest
  sexily
shabbiness
shabby *adjective*
  shabbier
  shabbiest
  shabbily
shack *noun*
  shacks
shade *noun*
  shades
shade *verb*
  shades
  shading
  shaded
shadow *noun*
  shadows
shadow *verb*
  shadows
  shadowing
  shadowed
shadowy
shady *adjective*
  shadier
  shadiest
shaft *noun*
  shafts
shaggy *adjective*
  shaggier
  shaggiest
  shaggily

★ A **sett** is a badger's burrow.
☆ To **sew** is to work with a needle and thread. **!** sow.

shake verb
shakes
shaking
shook
shaken
★ **shake** noun
shakes
shaky adjective
shakier
shakiest
shakily
shall verb
should
shallow adjective
shallower
shallowest
shallowly
sham noun
shams
shamble verb
shambles
shambling
shambled
shambles noun
shame verb
shames
shaming
shamed
shame noun
shameful adjective
shamefully
shameless adjective
shamelessly
shampoo noun
shampoos
shampoo verb
shampoos
shampooing
shampooed
shamrock

shandy noun
shandies
shan't verb
shanty noun
shanties
shape noun
shapes
shape verb
shapes
shaping
shaped
shapeless adjective
shapelessly
shapely adjective
shapelier
shapeliest
share noun
shares
share verb
shares
sharing
shared
shark noun
sharks
sharp adjective
sharper
sharpest
sharply
sharp noun
sharps
sharpen verb
sharpens
sharpening
sharpened
sharpener noun
sharpeners
sharpness
shatter verb
shatters
shattering
shattered

shave verb
shaves
shaving
shaved
shave noun
shaves
shaver noun
shavers
shavings plural noun
shawl noun
shawls
she
sheaf noun
sheaves
☆ **shear** verb
shears
shearing
sheared
shorn
shearer noun
shearers
shears plural noun
sheath noun
sheaths
sheathe verb
sheathes
sheathing
sheathed
shed noun
sheds
shed verb
sheds
shedding
shed
she'd verb
sheen
sheep noun
sheep
sheepdog noun
sheepdogs

- -

★ To **shake** is to tremble or quiver. ! ~~sheikh~~.
☆ To **shear** is to cut wool from a sheep. ! ~~sheer~~.

sheepish adjective
sheepishly
★ **sheer** adjective
sheerer
sheerest
sheet noun
sheets
sheikh noun
sheikhs
shelf noun
shelves
shell noun
shells
shell verb
shells
shelling
shelled
she'll verb
shellfish noun
shellfish
shelter noun
shelters
shelter verb
shelters
sheltering
sheltered
shelve verb
shelves
shelving
shelved
shepherd noun
shepherds
sherbet noun
sherbets
sheriff noun
sheriffs
sherry noun
sherries
she's verb
shield noun
shields

shield verb
shields
shielding
shielded
shift noun
shifts
shift verb
shifts
shifting
shifted
shilling noun
shillings
shimmer verb
shimmers
shimmering
shimmered
shin noun
shins
shine verb
shines
shining
shone
shined
shine noun
shingle
shiny adjective
shinier
shiniest

-ship
-ship makes nouns,
e.g. friendship. Other
noun suffixes are
-dom, -hood, -ment,
and -ness.

ship noun
ships
ship verb
ships
shipping
shipped

shipping
shipwreck noun
shipwrecks
shipwrecked
shipyard noun
shipyards
shire noun
shires
shirk verb
shirks
shirking
shirked
shirt noun
shirts
shiver verb
shivers
shivering
shivered
shiver noun
shivers
shivery
shoal noun
shoals
shock verb
shocks
shocking
shocked
shock noun
shocks
shoddy adjective
shoddier
shoddiest
shoddily
shoe noun
shoes
shoelace noun
shoelaces
shoestring noun
shoestrings
shone see shine
shook see shake

★ You use sheer in e.g. sheer joy. ! shear.

shoot verb
shoots
shooting
shot
★ **shoot** noun
shoots
shop noun
shops
shop verb
shops
shopping
shopped
shopkeeper noun
shopkeepers
shoplifter noun
shoplifters
shopper noun
shoppers
shopping
shore noun
shores
shorn see shear
short adjective
shorter
shortest
shortly
shortness
shortage noun
shortages
shortbread
shortcake noun
shortcakes
shortcoming noun
shortcomings
shorten verb
shortens
shortening
shortened
shorthand

short-handed
shortly
shorts plural noun
short-sighted
shot noun
shots
shot see shoot
shotgun noun
shotguns
should
shoulder noun
shoulders
shoulder verb
shoulders
shouldering
shouldered
shout verb
shouts
shouting
shouted
shout noun
shouts
shove verb
shoves
shoving
shoved
shovel noun
shovels
shovel verb
shovels
shovelling
shovelled
show verb
shows
showing
showed
shown
show noun
shows
shower noun
showers

shower verb
showers
showering
showered
showery
showjumper noun
showjumpers
showjumping
showman noun
showmen
showmanship
showroom noun
showrooms
showiness
showy adjective
showier
showiest
showily
shrank see shrink
shrapnel
shred noun
shreds
shred verb
shreds
shredding
shredded
shrew noun
shrews
shrewd adjective
shrewder
shrewdest
shrewdly
shrewdness
shriek verb
shrieks
shrieking
shrieked
shriek noun
shrieks

. . . .

★ To shoot is to fire at someone with a gun. ! chute.

shrill adjective
  shriller
  shrillest
  shrilly
shrillness
shrimp noun
  shrimps
shrine noun
  shrines
shrink verb
  shrinks
  shrinking
  shrank
  shrunk
shrinkage
shrivel verb
  shrivels
  shrivelling
  shrivelled
shroud noun
  shrouds
shroud verb
  shrouds
  shrouding
  shrouded
Shrove Tuesday
shrub noun
  shrubs
shrubbery noun
  shrubberies
shrug verb
  shrugs
  shrugging
  shrugged
shrug noun
  shrugs
shrunk see shrink
shrunken adjective
shudder verb
  shudders
  shuddering
  shuddered

shudder noun
  shudders
shuffle verb
  shuffles
  shuffling
  shuffled
shuffle noun
  shuffles
shunt verb
  shunts
  shunting
  shunted
shunter noun
  shunters
shut verb
  shuts
  shutting
  shut
shutter noun
  shutters
shuttle noun
  shuttles
shuttlecock noun
  shuttlecocks
shy adjective
  shyer
  shyest
  shyly
Siamese
sick adjective
  sicker
  sickest
sicken verb
  sickens
  sickening
  sickened
sickly adjective
  sicklier
  sickliest
sickness noun
  sicknesses

side noun
  sides
side verb
  sides
  siding
  sided
sideboard noun
  sideboards
sidecar noun
  sidecars
sideline noun
  sidelines
sideshow noun
  sideshows
sideways
siding noun
  sidings
siege noun
  sieges
sieve noun
  sieves
sift verb
  sifts
  sifting
  sifted
sigh verb
  sighs
  sighing
  sighed
sigh noun
  sighs
★ **sight** noun
  sights
sight verb
  sights
  sighting
  sighted
sightseer noun
  sightseers
sightseeing

· ·

★ A **sight** is something you see. ! site.

sign verb
signs
signing
signed
sign noun
signs
signal noun
signals
signal verb
signals
signalling
signalled
signaller noun
signallers
signalman noun
signalmen
signature noun
signatures
★ **signet** noun
signets
significance
significant adjective
significantly
signify verb
signifies
signifying
signified
signing
signpost noun
signposts
Sikh noun
Sikhs
silence noun
silences
silence verb
silences
silencing
silenced
silencer noun
silencers

silent adjective
silently
silhouette noun
silhouettes
silicon
silk
silken
silkworm noun
silkworms
silky adjective
silkier
silkiest
silkily
sill noun
sills
silliness
silly adjective
sillier
silliest
sillily
silver
silvery
similar adjective
similarly
similarity
simile noun
similes
simmer verb
simmers
simmering
simmered
simple adjective
simpler
simplest
simplicity
simplification
simplify verb
simplifies
simplifying
simplified

simply
simulate verb
simulates
simulating
simulated
simulation noun
simulations
simulator noun
simulators
simultaneous
adjective
simultaneously
sin noun
sins
sin verb
sins
sinning
sinned
since preposition,
adverb, and
conjunction
sincere adjective
sincerer
sincerest
sincerely
sincerity
sinew noun
sinews
sinful adjective
sinfully
sinfulness
sing verb
sings
singing
sang
sung
singer noun
singers
singe verb
singes
singeing
singed

- -

★ A **signet** is a seal worn in a ring. ! cygnet.

single *adjective*
  singly
single *noun*
  singles
single *verb*
  singles
  singling
  singled
single-handed
singular *adjective*
  singularly
singular *noun*
  singulars
sinister *adjective*
  sinisterly
sink *verb*
  sinks
  sinking
  sank *or* sunk
  sunk
sink *noun*
  sinks
sinner *noun*
  sinners
sinus *noun*
  sinuses
sip *verb*
  sips
  sipping
  sipped
siphon *noun*
  siphons
siphon *verb*
  siphons
  siphoning
  siphoned
sir
siren *noun*
  sirens
sister *noun*
  sisters

sisterly
sister-in-law *noun*
  sisters-in-law
sit *verb*
  sits
  sitting
  sat
sitter *noun*
  sitters
★ **site** *noun*
  sites
site *verb*
  sites
  siting
  sited
sit-in *noun*
  sit-ins
situated
situation *noun*
  situations
six *noun*
  sixes
sixpence *noun*
  sixpences
sixteen *noun*
  sixteens
sixteenth
sixth
sixthly
sixtieth
sixty *noun*
  sixties
size *noun*
  sizes
size *verb*
  sizes
  sizing
  sized
sizeable

sizzle *verb*
  sizzles
  sizzling
  sizzled
skate *verb*
  skates
  skating
  skated
☆ **skate** *noun*
  skates *or* skate
skateboard *noun*
  skateboards
skater *noun*
  skaters
skeletal *adjective*
  skeletally
skeleton *noun*
  skeletons
sketch *noun*
  sketches
sketch *verb*
  sketches
  sketching
  sketched
sketchy *adjective*
  sketchier
  sketchiest
  sketchily
skewer *noun*
  skewers
ski *verb*
  skis
  skiing
  skied
  ski'd
ski *noun*
  skis

★ A **site** is a place where something will be built. **! sight.**
☆ The plural is **skate** when you mean the fish.

skid verb
skids
skidding
skidded
skid noun
skids
skier noun
skiers
skilful adjective
skilfully
skill noun
skills
skilled
skim verb
skims
skimming
skimmed
skimp verb
skimps
skimping
skimped
skimpy adjective
skimpier
skimpiest
skimpily
skin noun
skins
skin verb
skins
skinning
skinned
skinny adjective
skinnier
skinniest
skint
skip verb
skips
skipping
skipped
skip noun
skips

skipper noun
skippers
skirt noun
skirts
skirt verb
skirts
skirting
skirted
skirting noun
skirtings
skit noun
skits
skittish adjective
skittishly
skittle noun
skittles
skull noun
skulls
skunk noun
skunks
sky noun
skies
skylark noun
skylarks
skylight noun
skylights
skyscraper noun
skyscrapers
slab noun
slabs
slack adjective
slacker
slackest
slackly
slacken verb
slackens
slackening
slackened
slackness

slacks plural noun
slag heap noun
slag heaps
slain see slay
slam verb
slams
slamming
slammed
slang
slant verb
slants
slanting
slanted
slant noun
slants
slap verb
slaps
slapping
slapped
slap noun
slaps
slapstick
slash verb
slashes
slashing
slashed
slash noun
slashes
slat noun
slats
slate noun
slates
slaty adjective
slatier
slatiest
slaughter verb
slaughters
slaughtering
slaughtered
slaughter noun

slaughterhouse
noun
slaughterhouses
slave noun
slaves
slave verb
slaves
slaving
slaved
slavery
★ **slay** verb
slays
slaying
slew
slain
sled noun
sleds
sledge noun
sledges
sledgehammer
noun
sledgehammers
sleek adjective
sleeker
sleekest
sleekly
sleep verb
sleeps
sleeping
slept
sleep noun
sleeper noun
sleepers
sleepiness
sleepless
sleepwalker noun
sleepwalkers
sleepwalking
sleepy adjective
sleepier
sleepiest
sleepily

sleet
sleeve noun
sleeves
sleeveless
☆ **sleigh** noun
sleighs
slender adjective
slenderer
slenderest
slept see sleep
slew see slay
slice noun
slices
slice verb
slices
slicing
sliced
slick adjective
slicker
slickest
slickly
slick noun
slicks
slide verb
slides
sliding
slid
slide noun
slides
slight adjective
slighter
slightest
slightly
slim adjective
slimmer
slimmest
slimly
slim verb
slims
slimming
slimmed

slime
slimmer noun
slimmers
slimy adjective
slimier
slimiest
sling verb
slings
slinging
slung
sling noun
slings
slink verb
slinks
slinking
slunk
slip verb
slips
slipping
slipped
slip noun
slips
slipper noun
slippers
slippery
slipshod
slit noun
slits
slit verb
slits
slitting
slit
slither verb
slithers
slithering
slithered
sliver noun
slivers
slog verb
slogs
slogging
slogged

★ To **slay** people is to kill them. ! sleigh.
☆ A **sleigh** is a vehicle for sliding on snow. ! slay.

slog noun
  slogs
slogan noun
  slogans
slop verb
  slops
  slopping
  slopped
slope verb
  slopes
  sloping
  sloped
slope noun
  slopes
sloppiness
sloppy adjective
  sloppier
  sloppiest
  sloppily
slops plural noun
slosh verb
  sloshes
  sloshing
  sloshed
slot noun
  slots
sloth noun
  sloths
slouch verb
  slouches
  slouching
  slouched
slovenly
slow adjective
  slower
  slowest
  slowly
slow verb
  slows
  slowing
  slowed

slowcoach noun
  slowcoaches
slowness
sludge
slug noun
  slugs
slum noun
  slums
slumber
slumber verb
  slumbers
  slumbering
  slumbered
slump verb
  slumps
  slumping
  slumped
slump noun
  slumps
slung see **sling**
slunk see **slink**
slur noun
  slurs
slush
slushy adjective
  slushier
  slushiest
  slushily
sly adjective
  slyer
  slyest
  slyly
slyness
smack verb
  smacks
  smacking
  smacked
smack noun
  smacks
small adjective
  smaller
  smallest

smallpox
smart adjective
  smarter
  smartest
  smartly
smart verb
  smarts
  smarting
  smarted
smarten verb
  smartens
  smartening
  smartened
smartness
smash verb
  smashes
  smashing
  smashed
smash noun
  smashes
smashing
smear verb
  smears
  smearing
  smeared
smear noun
  smears
smell verb
  smells
  smelling
  smelt or smelled
smell noun
  smells
smelly adjective
  smellier
  smelliest
smelt verb
  smelts
  smelting
  smelted

smile noun
smiles
smile verb
smiles
smiling
smiled
smith noun
smiths
smithereens plural
noun
smock noun
smocks
smog
smoke noun
smoke verb
smokes
smoking
smoked
smokeless
smoker noun
smokers
smoky adjective
smokier
smokiest
smooth adjective
smoother
smoothest
smoothly
smooth verb
smooths
smoothing
smoothed
smoothness
smother verb
smothers
smothering
smothered
smoulder verb
smoulders
smouldering
smouldered

smudge verb
smudges
smudging
smudged
smudge noun
smudges
smuggle verb
smuggles
smuggling
smuggled
smuggler noun
smugglers
smut noun
smuts
smutty adjective
smuttier
smuttiest
smuttily
snack noun
snacks
snag noun
snags
snail noun
snails
snake noun
snakes
snaky adjective
snakier
snakiest
snap verb
snaps
snapping
snapped
snap noun
snaps
snappy adjective
snappier
snappiest
snappily
snapshot noun
snapshots

snare noun
snares
snare verb
snares
snaring
snared
snarl verb
snarls
snarling
snarled
snarl noun
snarls
snatch verb
snatches
snatching
snatched
snatch noun
snatches
sneak verb
sneaks
sneaking
sneaked
sneak noun
sneaks
sneaky adjective
sneakier
sneakiest
sneakily
sneer verb
sneers
sneering
sneered
sneeze verb
sneezes
sneezing
sneezed
sneeze noun
sneezes
sniff verb
sniffs
sniffing
sniffed

sniff noun
  sniffs
snigger verb
  sniggers
  sniggering
  sniggered
snigger noun
  sniggers
snip verb
  snips
  snipping
  snipped
snip noun
  snips
snipe verb
  snipes
  sniping
  sniped
sniper noun
  snipers
snippet noun
  snippets
snivel verb
  snivels
  snivelling
  snivelled
snob noun
  snobs
snobbery
snobbish adjective
  snobbishly
snooker
snoop verb
  snoops
  snooping
  snooped
snooper noun
  snoopers
snore verb
  snores
  snoring
  snored

snorkel noun
  snorkels
snort verb
  snorts
  snorting
  snorted
snort noun
  snorts
snout noun
  snouts
snow noun
snow verb
  snows
  snowing
  snowed
snowball noun
  snowballs
snowdrop noun
  snowdrops
snowflake noun
  snowflakes
snowman noun
  snowmen
snowplough noun
  snowploughs
snowshoe noun
  snowshoes
snowstorm noun
  snowstorms
snowy adjective
  snowier
  snowiest
snub verb
  snubs
  snubbing
  snubbed
snuff
snug adjective
  snugger
  snuggest
  snugly

snuggle verb
  snuggles
  snuggling
  snuggled
soak verb
  soaks
  soaking
  soaked
so-and-so noun
  so-and-so's
soap noun
  soaps
soapiness noun
soapy adjective
  soapier
  soapiest
  soapily
★ **soar** verb
  soars
  soaring
  soared
sob verb
  sobs
  sobbing
  sobbed
sob noun
  sobs
sober adjective
  soberly
sobriety
so-called
soccer
sociability
sociable adjective
  sociably
social adjective
  socially
socialism
socialist noun
  socialists

★ To **soar** is to rise or fly high. ! ~~sore~~.

society *noun*
  societies
sociological
  adjective
  sociologically
sociologist *noun*
  sociologists
sociology
sock *noun*
  socks
sock *verb*
  socks
  socking
  socked
socket *noun*
  sockets
soda
sodium
sofa *noun*
  sofas
soft *adjective*
  softer
  softest
  softly
soften *verb*
  softens
  softening
  softened
softness
software
soggy *adjective*
  soggier
  soggiest
  soggily
soil *noun*
soil *verb*
  soils
  soiling
  soiled

solar
sold see **sell**
solder *noun*
solder *verb*
  solders
  soldering
  soldered
soldier *noun*
  soldiers
★ **sole** *noun*
  soles
sole *adjective*
  solely
solemn *adjective*
  solemnly
solemnity
solicitor *noun*
  solicitors
solid *adjective*
  solidly
solid *noun*
  solids
solidify *verb*
  solidifies
  solidifying
  solidified
solidity
soliloquy *noun*
  soliloquies
solitary
solitude
solo *noun*
  solos
soloist *noun*
  soloists
solstice *noun*
  solstices

solubility
soluble *adjective*
  solubly
solution *noun*
  solutions
solve *verb*
  solves
  solving
  solved
solvent *adjective* and
  noun
  solvents
sombre *adjective*
  sombrely
☆ **some** *adjective* and
  pronoun
somebody
somehow
someone
somersault *noun*
  somersaults
something
sometime
sometimes
somewhat
somewhere
❍ **son** *noun*
  sons
sonar *noun*
  sonars
song *noun*
  songs
songbird *noun*
  songbirds
sonic *adjective*
  sonically
sonnet *noun*
  sonnets

· ·

★ A **sole** is a fish or a part of a shoe. ! **soul**
☆ You use **some** in e.g. *Have some cake.* ! **sum**.
❍ A **son** is a male child. ! **sun**.

soon *adverb*
sooner
soonest
soot
soothe *verb*
soothes
soothing
soothed
sooty *adjective*
sootier
sootiest
sophisticated
sophistication
sopping
soppy *adjective*
soppier
soppiest
soppily
soprano *noun*
sopranos
sorcerer *noun*
sorcerers
sorceress *noun*
sorceresses
sorcery
★ **sore** *adjective*
sorer
sorest
sorely
sore *noun*
sores
soreness
sorrow *noun*
sorrows
sorrowful *adjective*
sorrowfully
sorry *adjective*
sorrier
sorriest

sort *noun*
sorts
sort *verb*
sorts
sorting
sorted
sought see seek
☆ **soul** *noun*
souls
sound *noun*
sounds
sound *verb*
sounds
sounding
sounded
sound *adjective*
sounder
soundest
soundly
soundness
soundtrack *noun*
soundtracks
soup *noun*
soups
sour *adjective*
sourer
sourest
sourly
✪ **source** *noun*
sources
sourness
south *adjective* and
adverb
✳ **south** *noun*
south-east *noun* and
adjective
southerly *adjective*
and *noun*
southerlies
southern *adjective*

southerner *noun*
southerners
southward *adjective*
and *adverb*
southwards *adverb*
south-west *noun* and
adjective
souvenir *noun*
souvenirs
sovereign *noun*
sovereigns
✱ **sow** *verb*
sows
sowing
sowed
sown
sow *noun*
sows
sower *noun*
sowers
soya bean *noun*
soya beans
space *noun*
spaces
space *verb*
spaces
spacing
spaced
spacecraft *noun*
spacecraft
spaceman *noun*
spacemen
spaceship *noun*
spaceships
spacewoman *noun*
spacewomen
spacious *adjective*
spaciously

- -

★ You use **sore** in e.g. *I've got a sore tooth.* ! **soar.**
☆ A **soul** is a person's spirit. ! **sole.**
✪ The **source** is where something comes from. ! **sauce.**
✳ You use a capital S in the **South,** when you mean a particular region.
✱ To **sow** is to put seed in the ground. ! **sew.**

spaciousness
spade *noun*
  spades
spaghetti
span *verb*
  spans
  spanning
  spanned
span *noun*
  spans
spaniel *noun*
  spaniels
spank *verb*
  spanks
  spanking
  spanked
spanner *noun*
  spanners
spar *noun*
  spars
spar *verb*
  spars
  sparring
  sparred
spare *verb*
  spares
  sparing
  spared
spare *adjective* and
  noun
  spares
sparing *adjective*
  sparingly
spark *noun*
  sparks
spark *verb*
  sparks
  sparking
  sparked

sparkle *verb*
  sparkles
  sparkling
  sparkled
sparkler *noun*
  sparklers
sparrow *noun*
  sparrows
sparse *adjective*
  sparser
  sparsest
  sparsely
sparseness
spastic *noun*
  spastics
spat see **spit**
spatter *verb*
  spatters
  spattering
  spattered
spawn *noun*
spawn *verb*
  spawns
  spawning
  spawned
speak *verb*
  speaks
  speaking
  spoke
  spoken
speaker *noun*
  speakers
spear *noun*
  spears
spear *verb*
  spears
  spearing
  speared

special *adjective*
  specially
specialist *noun*
  specialists
speciality *noun*
  specialities
specialization
specialize *verb*
  specializes
  specializing
  specialized
species *noun*
  species
specific *adjective*
  specifically
specification *noun*
  specifications
specify *verb*
  specifies
  specifying
  specified
specimen *noun*
  specimens
speck *noun*
  specks
speckled
spectacle *noun*
  spectacles
spectacular
  adjective
  spectacularly
spectator *noun*
  spectators
spectre *noun*
  spectres
spectrum *noun*
  spectra
speech *noun*
  speeches
speechless

speed *noun*
  speeds
★ speed *verb*
  speeds
  speeding
  sped *or* speeded
speedboat *noun*
  speedboats
speedometer *noun*
  speedometers
speedway *noun*
  speedways
speedy *adjective*
  speedier
  speediest
  speedily
spell *verb*
  spells
  spelling
  spelt
  spelled
spell *noun*
  spells
spelling *noun*
  spellings
spend *verb*
  spends
  spending
  spent
sperm *noun*
  sperms *or* sperm
sphere *noun*
  spheres
spherical *adjective*
  spherically
spice *noun*
  spices
spicy *adjective*
  spicier
  spiciest
spider *noun*
  spiders

spied *see* spy
spike *noun*
  spikes
spiky *adjective*
  spikier
  spikiest
☆ spill *verb*
  spills
  spilling
  spilt *or* spilled
spill *noun*
  spills
spin *verb*
  spins
  spinning
  spun
spin *noun*
  spins
spinach
spindle *noun*
  spindles
spin-drier *noun*
  spin-driers
spine *noun*
  spines
spinal
spin-off *noun*
  spin-offs
spinster *noun*
  spinsters
spiny *adjective*
  spiniest
  spiniest
spiral *adjective*
  spirally
spire *noun*
  spires
spirit *noun*
  spirits
spiritual *adjective*
  spiritually

spiritual *noun*
  spirituals
spiritualism
spiritualist *noun*
  spiritualists
spit *verb*
  spits
  spitting
  spat
spit *noun*
  spits
spite
spiteful *adjective*
  spitefully
spittle
splash *verb*
  splashes
  splashing
  splashed
splash *noun*
  splashes
splashdown *noun*
  splashdowns
splendid *adjective*
  splendidly
splendour
splint *noun*
  splints
splinter *noun*
  splinters
splinter *verb*
  splinters
  splintering
  splintered
split *verb*
  splits
  splitting
  split
split *noun*
  splits

. . . .

★ You use sped in e.g. *Cars sped past* and speeded in e.g. *They speeded up the process.*

☆ You use spilled in e.g. *I spilled the milk.* You use spilt in e.g. *I can see spilt milk.* You use spilled or spilt in e.g. *I have spilled/spilt the milk.*

splutter verb
  splutters
  spluttering
  spluttered
★ **spoil** verb
  spoils
  spoiling
  spoilt or spoiled
spoils plural noun
spoilsport noun
  spoilsports
spoke noun
  spokes
spoke see speak
spoken see speak
spokesperson noun
  spokespersons
sponge noun
  sponges
sponge verb
  sponges
  sponging
  sponged
sponger noun
  spongers
sponginess noun
spongy adjective
  spongier
  spongiest
  spongily
sponsor noun
  sponsors
sponsorship noun
  sponsorships
spontaneity
spontaneous
  adjective
  spontaneously
spooky adjective
  spookier
  spookiest
  spookily

spool noun
  spools
spoon noun
  spoons
spoon verb
  spoons
  spooning
  spooned
spoonful noun
  spoonfuls
sport noun
  sports
sporting
sportsman noun
  sportsmen
sportsmanship
sportswoman noun
  sportswomen
spot noun
  spots
spot verb
  spots
  spotting
  spotted
spotless adjective
  spotlessly
spotlight noun
  spotlights
spotter noun
  spotters
spotty adjective
  spottier
  spottiest
  spottily
spout noun
  spouts
spout verb
  spouts
  spouting
  spouted

sprain verb
  sprains
  spraining
  sprained
sprain noun
  sprains
sprang see spring
sprawl verb
  sprawls
  sprawling
  sprawled
spray verb
  sprays
  spraying
  sprayed
spray noun
  sprays
spread verb
  spreads
  spreading
  spread
spread noun
  spreads
spreadsheet noun
  spreadsheets
sprightliness
sprightly adjective
  sprightlier
  sprightliest
spring verb
  springs
  springing
  sprang
  sprung
spring noun
  springs
springboard noun
  springboards

★ You use spoiled in e.g. *They spoiled the party.* You use spoilt in e.g. *a spoilt child.* You use spoiled or spoilt in e.g. *They have spoiled/spoilt the party.*

spring-clean *verb*
spring-cleans
spring-cleaning
spring-cleaned
springtime
springy *adjective*
springier
springiest
sprinkle *verb*
sprinkles
sprinkling
sprinkled
sprinkler *noun*
sprinklers
sprint *verb*
sprints
sprinting
sprinted
sprinter *noun*
sprinters
sprout *verb*
sprouts
sprouting
sprouted
sprout *noun*
sprouts
spruce *noun*
spruces
spruce *adjective*
sprucer
sprucest
sprung see **spring**
spud *noun*
spuds
spun see **spin**
spur *noun*
spurs
spur *verb*
spurs
spurring
spurred

spurt *verb*
spurts
spurting
spurted
spurt *noun*
spurts
spy *noun*
spies
spy *verb*
spies
spying
spied
squabble *verb*
squabbles
squabbling
squabbled
squabble *noun*
squabbles
squad *noun*
squads
squadron *noun*
squadrons
squalid *adjective*
squalidly
squall *noun*
squalls
squally *adjective*
squallier
squalliest
squalor
squander *verb*
squanders
squandering
squandered
square *adjective*
squarely
square *noun*
squares
square *verb*
squares
squaring
squared

squareness
squash *verb*
squashes
squashing
squashed
squash *noun*
squashes
squat *verb*
squats
squatting
squatted
squat *adjective*
squatter
squattest
squatly
squatter *noun*
squatters
squaw *noun*
squaws
squawk *verb*
squawks
squawking
squawked
squawk *noun*
squawks
squeak *verb*
squeaks
squeaking
squeaked
squeak *noun*
squeaks
squeaky *adjective*
squeakier
squeakiest
squeakily
squeal *verb*
squeals
squealing
squealed
squeal *noun*
squeals

squeeze verb
squeezes
squeezing
squeezed
squeeze noun
squeezes
squeezer noun
squeezers
squelch verb
squelches
squelching
squelched
squelch noun
squelches
squid noun
squid or squids
squint verb
squints
squinting
squinted
squint noun
squints
squire noun
squires
squirm verb
squirms
squirming
squirmed
squirrel noun
squirrels
squirt verb
squirts
squirting
squirted
stab verb
stabs
stabbing
stabbed
stab noun
stabs
stability

stabilize verb
stabilizes
stabilizing
stabilized
stabilizer noun
stabilizers
stable adjective
stabler
stablest
stably
stable noun
stables
stack verb
stacks
stacking
stacked
stack noun
stacks
stadium noun
stadiums or stadia
staff noun
staffs
stag noun
stags
stage noun
stages
stage verb
stages
staging
staged
stagecoach noun
stagecoaches
stagger verb
staggers
staggering
staggered
stagnant adjective
stagnantly
stain noun
stains

stain verb
stains
staining
stained
stainless
★ **stair** noun
stairs
staircase noun
staircases
☆ **stake** noun
stakes
stake verb
stakes
staking
staked
stalactite noun
stalactites
stalagmite noun
stalagmites
stale adjective
staler
stalest
stalk noun
stalks
stalk verb
stalks
stalking
stalked
stall noun
stalls
stall verb
stalls
stalling
stalled
stallion noun
stallions
stalls plural noun
stamen noun
stamens
stamina

- -

★ A **stair** is one of a set of steps. ! stare.
☆ A **stake** is a pointed stick or post. ! steak.

stammer verb
stammers
stammering
stammered
stammer noun
stammers
stamp noun
stamps
stamp verb
stamps
stamping
stamped
stampede noun
stampedes
stand verb
stands
standing
stood
stand noun
stands
standard adjective
and noun
standards
standardize verb
standardizes
standardizing
standardized
standby noun
standbys
standstill noun
standstills
stank see **stink**
stanza noun
stanzas
staple noun
staples
staple adjective
stapler noun
staplers

star noun
stars
starry adjective
starrier
starriest
starrily
star verb
stars
starring
starred
starboard
starch noun
starches
starchy adjective
starchier
starchiest
★ **stare** verb
stares
staring
stared
starfish noun
starfish or starfishes
starling noun
starlings
start verb
starts
starting
started
start noun
starts
starter noun
starters
startle verb
startles
startling
startled
starvation
starve verb
starves
starving
starved

state noun
states
state verb
states
stating
stated
stateliness
stately adjective
statelier
stateliest
statement noun
statements
statesman noun
statesmen
statesmanship
stateswoman noun
stateswomen
static adjective
statically
station noun
stations
station verb
stations
stationing
stationed
☆ **stationary** adjective
✪ **stationery** noun
stationmaster noun
stationmasters
statistic noun
statistics
statistical adjective
statistically
statistician noun
statisticians
statistics
statue noun
statues
status noun
statuses

★ To **stare** is to look at something without moving your eyes. ! **stair**.
☆ **Stationary** means 'not moving'. ! **stationery**.
✪ **Stationery** means 'paper and envelopes'. ! **stationary**.

staunch adjective
stauncher
staunchest
staunchly
stave noun
staves
stave verb
staves
staving
staved
stove
stay verb
stays
staying
stayed
stay noun
stays
steadiness
steady adjective
steadier
steadiest
steadily
steady verb
steadies
steadying
steadied
★ **steak** noun
steaks
☆ **steal** verb
steals
stealing
stole
stolen
stealth
stealthy adjective
stealthier
stealthiest
stealthily
steam noun

steam verb
steams
steaming
steamed
steamy adjective
steamier
steamiest
steamily
steamer noun
steamers
steamroller noun
steamrollers
steamship noun
steamships
steed noun
steeds
steel noun
○ **steel** verb
steels
steeling
steeled
steely adjective
steelier
steeliest
steep adjective
steeper
steepest
steeply
steepness
steeple noun
steeples
steeplechase noun
steeplechases
steeplejack noun
steeplejacks
steer verb
steers
steering
steered
steer noun
steers

stem noun
stems
stem verb
stems
stemming
stemmed
stench noun
stenches
stencil noun
stencils
✳ **step** noun
steps
step verb
steps
stepping
stepped
stepchild noun
stepchildren
stepfather noun
stepfathers
stepladder noun
stepladders
stepmother noun
stepmothers
✴ **steppe** noun
steppes
stereo adjective and noun
stereos
stereophonic adjective
stereophonically
sterile
sterility
sterilization
sterilize verb
sterilizes
sterilizing
sterilized
sterling

★ A **steak** is a thick slice of meat. ! stake.
☆ To **steal** is to take something that is not yours. ! steel.
○ To **steel** yourself is to find courage to do something hard. ! steal.
✳ A **step** is a movement of the feet or part of a stair. ! steppe.
✴ A **steppe** is a grassy plain. ! step.

stern noun
  sterns
stern adjective
  sterner
  sternest
  sternly
sternness
stethoscope noun
  stethoscopes
stew verb
  stews
  stewing
  stewed
stew noun
  stews
steward noun
  stewards
stewardess noun
  stewardesses
stick verb
  sticks
  sticking
  stuck
stick noun
  sticks
sticker noun
  stickers
stickiness
stickleback noun
  sticklebacks
sticky adjective
  stickier
  stickiest
  stickily
stiff adjective
  stiffer
  stiffest
  stiffly
stiffen verb
  stiffens
  stiffening
  stiffened

stiffness
stifle verb
  stifles
  stifling
  stifled
stile noun
  stiles
still adjective
  stiller
  stillest
still adverb
still verb
  stills
  stilling
  stilled
stillness
stilts
stimulant noun
  stimulants
stimulate verb
  stimulates
  stimulating
  stimulated
stimulation
stimulus noun
  stimuli
sting noun
  stings
sting verb
  stings
  stinging
  stung
stingy adjective
  stingier
  stingiest
  stingily
stink noun
  stinks
stink verb
  stinks
  stinking

  stank
  stunk
stir verb
  stirs
  stirring
  stirred
stir noun
  stirs
stirrup noun
  stirrups
stitch noun
  stitches
stoat noun
  stoats
stock noun
  stocks
stock verb
  stocks
  stocking
  stocked
stockade noun
  stockades
stockbroker noun
  stockbrokers
stocking noun
  stockings
stockpile noun
  stockpiles
stocks plural noun
stocky adjective
  stockier
  stockiest
  stockily
stodgy adjective
  stodgier
  stodgiest
  stodgily
stoke verb
  stokes
  stoking
  stoked

stole noun
stoles
stole see **steal**
stolen see **steal**
stomach noun
stomachs
stomach verb
stomachs
stomaching
stomached
stone noun
stones or stone
stone verb
stones
stoning
stoned
stony adjective
stonier
stoniest
stood see **stand**
stool noun
stools
stoop verb
stoops
stooping
stooped
stop verb
stops
stopping
stopped
stop noun
stops
stoppage noun
stoppages
stopper noun
stoppers
stopwatch noun
stopwatches
storage

store verb
stores
storing
stored
store noun
stores
★ **storey** noun
storeys
stork noun
storks
storm noun
storms
storm verb
storms
storming
stormed
stormy adjective
stormier
stormiest
stormily
☆ **story** noun
stories
stout adjective
stouter
stoutest
stoutly
stoutness
stove noun
stoves
stove see **stave**
stow verb
stows
stowing
stowed
stowaway noun
stowaways
straddle verb
straddles
straddling
straddled

straggle verb
straggles
straggling
straggled
straggler noun
stragglers
straggly adjective
stragglier
straggliest
○ **straight** adjective
straighter
straightest
straighten verb
straightens
straightening
straightened
straightforward adjective
straightforwardly
strain verb
strains
straining
strained
strain noun
strains
strainer noun
strainers
✳ **strait** noun
straits
✴ **straits** plural noun
strand noun
strands
stranded
strange adjective
stranger
strangest
strangely
strangeness
stranger noun
strangers

. . . .

★ A **storey** is a floor of a building. ! story.
☆ You use **story** in e.g. read me a story. ! storey.
○ **Straight** means 'not curving or bending'. ! strait.
✳ A **strait** is a narrow stretch of water. ! straight.
✴ You use **straits** in the phrase in dire straits.

strangle verb
 strangles
 strangling
 strangled
strangler noun
 stranglers
strangulation
strap noun
 straps
strap verb
 straps
 strapping
 strapped
strategic adjective
 strategically
strategist noun
 strategists
strategy noun
 strategies
stratum noun
 strata
straw noun
 straws
strawberry noun
 strawberries
stray verb
 strays
 straying
 strayed
stray adjective
streak noun
 streaks
streak verb
 streaks
 streaking
 streaked
streaky adjective
 streakier
 streakiest
 streakily
stream noun
 streams

stream verb
 streams
 streaming
 streamed
streamer noun
 streamers
streamline verb
 streamlines
 streamlining
 streamlined
street noun
 streets
strength noun
 strengths
strengthen verb
 strengthens
 strengthening
 strengthened
strenuous adjective
 strenuously
stress noun
 stresses
stress verb
 stresses
 stressing
 stressed
stretch verb
 stretches
 stretching
 stretched
stretch noun
 stretches
stretcher noun
 stretchers
strew verb
 strews
 strewing
 strewed
 strewn
stricken

strict adjective
 stricter
 strictest
 strictly
strictness
stride verb
 strides
 striding
 strode
 stridden
stride noun
 strides
strife
strike verb
 strikes
 striking
 struck
strike noun
 strikes
striker noun
 strikers
striking adjective
 strikingly
string noun
 strings
string verb
 strings
 stringing
 strung
stringiness
stringy adjective
 stringier
 stringiest
 stringily
strip verb
 strips
 stripping
 stripped
strip noun
 strips

stripe noun
  stripes
striped
stripy adjective
  stripier
  stripiest
strive verb
  strives
  striving
  strove
  striven
strobe noun
  strobes
strode see **stride**
stroke noun
  strokes
stroke verb
  strokes
  stroking
  stroked
stroll verb
  strolls
  strolling
  strolled
stroll noun
  strolls
strong adjective
  stronger
  strongest
  strongly
stronghold noun
  strongholds
strove see **strive**
struck see **strike**
structural adjective
  structurally
structure noun
  structures
struggle verb
  struggles
  struggling
  struggled

struggle noun
  struggles
strum verb
  strums
  strumming
  strummed
strung see **string**
strut verb
  struts
  strutting
  strutted
strut noun
  struts
stub verb
  stubs
  stubbing
  stubbed
stub noun
  stubs
stubble
stubborn adjective
  stubbornly
stubbornness
stuck see **stick**
stuck-up
stud noun
  studs
student noun
  students
studio noun
  studios
studious adjective
  studiously
study verb
  studies
  studying
  studied
study noun
  studies
stuff noun

stuff verb
  stuffs
  stuffing
  stuffed
stuffiness
stuffing noun
  stuffings
stuffy adjective
  stuffier
  stuffiest
  stuffily
stumble verb
  stumbles
  stumbling
  stumbled
stump noun
  stumps
stump verb
  stumps
  stumping
  stumped
stun verb
  stuns
  stunning
  stunned
stung see **sting**
stunk see **stink**
stunt noun
  stunts
stupendous adjective
  stupendously
stupid adjective
  stupider
  stupidest
  stupidly
stupidity
sturdiness
sturdy adjective
  sturdier
  sturdiest
  sturdily

stutter verb
stutters
stuttering
stuttered
stutter noun
stutters
★ **sty** noun
sties
style noun
styles
style verb
styles
styling
styled
stylish adjective
stylishly
stylus noun
styluses
subcontinent noun
subcontinents
subdivide verb
subdivides
subdividing
subdivided
subdivision noun
subdivisions
subdue verb
subdues
subduing
subdued
subject adjective and
noun
subjects
subject verb
subjects
subjecting
subjected
subjective adjective
subjectively
submarine noun
submarines

submerge verb
submerges
submerging
submerged
submersion
submission noun
submissions
submissive
adjective
submissively
submit verb
submits
submitting
submitted
subordinate
adjective and noun
subordinates
subordinate verb
subordinates
subordinating
subordinated
subordination
subscribe verb
subscribes
subscribing
subscribed
subscriber noun
subscribers
subscription noun
subscriptions
subsequent adjective
subsequently
subside verb
subsides
subsiding
subsided
subsidence
subsidize verb
subsidizes
subsidizing
subsidized

subsidy noun
subsidies
substance noun
substances
substantial adjective
substantially
substitute verb
substitutes
substituting
substituted
substitute noun
substitutes
substitution noun
substitutions
subtle adjective
subtler
subtlest
subtly
subtlety noun
subtleties
subtract verb
subtracts
subtracting
subtracted
subtraction noun
subtractions
suburb noun
suburbs
suburban
suburbia
subway noun
subways
succeed verb
succeeds
succeeding
succeeded
success noun
successes
successful adjective
successfully

★ A **sty** is a place for pigs or a swelling on the eye. In the second meaning you can also use *stye*, plural *styes*.

succession noun
  successions
successive adjective
  successively
successor noun
  successors
such
suck verb
  sucks
  sucking
  sucked
suck noun
  sucks
suction
sudden adjective
  suddenly
suddenness
suds plural noun
sue verb
  sues
  suing
  sued
suede
suet
suffer verb
  suffers
  suffering
  suffered
sufficiency
sufficient adjective
  sufficiently
suffix noun
  suffixes
suffocate verb
  suffocates
  suffocating
  suffocated
suffocation
sugar
sugary

suggest verb
  suggests
  suggesting
  suggested
suggestion noun
  suggestions
suicidal adjective
  suicidally
suicide noun
  suicides
★ **suit** noun
  suits
suit verb
  suits
  suiting
  suited
suitability
suitable adjective
  suitably
suitcase noun
  suitcases
☆ **suite** noun
  suites
suitor noun
  suitors
sulk verb
  sulks
  sulking
  sulked
sulkiness
sulky adjective
  sulkier
  sulkiest
  sulkily
sullen adjective
  sullenly
sullenness
sulphur
sulphuric acid
sultan noun
  sultans

sultana noun
  sultanas
○ **sum** noun
  sums
sum verb
  sums
  summing
  summed
summarize verb
  summarizes
  summarizing
  summarized
summary noun
  summaries
summer noun
  summers
summertime
summit noun
  summits
summon verb
  summons
  summoning
  summoned
summons noun
  summonses
✳ **sun** noun
  suns
sun verb
  suns
  sunning
  sunned
sunbathe verb
  sunbathes
  sunbathing
  sunbathed
sunburn
sunburned or
sunburnt
✱ **sundae** noun
  sundaes

. . . .

★ A **suit** is a set of matching clothes. ! **suite**.
☆ A **suite** is a set of furniture or a group of rooms. ! **suit**.
○ A **sum** is an amount or total. ! **some**.
✳ A **sun** is a large star. ! **son**.
✱ A **sundae** is a cocktail of fruit and ice cream. ! **Sunday**.

★ **Sunday** noun
Sundays
sundial noun
sundials
sunflower noun
sunflowers
sung see sing
sunglasses
sunk see sink
sunlight
sunlit
sunny adjective
sunnier
sunniest
sunnily
sunrise noun
sunrises
sunset noun
sunsets
sunshade noun
sunshades
sunshine
sunspot noun
sunspots
sunstroke
suntan noun
suntans
suntanned
super

super-
super- makes words
meaning 'very good'
or 'extra', e.g.
supermarket,
supermodel. They
are normally spelt
joined up.

superb adjective
superbly
superficial adjective
superficially

superfluous adjective
superfluously
superintend verb
superintends
superintending
superintended
superintendent
noun
superintendents
superior adjective
and noun
superiors
superiority
superlative adjective
superlatively
superlative noun
superlatives
supermarket noun
supermarkets
supernatural
adjective
supernaturally
supersonic adjective
supersonically
superstition noun
superstitions
superstitious
adjective
superstitiously
supervise verb
supervises
supervising
supervised
supervision
supervisor
supper noun
suppers
supple adjective
suppler
supplest
supplely

supplement noun
supplements
supplementary
suppleness
supply verb
supplies
supplying
supplied
supplier noun
suppliers
supply noun
supplies
support verb
supports
supporting
supported
support noun
supports
supporter noun
supporters
suppose verb
supposes
supposing
supposed
supposedly
supposition noun
suppositions
suppress verb
suppresses
suppressing
suppressed
suppression
supremacy
supreme adjective
supremely
sure adjective
surer
surest
surely
surf noun

- -

★ **Sunday** is a day of the week. ! sundae.

surf verb
  surfs
  surfing
  surfed
surface noun
  surfaces
surface verb
  surfaces
  surfacing
  surfaced
surfboard noun
  surfboards
surfer noun
  surfers
surge verb
  surges
  surging
  surged
surge noun
  surges
surgeon noun
  surgeons
surgery noun
  surgeries
surgical adjective
  surgically
surname noun
  surnames
surpass verb
  surpasses
  surpassing
  surpassed
surplus noun
  surpluses
surprise verb
  surprises
  surprising
  surprised
surprise noun
  surprises

surrender verb
  surrenders
  surrendering
  surrendered
surrender noun
  surrenders
surround verb
  surrounds
  surrounding
  surrounded
surroundings plural
  noun
survey noun
  surveys
survey verb
  surveys
  surveying
  surveyed
surveyor noun
  surveyors
survival
survive verb
  survives
  surviving
  survived
survivor noun
  survivors
suspect verb
  suspects
  suspecting
  suspected
suspect noun
  suspects
suspend verb
  suspends
  suspending
  suspended
suspense
suspension noun
  suspensions

suspicion noun
  suspicions
suspicious adjective
  suspiciously
sustain verb
  sustains
  sustaining
  sustained
swagger verb
  swaggers
  swaggering
  swaggered
swallow verb
  swallows
  swallowing
  swallowed
swallow noun
  swallows
swam see swim
swamp verb
  swamps
  swamping
  swamped
swamp noun
  swamps
swampy adjective
  swampier
  swampiest
swan noun
  swans
swank verb
  swanks
  swanking
  swanked
swap verb
  swaps
  swapping
  swapped
swap noun
  swaps
swarm noun
  swarms

swarm *verb*
swarms
swarming
swarmed
swastika *noun*
swastikas
★ **swat** *verb*
swats
swatting
swatted
swatter *noun*
swatters
sway *verb*
sways
swaying
swayed
swear *verb*
swears
swearing
swore
sworn
sweat *verb*
sweats
sweating
sweated
sweat *noun*
sweater *noun*
sweaters
sweatshirt *noun*
sweatshirts
sweaty *adjective*
sweatier
sweatiest
sweatily
swede *noun*
swedes
sweep *verb*
sweeps
sweeping
swept
sweep *noun*
sweeps

sweeper *noun*
sweepers
sweet *adjective*
sweeter
sweetest
sweetly
sweet *noun*
sweets
sweetcorn
sweeten *verb*
sweetens
sweetening
sweetened
sweetener *noun*
sweeteners
sweetheart *noun*
sweethearts
sweetness
swell *verb*
swells
swelling
swelled
swollen
swell *noun*
swells
swelling *noun*
swellings
swelter *verb*
swelters
sweltering
sweltered
swept see **sweep**
swerve *verb*
swerves
swerving
swerved
swerve *noun*
swerves
swift *adjective*
swifter
swiftest
swiftly

swift *noun*
swifts
swiftness
swill *verb*
swills
swilling
swilled
swill *noun*
swim *verb*
swims
swimming
swam
swum
swim *noun*
swims
swimmer *noun*
swimmers
swimsuit *noun*
swimsuits
swindle *verb*
swindles
swindling
swindled
swindler *noun*
swindlers
swindle *noun*
swindles
swine *noun*
swine or swines
swing *verb*
swings
swinging
swung
swing *noun*
swings
swipe *verb*
swipes
swiping
swiped

- -

★ To **swat** an insect is to hit it. ! **swot**.

swipe noun
  swipes
swirl verb
  swirls
  swirling
  swirled
swirl noun
  swirls
swish verb
  swishes
  swishing
  swished
swish noun
  swishes
Swiss roll noun
  Swiss rolls
switch verb
  switches
  switching
  switched
switch noun
  switches
switchboard noun
  switchboards
swivel verb
  swivels
  swivelling
  swivelled
swollen see swell
swoon verb
  swoons
  swooning
  swooned
swoop verb
  swoops
  swooping
  swooped
swoop noun
  swoops

swop verb
  swops
  swopping
  swopped
sword noun
  swords
swore see swear
sworn see swear
★ **swot** verb
  swots
  swotting
  swotted
swot noun
  swots
swum see swim
swung see swing
sycamore noun
  sycamores
syllabic adjective
  syllabically
syllable noun
  syllables
syllabus noun
  syllabuses
symbol noun
  symbols
symbolic adjective
  symbolically
symbolism
symbolize verb
  symbolizes
  symbolizing
  symbolized
symmetrical
  adjective
  symmetrically
symmetry
sympathetic
  adjective
  sympathetically

sympathize verb
  sympathizes
  sympathizing
  sympathized
sympathy noun
  sympathies
symphonic adjective
  symphonically
symphony noun
  symphonies
symptom noun
  symptoms
symptomatic
  adjective
  symptomatically
synagogue noun
  synagogues
synchronization
synchronize verb
  synchronizes
  synchronizing
  synchronized
syncopated
synonym noun
  synonyms
synonymous
  adjective
  synonymously
synthesis noun
  syntheses
synthesize verb
  synthesizes
  synthesizing
  synthesized
synthesizer noun
  synthesizers
synthetic adjective
  synthetically
syringe noun
  syringes

. . . .

★ To **swot** is to study hard. ! swat.

syrup noun
  syrups
syrupy
system noun
  systems
systematic adjective
  systematically

Tt

-t
See the note at -ed.

tab noun
  tabs
tabby noun
  tabbies
table noun
  tables
tablecloth noun
  tablecloths
tablespoon noun
  tablespoons
tablespoonful noun
  tablespoonfuls
tablet noun
  tablets
tack noun
  tacks
tack verb
  tacks
  tacking
  tacked
tackle verb
  tackles
  tackling
  tackled

tackle noun
  tackles
tacky adjective
  tackier
  tackiest
  tackily
tact
tactful adjective
  tactfully
tactical adjective
  tactically
tactics plural noun
tactless adjective
  tactlessly
tadpole noun
  tadpoles
tag noun
  tags
tag verb
  tags
  tagging
  tagged
★ **tail** noun
  tails
tail verb
  tails
  tailing
  tailed
tailback noun
  tailbacks
tailless
tailor noun
  tailors
take verb
  takes
  taking
  took
  taken
takeaway noun
  takeaways
takings plural noun

talc
talcum powder
☆ **tale** noun
  tales
talent noun
  talents
talented
talk verb
  talks
  talking
  talked
talk noun
  talks
talkative adjective
  talkatively
talker noun
  talkers
tall adjective
  taller
  tallest
tally verb
  tallies
  tallying
  tallied
Talmud
talon noun
  talons
tambourine noun
  tambourines
tame adjective
  tamer
  tamest
  tamely
tame verb
  tames
  taming
  tamed
tameness
tamer noun
  tamers

. . . .

★ A **tail** is a part at the back of an animal. ! **tale**.
☆ A **tale** is a story. ! **tail**.

tamper verb
tampers
tampering
tampered
tampon noun
tampons
tan noun
tans
tan verb
tans
tanning
tanned
tandem noun
tandems
tang noun
tangs
tangent noun
tangents
tangerine noun
tangerines
tangle verb
tangles
tangling
tangled
tangle noun
tangles
tank noun
tanks
tankard noun
tankards
tanker noun
tankers
tanner noun
tanners
tantalize verb
tantalizes
tantalizing
tantalized
tantrum noun
tantrums
tap noun
taps

tap verb
taps
tapping
tapped
tap dance noun
tap dances
tap dancer noun
tap dancers
tap dancing
tape noun
tapes
tape verb
tapes
taping
taped
tape-measure noun
tape-measures
taper verb
tapers
tapering
tapered
taper noun
tapers
tape recorder noun
tape recorders
tapestry noun
tapestries
tapeworm noun
tapeworms
tapioca
tar noun
tar verb
tars
tarring
tarred
tarantula noun
tarantulas
target noun
targets

target verb
targets
targeting
targeted
tarmac
tarmacadam
tarnish verb
tarnishes
tarnishing
tarnished
tarpaulin noun
tarpaulins
tarry adjective
tarrier
tarriest
tart noun
tarts
tart adjective
tarter
tartest
tartly
tartan noun
tartans
task noun
tasks
tassel noun
tassels
taste verb
tastes
tasting
tasted
taste noun
tastes
tasteful adjective
tastefully
tasteless adjective
tastelessly
tasty adjective
tastier
tastiest
tastily
tattered

tatters *plural noun*
tattoo *noun*
  tattoos
tattoo *verb*
  tattoos
  tattooing
  tattooed
tatty *adjective*
  tattier
  tattiest
  tattily
taught see **teach**
taunt *verb*
  taunts
  taunting
  taunted
taunt *noun*
  taunts
taut *adjective*
  tauter
  tautest
  tautly
tautness
tavern *noun*
  taverns
tawny *adjective*
  tawnier
  tawniest
tax *noun*
  taxes
tax *verb*
  taxes
  taxing
  taxed
taxable
taxation
taxi *noun*
  taxis
taxi *verb*
  taxis
  taxiing
  taxied

taxpayer *noun*
  taxpayers
★ **tea** *noun*
  teas
teabag *noun*
  teabags
teacake *noun*
  teacakes
teach *verb*
  teaches
  teaching
  taught
teacher *noun*
  teachers
tea cloth or
  tea towel *noun*
  tea cloths or
  tea towels
teacup *noun*
  teacups
teak
☆ **team** *noun*
  teams
teapot *noun*
  teapots
tear *verb*
  tears
  tearing
  tore
  torn
○ **tear** *noun*
  tears
tearful *adjective*
  tearfully
tear gas
tease *verb*
  teases
  teasing
  teased
teaspoon *noun*
  teaspoons

teaspoonful *noun*
  teaspoonfuls
teat *noun*
  teats
tech *noun*
  techs
technical *adjective*
  technically
technicality *noun*
  technicalities
technician *noun*
  technicians
technique *noun*
  techniques
technological
  adjective
  technologically
technology *noun*
  technologies
teddy bear *noun*
  teddy bears
tedious *adjective*
  tediously
tediousness
tedium
✳ **tee** *noun*
  tees
✴ **teem** *verb*
  teems
  teeming
  teemed
teenage
teenager *noun*
  teenagers
teens
teeth see **tooth**
teetotal
teetotaller *noun*
  teetotallers

· ·

★ **Tea** is a hot drink. **! tee.**
☆ You use **team** in e.g. *a football team.* **! teem.**
○ A **tear** is a drop of water from an eye and rhymes with 'here', or a split in something and rhymes with 'hair'.
✳ A **tee** is part of a golf course. **! tea.**
✴ You use **teem** in e.g. *a place teeming with people.* **! team.**

telecommunications
plural noun
telegram noun
telegrams
telegraph noun
telegraphs
telegraphic adjective
telegraphically
telegraphy
telepathic adjective
telepathically
telepathy
telephone noun
telephones
telephone verb
telephones
telephoning
telephoned
telephonist noun
telephonists
telescope noun
telescopes
telescopic adjective
telescopically
teletext
televise verb
televises
televising
televised
television noun
televisions
tell verb
tells
telling
told
tell-tale adjective
and noun
tell-tales
telly noun
tellies
temper noun
tempers

temperate
temperature noun
temperatures
tempest noun
tempests
tempestuous
adjective
tempestuously
temple noun
temples
tempo noun
tempos
temporary adjective
temporarily
tempt verb
tempts
tempting
tempted
temptation noun
temptations
tempter noun
tempters
temptress noun
temptresses
ten noun
tens
tenancy noun
tenancies
tenant noun
tenants
tend verb
tends
tending
tended
tendency noun
tendencies
tender adjective
tenderer
tenderest
tenderly
tender noun
tenders

tender verb
tenders
tendering
tendered
tenderness
tendon noun
tendons
tendril noun
tendrils
tennis
tenor noun
tenors
tenpin bowling
tense adjective
tenser
tensest
tensely
tense noun
tenses
tension noun
tensions
tent noun
tents
tentacle noun
tentacles
tenth
tenthly
tepid
term noun
terms
term verb
terms
terming
termed
terminal noun
terminals
terminate verb
terminates
terminating
terminated

termination noun
terminations
terminus noun
termini
terrace noun
terraces
terrapin noun
terrapins
terrible adjective
terribly
terrier noun
terriers
terrific adjective
terrifically
terrify verb
terrifies
terrifying
terrified
territorial adjective
territorially
territory noun
territories
terror noun
terrors
terrorism
terrorist adjective
and noun
terrorists
terrorize verb
terrorizes
terrorizing
terrorized
tessellation noun
tessellations
test noun
tests
test verb
tests
testing
tested
testament noun
testaments

testicle noun
testicles
testify verb
testifies
testifying
testified
testimonial noun
testimonials
testimony noun
testimonies
testy adjective
testier
testiest
tether verb
tethers
tethering
tethered
tether noun
tethers
text noun
texts
textbook noun
textbooks
textile noun
textiles
texture noun
textures
than
thank verb
thanks
thanking
thanked
thankful adjective
thankfully
thankless adjective
thanklessly
thanks plural noun
that adjective,
pronoun, and
conjunction
thatch noun

thatch verb
thatches
thatching
thatched
thatcher noun
thatchers
thaw verb
thaws
thawing
thawed
theatre noun
theatres
theatrical adjective
theatrically
thee
theft noun
thefts
★ **their**
☆ **theirs**
them
theme noun
themes
theme park noun
theme parks
themselves
then
theologian noun
theologians
theological adjective
theologically
theology
theorem noun
theorems
theoretical adjective
theoretically
theory noun
theories
therapist noun
therapists

- -

★ You use their in e.g. *this is their house.* ! ~~there, they're.~~
☆ You use theirs in e.g. *the house is theirs.* Note that there is no apostrophe in this word.

therapy *noun*
　therapies
★ **there** *adverb*
thereabouts
therefore
thermal *adjective*
　thermally
thermometer *noun*
　thermometers
Thermos *noun*
　Thermoses
thermostat *noun*
　thermostats
thermostatic
　adjective
　thermostatically
thesaurus *noun*
　thesauri *or*
　thesauruses
these
they
they'd *verb*
they'll *verb*
☆ **they're** *verb*
they've *verb*
thick *adjective*
　thicker
　thickest
　thickly
thicken *verb*
　thickens
　thickening
　thickened
thicket *noun*
　thickets
thickness *noun*
　thicknesses
thief *noun*
　thieves

thigh *noun*
　thighs
thimble *noun*
　thimbles
thin *adjective*
　thinner
　thinnest
　thinly
thin *verb*
　thins
　thinning
　thinned
thine
thing *noun*
　things
think *verb*
　thinks
　thinking
　thought
thinker *noun*
　thinkers
thinness
third
thirdly
Third World
thirst
thirsty *adjective*
　thirstier
　thirstiest
　thirstily
thirteen
thirteenth
thirtieth
thirty *noun*
　thirties
this
thistle *noun*
　thistles
thorn *noun*
　thorns

thorny *adjective*
　thornier
　thorniest
thorough *adjective*
　thoroughly
thoroughness
those
thou
though
thought *noun*
　thoughts
thought see **think**
thoughtful *adjective*
　thoughtfully
thoughtfulness
thoughtless *adjective*
　thoughtlessly
thoughtlessness
thousand *noun*
　thousands
thousandth
✪ **thrash** *verb*
　thrashes
　thrashing
　thrashed
thread *noun*
　threads
thread *verb*
　threads
　threading
　threaded
threadbare
threat *noun*
　threats
threaten *verb*
　threatens
　threatening
　threatened
three *noun*
　threes

. . . .

★ You use **there** in e.g. *Look over there.* ! their, they're.
☆ **They're** is short for *they are.* ! their, there.
✪ To **thrash** someone is to beat them. ! thresh.

three-dimensional *adjective*
three-dimensionally
★ **thresh** *verb*
threshes
threshing
threshed
threshold *noun*
thresholds
threw see **throw**
thrift
thrifty *adjective*
thriftier
thriftiest
thriftily
thrill *noun*
thrills
thrill *verb*
thrills
thrilling
thrilled
thriller *noun*
thrillers
thrive *verb*
thrives
thriving
thrived *or* throve
or thriven
throat *noun*
throats
throb *verb*
throbs
throbbing
throbbed
throb *noun*
throbs
throne *noun*
thrones
throng *noun*
throngs

throttle *verb*
throttles
throttling
throttled
throttle *noun*
throttles
through
throughout
throve see **thrive**
throw *verb*
throws
throwing
threw
thrown
throw *noun*
throws
thrush *noun*
thrushes
thrust *verb*
thrusts
thrusting
thrust
thud *noun*
thuds
thud *verb*
thuds
thudding
thudded
thumb *noun*
thumbs
thump *verb*
thumps
thumping
thumped
thump *noun*
thumps
thunder *noun*
thunder *verb*
thunders
thundering
thundered

thunderous *adjective*
thunderously
thunderstorm *noun*
thunderstorms
Thursday *noun*
Thursdays
thus
thy
tick *verb*
ticks
ticking
ticked
tick *noun*
ticks
ticket *noun*
tickets
tickle *verb*
tickles
tickling
tickled
ticklish *adjective*
ticklishly
tidal
tiddler *noun*
tiddlers
tiddlywink *noun*
tiddlywinks
tide *noun*
tides
tide *verb*
tides
tiding
tided
tidiness
tidy *adjective*
tidier
tidiest
tidily
tie *verb*
ties
tying
tied

- -

★ To **thresh** corn is to beat it to separate the grain. ! **thrash.**

tie *noun*
ties
tie-break *noun*
tie-breaks
tiger *noun*
tigers
tight *adjective*
tighter
tightest
tightly
tighten *verb*
tightens
tightening
tightened
tightness
tightrope *noun*
tightropes
tights *plural noun*
tigress *noun*
tigresses
tile *noun*
tiles
tiled
till *preposition* and
conjunction
till *noun*
tills
till *verb*
tills
tilling
tilled
tiller *noun*
tillers
tilt *verb*
tilts
tilting
tilted
tilt *noun*
tilts
timber *noun*
timbers

time *noun*
times
time *verb*
times
timing
timed
timer *noun*
timers
times
timetable *noun*
timetables
timid *adjective*
timidly
timidity
timing
timpani *plural noun*
tin *noun*
tins
tin *verb*
tins
tinning
tinned
tingle *verb*
tingles
tingling
tingled
tingle *noun*
tingles
tinker *verb*
tinkers
tinkering
tinkered
tinker *noun*
tinkers
tinkle *verb*
tinkles
tinkling
tinkled
tinkle *noun*
tinkles

tinny *adjective*
tinnier
tinniest
tinnily
tinsel
tint *noun*
tints
tint *verb*
tints
tinting
tinted
tiny *adjective*
tinier
tiniest
tip *verb*
tips
tipping
tipped
tip *noun*
tips
tiptoe *verb*
tiptoes
tiptoeing
tiptoed
tiptoe *noun*
★ **tire** *verb*
tires
tiring
tired
tired
tireless *adjective*
tirelessly
tiresome *adjective*
tiresomely
tissue *noun*
tissues
tit *noun*
tits
titbit *noun*
titbits

· ·

★ To **tire** is to become tired. **!** tyre.

title *noun*
titles
titter *verb*
titters
tittering
tittered
★ **to** *preposition*
toad *noun*
toads
toadstool *noun*
toadstools
toast *verb*
toasts
toasting
toasted
toast *noun*
toasts
toaster *noun*
toasters
tobacco *noun*
tobaccos
tobacconist *noun*
tobacconists
toboggan *noun*
toboggans
tobogganing
today
toddler *noun*
toddlers
☆ **toe** *noun*
toes
toffee *noun*
toffees
toga *noun*
togas
together
toil *verb*
toils
toiling
toiled

toilet *noun*
toilets
token *noun*
tokens
told see **tell**
tolerable *adjective*
tolerably
tolerance
tolerant *adjective*
tolerantly
tolerate *verb*
tolerates
tolerating
tolerated
toll *noun*
tolls
toll *verb*
tolls
tolling
tolled
tomahawk *noun*
tomahawks
tomato *noun*
tomatoes
tomb *noun*
tombs
tomboy *noun*
tomboys
tombstone *noun*
tombstones
tomcat *noun*
tomcats
tommy-gun *noun*
tommy-guns
tomorrow
tom-tom *noun*
tom-toms
○ **ton** *noun*
tons
tonal *adjective*
tonally

tone *noun*
tones
tone *verb*
tones
toning
toned
tone-deaf
tongs *plural noun*
tongue *noun*
tongues
tonic *noun*
tonics
tonight
✳ **tonne** *noun*
tonnes
tonsillitis
tonsils *plural noun*
✸ **too** *adverb*
took see **take**
tool *noun*
tools
tooth *noun*
teeth
toothache
toothbrush *noun*
toothbrushes
toothed
toothpaste *noun*
toothpastes
top *noun*
tops
top *verb*
tops
topping
topped
topic *noun*
topics
topical *adjective*
topically
topicality

★ You use **to** in e.g. *go to bed* or *I want to stay*. ! **too, two**.
☆ A **toe** is a part of a foot. ! **tow**.
○ A **ton** is a non-metric unit of weight. ! **tonne**.
✳ A **tonne** is a metric unit of weight. ! **ton**.
✸ You use **too** in e.g. *it's too late* or *I want to come too*. ! **to, two**.

topless
topmost
topping noun
  toppings
topple verb
  topples
  toppling
  toppled
topsy-turvy
torch noun
  torches
tore see **tear**
toreador noun
  toreadors
torment verb
  torments
  tormenting
  tormented
torment noun
  torments
tormentor noun
  tormentors
torn see **tear**
tornado noun
  tornadoes
torpedo noun
  torpedoes
torpedo verb
  torpedoes
  torpedoing
  torpedoed
torrent noun
  torrents
torrential adjective
  torrentially
torso noun
  torsos
tortoise noun
  tortoises

torture verb
  tortures
  torturing
  tortured
torture noun
  tortures
torturer noun
  torturers
Tory noun
  Tories
toss verb
  tosses
  tossing
  tossed
toss noun
  tosses
total noun
  totals
total adjective
  totally
total verb
  totals
  totalling
  totalled
totalitarian
totem pole noun
  totem poles
totter verb
  totters
  tottering
  tottered
touch verb
  touches
  touching
  touched
touch noun
  touches
touchy adjective
  touchier
  touchiest
  touchily

tough adjective
  tougher
  toughest
  toughly
toughen verb
  toughens
  toughening
  toughened
toughness
tour noun
  tours
tourism
tourist noun
  tourists
tournament noun
  tournaments
★ **tow** verb
  tows
  towing
  towed
tow noun
toward or **towards**
towel noun
  towels
towelling
tower noun
  towers
tower verb
  towers
  towering
  towered
town noun
  towns
towpath noun
  towpaths
toxic adjective
  toxically
toy noun
  toys

· ·

★ To **tow** something is to pull it along. ! **toe**.

toy *verb*
toys
toying
toyed
toyshop *noun*
toyshops
trace *noun*
traces
trace *verb*
traces
tracing
traced
traceable
track *noun*
tracks
track *verb*
tracks
tracking
tracked
tracker *noun*
trackers
tracksuit *noun*
tracksuits
tract *noun*
tracts
traction
tractor *noun*
tractors
trade *noun*
trades
trade *verb*
trades
trading
traded
trademark *noun*
trademarks
trader *noun*
traders
tradesman *noun*
tradesmen

trade union *noun*
trade unions
tradition *noun*
traditions
traditional *adjective*
traditionally
traffic *noun*
traffic *verb*
traffics
trafficking
trafficked
tragedy *noun*
tragedies
tragic *adjective*
tragically
trail *noun*
trails
trail *verb*
trails
trailing
trailed
trailer *noun*
trailers
train *noun*
trains
train *verb*
trains
training
trained
trainer *noun*
trainers
traitor *noun*
traitors
tram *noun*
trams
tramp *noun*
tramps
tramp *verb*
tramps
tramping
tramped

trample *verb*
tramples
trampling
trampled
trampoline *noun*
trampolines
trance *noun*
trances
tranquil *adjective*
tranquilly
★ **tranquillity**
tranquillizer *noun*
tranquillizers
transact *verb*
transacts
transacting
transacted
transaction *noun*
transactions
transatlantic
transfer *verb*
transfers
transferring
transferred
transfer *noun*
transfers
transferable
transference
transform *verb*
transforms
transforming
transformed
transformation
noun
transformations
transformer *noun*
transformers
transfusion *noun*
transfusions
transistor *noun*
transistors

★ Note that there are two ls in this word.

transition *noun*
transitions
transitional *adjective*
transitionally
transitive *adjective*
transitively
translate *verb*
translates
translating
translated
translation *noun*
translations
translator *noun*
translators
translucent
transmission *noun*
transmissions
transmit *verb*
transmits
transmitting
transmitted
transmitter *noun*
transmitters
transparency *noun*
transparencies
transparent *adjective*
transparently
transpire *verb*
transpires
transpiring
transpired
transplant *verb*
transplants
transplanting
transplanted
transplant *noun*
transplants

transplantation *noun*
transplantations
transport *verb*
transports
transporting
transported
transportation
transport
transporter *noun*
transporters
trap *verb*
traps
trapping
trapped
trap *noun*
traps
trapdoor *noun*
trapdoors
trapeze *noun*
trapezes
trapezium *noun*
trapeziums
trapezoid *noun*
trapezoids
trapper *noun*
trappers
trash
trashy *adjective*
trashier
trashiest
trashily
travel *verb*
travels
travelling
travelled
travel *noun*
traveller *noun*
travellers

traveller's cheque *noun*
traveller's cheques
trawler *noun*
trawlers
tray *noun*
trays
treacherous *adjective*
treacherously
treachery
treacle
tread *verb*
treads
treading
trod
trodden
tread *noun*
treads
treason
treasure *noun*
treasures
treasure *verb*
treasures
treasuring
treasured
treasurer *noun*
treasurers
treasury *noun*
treasuries
treat *verb*
treats
treating
treated
treat *noun*
treats
treatment *noun*
treatments
treaty *noun*
treaties

treble *adjective* and
  noun
  trebles
treble *verb*
  trebles
  trebling
  trebled
tree *noun*
  trees
trek *verb*
  treks
  trekking
  trekked
trek *noun*
  treks
trellis *noun*
  trellises
tremble *verb*
  trembles
  trembling
  trembled
tremble *noun*
  trembles
tremendous
  adjective
  tremendously
tremor *noun*
  tremors
trench *noun*
  trenches
trend *noun*
  trends
trendiness
trendy *adjective*
  trendier
  trendiest
  trendily
trespass *verb*
  trespasses
  trespassing
  trespassed

trespasser *noun*
  trespassers
trestle *noun*
  trestles
trial *noun*
  trials
triangle *noun*
  triangles
triangular
tribal *adjective*
  tribally
tribe *noun*
  tribes
tribesman *noun*
  tribesmen
tributary *noun*
  tributaries
tribute *noun*
  tributes
trick *noun*
  tricks
trick *verb*
  tricks
  tricking
  tricked
trickery
trickster *noun*
  tricksters
trickle *verb*
  trickles
  trickling
  trickled
trickle *noun*
  trickles
tricky *adjective*
  trickier
  trickiest
  trickily
tricycle *noun*
  tricycles

tried see try
trifle *noun*
  trifles
trifle *verb*
  trifles
  trifling
  trifled
trifling
trigger *noun*
  triggers
trigger *verb*
  triggers
  triggering
  triggered
trillion *noun*
  trillions
trim *adjective*
  trimmer
  trimmest
  trimly
trim *verb*
  trims
  trimming
  trimmed
trim *noun*
  trims
★ Trinity
trio *noun*
  trios
trip *verb*
  trips
  tripping
  tripped
trip *noun*
  trips
tripe
triple *adjective*
  triply
triple *noun*
  triples

★ You use a capital T when you mean the three persons of God in Christianity.

triple verb
triples
tripling
tripled
triplet noun
triplets
tripod noun
tripods
triumph noun
triumphs
triumphant adjective
triumphantly
trivial adjective
trivially
triviality noun
trivialities
trod see tread
trodden see tread
troll noun
trolls
trolley noun
trolleys
trombone noun
trombones
troop noun
troops
troop verb
troops
trooping
trooped
troops plural noun
trophy noun
trophies
tropic noun
tropics
tropical adjective
trot verb
trots
trotting
trotted
trot noun
trots

trouble noun
troubles
trouble verb
troubles
troubling
troubled
troublesome
trough noun
troughs
trousers plural noun
trout noun
trout
trowel noun
trowels
truancy noun
truancies
truant noun
truants
truce noun
truces
truck noun
trucks
trudge verb
trudges
trudging
trudged
true adjective
truer
truest
truly
trump noun
trumps
trump verb
trumps
trumping
trumped
trumpet noun
trumpets
trumpet verb
trumpets
trumpeting
trumpeted

trumpeter noun
trumpeters
truncheon noun
truncheons
trundle verb
trundles
trundling
trundled
trunk noun
trunks
trunks plural noun
trust verb
trusts
trusting
trusted
trust
trustful adjective
trustfully
trustworthy adjective
trustworthily
trusty adjective
trustier
trustiest
trustily
truth noun
truths
truthful adjective
truthfully
truthfulness
try verb
tries
trying
tried
try noun
tries
T-shirt noun
T-shirts
tub noun
tubs

tuba noun
tubas
tube noun
tubes
tuber noun
tubers
tubing
tubular
tuck verb
tucks
tucking
tucked
tuck noun
tucks
Tuesday noun
Tuesdays
tuft noun
tufts
tug noun
tugs
tug verb
tugs
tugging
tugged
tulip noun
tulips
tumble verb
tumbles
tumbling
tumbled
tumble noun
tumbles
tumble-drier noun
tumble-driers
tumbler noun
tumblers
tummy noun
tummies
tumour noun
tumours

tumult
tumultuous adjective
tumultuously
tuna noun
tuna or tunas
tundra
tune noun
tunes
tune verb
tunes
tuning
tuned
tuneful adjective
tunefully
tunic noun
tunics
tunnel noun
tunnels
tunnel verb
tunnels
tunnelling
tunnelled
turban noun
turbans
turbine noun
turbines
turbulence
turbulent adjective
turbulently
turf noun
turfs or turves
turkey noun
turkeys
Turkish bath noun
Turkish baths
Turkish delight
turmoil

turn verb
turns
turning
turned
turn
noun
turns
turncoat noun
turncoats
turnip noun
turnips
turnover noun
turnovers
turnstile noun
turnstiles
turntable noun
turntables
turpentine
turquoise
turret noun
turrets
turtle noun
turtles
tusk noun
tusks
tussle verb
tussles
tussling
tussled
tussle noun
tussles
tutor noun
tutors
tweak verb
tweaks
tweaking
tweaked
tweak noun
tweaks
tweed
tweezers plural noun

twelve *noun*
  twelves
twelfth
twentieth
twenty *noun*
  twenties
twice
twiddle *verb*
  twiddles
  twiddling
  twiddled
twiddle *noun*
  twiddles
twig *noun*
  twigs
twig *verb*
  twigs
  twigging
  twigged
twilight
twin *noun*
  twins
twin *verb*
  twins
  twinning
  twinned
twine
twinkle *verb*
  twinkles
  twinkling
  twinkled
twinkle *noun*
  twinkles
twirl *verb*
  twirls
  twirling
  twirled
twirl *noun*
  twirls
twist *verb*
  twists
  twisting
  twisted

twist *noun*
  twists
twister *noun*
  twisters
twitch *verb*
  twitches
  twitching
  twitched
twitch *noun*
  twitches
twitter *verb*
  twitters
  twittering
  twittered
★ two *adjective* and *noun*
  twos
tying see **tie**
type *noun*
  types
type *verb*
  types
  typing
  typed
typewriter *noun*
  typewriters
typewritten
typhoon *noun*
  typhoons
typical *adjective*
  typically
typist *noun*
  typists
tyranny *noun*
  tyrannies
tyrannical *adjective*
  tyrannically
tyrant *noun*
  tyrants
☆ tyre *noun*
  tyres

Uu

udder *noun*
  udders
ugliness
ugly *adjective*
  uglier
  ugliest
ulcer *noun*
  ulcers
ultimate *adjective*
  ultimately
ultraviolet
umbilical cord *noun*
  umbilical cords
umbrella *noun*
  umbrellas
umpire *noun*
  umpires

un-
un- makes words meaning 'not', e.g. **unable, unhappiness.** Some of these words have special meanings, e.g. **unprofessional.** See the note at **non-**.

unable
unaided
unanimity
unanimous *adjective*
  unanimously
unavoidable
  adjective
  unavoidably
unaware

★ You use **two** in e.g. *two people* or *there are two of them.* ! **to, too.**
☆ A **tyre** is a rubber cover for a wheel. ! **tire.**

unawares
unbearable *adjective*
  unbearably
unbelievable
  adjective
  unbelievably
unblock *verb*
  unblocks
  unblocking
  unblocked
unborn
uncalled for
uncanny *adjective*
  uncannier
  uncanniest
uncertain *adjective*
  uncertainly
uncertainty
uncle *noun*
  uncles
uncomfortable
  adjective
  uncomfortably
uncommon
  adjective
  uncommonly
unconscious
  adjective
  unconsciously
unconsciousness
uncontrollable
  adjective
  uncontrollably
uncountable
uncouth
uncover *verb*
  uncovers
  uncovering
  uncovered
undecided

undeniable *adjective*
  undeniably
under
underarm *adjective*
underclothes *plural*
  noun
underdeveloped
underdone
underfoot
undergo *verb*
  undergoes
  undergoing
  underwent
  undergone
undergraduate
  noun
  undergraduates
underground
  adjective and *noun*
  undergrounds
undergrowth
underhand
underlie *verb*
  underlies
  underlying
  underlay
  underlain
underline *verb*
  underlines
  underlining
  underlined
undermine *verb*
  undermines
  undermining
  undermined
underneath
  preposition
underpants *plural*
  noun
underpass *noun*
  underpasses

underprivileged
understand *verb*
  understands
  understanding
  understood
understandable
  adjective
  understandably
understanding
undertake *verb*
  undertakes
  undertaking
  undertook
  undertaken
undertaker *noun*
  undertakers
undertaking *noun*
  undertakings
underwater
underwear
underworld
undesirable
  adjective
  undesirably
undeveloped
undo *verb*
  undoes
  undoing
  undid
  undone
undoubted *adjective*
  undoubtedly
undress *verb*
  undresses
  undressing
  undressed
unearth *verb*
  unearths
  unearthing
  unearthed
unearthly

unease
uneasiness
uneasy *adjective*
  uneasier
  uneasiest
  uneasily
uneatable
unemployed
unemployment
uneven *adjective*
  unevenly
unevenness
unexpected *adjective*
  unexpectedly
unfair *adjective*
  unfairly
unfairness
unfaithful *adjective*
  unfaithfully
unfamiliar
unfamiliarity
unfasten *verb*
  unfastens
  unfastening
  unfastened
unfavourable
  adjective
  unfavourably
unfinished
unfit
unfold *verb*
  unfolds
  unfolding
  unfolded
unforgettable
  adjective
  unforgettably
unforgivable
  adjective
  unforgivably

unfortunate
  adjective
  unfortunately
unfreeze *verb*
  unfreezes
  unfreezing
  unfroze
  unfrozen
unfriendliness
unfriendly
ungrateful *adjective*
  ungratefully
unhappiness
unhappy *adjective*
  unhappier
  unhappiest
  unhappily
unhealthy *adjective*
  unhealthier
  unhealthiest
  unhealthily
unheard-of
unicorn *noun*
  unicorns
unification
uniform *noun*
  uniforms
uniform *adjective*
  uniformly
uniformed
uniformity
unify *verb*
  unifies
  unifying
  unified
unimportance
unimportant
uninhabited

unintentional
  adjective
  unintentionally
uninterested
uninteresting
union *noun*
  unions
unique *adjective*
  uniquely
uniqueness
unisex
unison
unit *noun*
  units
unite *verb*
  unites
  uniting
  united
unity *noun*
  unities
universal *adjective*
  universally
universe
university *noun*
  universities
unjust *adjective*
  unjustly
unkind *adjective*
  unkinder
  unkindest
  unkindly
unkindness
unknown
unleaded
unless
unlike
unlikely *adjective*
  unlikelier
  unlikeliest

unload *verb*
unloads
unloading
unloaded
unlock *verb*
unlocks
unlocking
unlocked
unlucky *adjective*
unluckier
unluckiest
unluckily
unmistakable
adjective
unmistakably
unnatural *adjective*
unnaturally
unnecessary
adjective
unnecessarily
unoccupied
unpack *verb*
unpacks
unpacking
unpacked
unpleasant *adjective*
unpleasantly
unpleasantness
unplug *verb*
unplugs
unplugging
unplugged
unpopular *adjective*
unpopularly
unpopularity
unravel *verb*
unravels
unravelling
unravelled
unreal

unreasonable
adjective
unreasonably
unrest
unroll *verb*
unrolls
unrolling
unrolled
unruliness
unruly *adjective*
unrulier
unruliest
unscrew *verb*
unscrews
unscrewing
unscrewed
unseemly
unseen
unselfish *adjective*
unselfishly
unselfishness
unsightly
unskilled
unsound *adjective*
unsoundly
unsteadiness
unsteady *adjective*
unsteadier
unsteadiest
unsteadily
unsuccessful
adjective
unsuccessfully
unsuitable *adjective*
unsuitably
unthinkable
adjective
unthinkably
untidiness

untidy *adjective*
untidier
untidiest
untidily
untie *verb*
unties
untying
untied
until
untimely
unto
untold
untoward
untrue *adjective*
untruly
untruthful *adjective*
untruthfully
unused
unusual *adjective*
unusually
unwanted
unwell
unwilling *adjective*
unwillingly
unwillingness
unwind *verb*
unwinds
unwinding
unwound
unwrap *verb*
unwraps
unwrapping
unwrapped
unzip *verb*
unzips
unzipping
unzipped
update *verb*
updates
updating
updated

upgrade verb
upgrades
upgrading
upgraded
upheaval noun
upheavals
uphill
uphold verb
upholds
upholding
upheld
upholstery
upkeep
uplands plural noun
upon
upper
upright adjective
uprightly
upright noun
uprights
uprising noun
uprisings
uproar noun
uproars
upset verb
upsets
upsetting
upset
upset noun
upsets
upshot
upside down
upstairs
upstart noun
upstarts
upstream adjective
uptake
uptight
upward adjective and
adverb

upwards adverb
uranium
urban
urbanization
urbanize verb
urbanizes
urbanizing
urbanized
urchin noun
urchins
Urdu
urge verb
urges
urging
urged
urge noun
urges
urgency
urgent adjective
urgently
urinary
urinate verb
urinates
urinating
urinated
urination
urine
urn noun
urns

-us
Most nouns ending in
-us come from Latin
words, e.g. **bonus** and
terminus. They
normally have plurals
ending in -uses, e.g.
bonuses and
terminuses. Some
more technical words
have plurals ending in
-i, e.g. **nucleus -
nuclei**.

usable
usage noun
usages
use verb
uses
using
used
use noun
uses
useful adjective
usefully
usefulness
useless adjective
uselessly
uselessness
user noun
users
user-friendly
adjective
user-friendlier
user-friendliest
usher noun
ushers
usher verb
ushers
ushering
ushered
usherette noun
usherettes
usual adjective
usually
usurp verb
usurps
usurping
usurped
usurper noun
usurpers
utensil noun
utensils
uterus noun
uteri

utilization
utilize *verb*
  utilizes
  utilizing
  utilized
utmost
utter *adjective*
utter *verb*
  utters
  uttering
  uttered
utterance *noun*
  utterances
utterly *adverb*
U-turn *noun*
  U-turns

vacancy *noun*
  vacancies
vacant *adjective*
  vacantly
vacate *verb*
  vacates
  vacating
  vacated
vacation *noun*
  vacations
vaccinate *verb*
  vaccinates
  vaccinating
  vaccinated
vaccination *noun*
  vaccinations
vaccine *noun*
  vaccines
vacuum *noun*
  vacuums

vagina *noun*
  vaginas
vague *adjective*
  vaguer
  vaguest
  vaguely
vagueness
★ vain *adjective*
  vainer
  vainest
  vainly
☆ vale *noun*
  vales
valentine *noun*
  valentines
valiant *adjective*
  valiantly
valid *adjective*
  validly
validity
valley *noun*
  valleys
valour
valuable *adjective*
  valuably
valuables *plural noun*
valuation *noun*
  valuations
value *noun*
  values
value *verb*
  values
  valuing
  valued
valueless
valuer *noun*
  valuers
valve *noun*
  valves

vampire *noun*
  vampires
van *noun*
  vans
vandal *noun*
  vandals
vandalism
✿ vane *noun*
  vanes
vanilla
vanish *verb*
  vanishes
  vanishing
  vanished
vanity
vanquish *verb*
  vanquishes
  vanquishing
  vanquished
vaporize *verb*
  vaporizes
  vaporizing
  vaporized
vapour *noun*
  vapours
variable *adjective*
  variably
variable *noun*
  variables
variation *noun*
  variations
varied
variety *noun*
  varieties
various *adjective*
  variously
varnish *noun*
  varnishes

- -

★ Vain means 'conceited' or 'proud'. ! vane, vein.
☆ A vale is a valley. ! veil.
✿ A vane is a pointer that shows which way the wind is blowing. ! vain, vein.

varnish *verb*
varnishes
varnishing
varnished
vary *verb*
varies
varying
varied
vase *noun*
vases
vast *adjective*
vastly
vastness
vat *noun*
vats
vault *verb*
vaults
vaulting
vaulted
vault *noun*
vaults
veal
vector *noun*
vectors
Veda
veer *verb*
veers
veering
veered
vegan *noun*
vegans
vegetable *noun*
vegetables
vegetarian *noun*
vegetarians
vegetate *verb*
vegetates
vegetating
vegetated
vegetation
vehicle *noun*
vehicles

★ **veil** *noun*
veils
veil *verb*
veils
veiling
veiled
☆ **vein** *noun*
veins
velocity *noun*
velocities
velvet
velvety
vendetta *noun*
vendettas
vendor *noun*
vendors
venerable *adjective*
venerably
venereal disease *noun*
venereal diseases
venetian blind *noun*
venetian blinds
vengeance
venison
Venn diagram *noun*
Venn diagrams
venom
venomous *adjective*
venomously
vent *noun*
vents
ventilate *verb*
ventilates
ventilating
ventilated
ventilation
ventilator *noun*
ventilators
ventriloquism

ventriloquist *noun*
ventriloquists
venture *verb*
ventures
venturing
ventured
venture *noun*
ventures
veranda *noun*
verandas
verb *noun*
verbs
verdict *noun*
verdicts
verge *verb*
verges
verging
verged
verge *noun*
verges
verification
verify *verb*
verifies
verifying
verified
vermin
verruca *noun*
verrucas
versatile
versatility
verse *noun*
verses
version *noun*
versions
versus
vertebra *noun*
vertebrae
vertebrate *noun*
vertebrates
vertex *noun*
vertices

· ·

★ A **veil** is a covering for the face. ! vale.
☆ A **vein** carries blood to the heart. ! vain, vane.

vertical adjective
vertically
very
Vesak
vessel noun
vessels
vest noun
vests
vested adjective
vested
vestment noun
vestments
vestry noun
vestries
vet noun
vets
veteran noun
veterans
veterinary
veto verb
vetoes
vetoing
vetoed
veto noun
vetoes
vex verb
vexes
vexing
vexed
vexation
via
viaduct noun
viaducts
vibrate verb
vibrates
vibrating
vibrated
vibration noun
vibrations
vicar noun
vicars

vicarage noun
vicarages
vice noun
vices
vice-president noun
vice-presidents
vice versa
vicinity noun
vicinities
vicious adjective
viciously
viciousness
victim noun
victims
victimize verb
victimizes
victimizing
victimized
victor noun
victors
Victorian adjective
and noun
Victorians
victorious adjective
victoriously
victory noun
victories
video noun
videos
video verb
videoes
videoing
videoed
videotape noun
videotapes
view noun
views
view verb
views
viewing
viewed

viewer noun
viewers
vigilance
vigilant adjective
vigilantly
vigorous adjective
vigorously
vigour
Viking noun
Vikings
vile adjective
viler
vilest
vilely
villa noun
villas
village noun
villages
villager noun
villagers
villain noun
villains
villainous adjective
villainously
villainy
vine noun
vines
vinegar
vineyard noun
vineyards
vintage noun
vintages
vinyl
viola noun
violas
violate verb
violates
violating
violated

violation *noun*
violations
violator *noun*
violators
violence
violent *adjective*
violently
violet *noun*
violets
violin *noun*
violins
violinist *noun*
violinists
viper *noun*
vipers
virgin *noun*
virgins
virginity
virtual *adjective*
virtually
virtue *noun*
virtues
virtuous *adjective*
virtuously
virus *noun*
viruses
visa *noun*
visas
visibility
visible *adjective*
visibly
vision *noun*
visions
visit *verb*
visits
visiting
visited
visit *noun*
visits
visitor *noun*
visitors

visor *noun*
visors
visual *adjective*
visually
visualize *verb*
visualizes
visualizing
visualized
vital *adjective*
vitally
vitality
vitamin *noun*
vitamins
vivid *adjective*
vividly
vividness
vivisection *noun*
vivisections
vixen *noun*
vixens
vocabulary *noun*
vocabularies
vocal *adjective*
vocally
vocalist *noun*
vocalists
vocation *noun*
vocations
vocational *adjective*
vocationally
vodka *noun*
vodkas
voice *noun*
voices
voice *verb*
voices
voicing
voiced
volcanic

volcano *noun*
volcanoes
vole *noun*
voles
volley *noun*
volleys
volleyball
volt *noun*
volts
voltage *noun*
voltages
volume *noun*
volumes
voluntary *adjective*
voluntarily
volunteer *verb*
volunteers
volunteering
volunteered
volunteer *noun*
volunteers
vomit *verb*
vomits
vomiting
vomited
vote *verb*
votes
voting
voted
vote *noun*
votes
voter *noun*
voters
vouch *verb*
vouches
vouching
vouched
voucher *noun*
vouchers
vow *noun*
vows

vow *verb*
vows
vowing
vowed
vowel *noun*
vowels
voyage *noun*
voyages
voyager *noun*
voyagers
vulgar *adjective*
vulgarly
vulnerable *adjective*
vulnerably
vulture *noun*
vultures
vulva *noun*
vulvas

Ww

wad *noun*
wads
waddle *verb*
waddles
waddling
waddled
waddle *noun*
waddles
wade *verb*
wades
wading
waded
wafer *noun*
wafers
wag *verb*
wags

wagging
wagged
wag *noun*
wags
wage *noun*
wages
wage *verb*
wages
waging
waged
wager *noun*
wagers
wager *verb*
wagers
wagering
wagered
waggle *verb*
waggles
waggling
waggled
wagon *noun*
wagons
wagtail *noun*
wagtails
wail *verb*
wails
wailing
wailed
★ wail *noun*
wails
☆ waist *noun*
waists
waistcoat *noun*
waistcoats
✪ wait *verb*
waits
waiting
waited
wait *noun*
waits
waiter *noun*

waiters
waitress *noun*
waitresses
✴ waive *verb*
waives
waiving
waived
wake *verb*
wakes
waking
woke
woken
wake *noun*
wakes
waken *verb*
wakens
wakening
wakened
walk *verb*
walks
walking
walked
walk *noun*
walks
walkabout *noun*
walkabouts
walker *noun*
walkers
walkie-talkie *noun*
walkie-talkies
Walkman *noun*
Walkmans
wall *noun*
walls
wall *verb*
walls
walling
walled
wallaby *noun*
wallabies

. . . .

★ A wail is a loud sad cry. ! whale.
☆ A person's waist is the narrow part around their middle. ! waste.
✪ To wait is to delay, pause, or rest. ! weight.
✴ To waive a right is to say you do not need it. ! wave.

wallet *noun*
wallets
wallflower *noun*
wallflowers
wallop *verb*
wallops
walloping
walloped
wallow *verb*
wallows
wallowing
wallowed
wallpaper *noun*
wallpapers
walnut *noun*
walnuts
walrus *noun*
walruses
waltz *noun*
waltzes
waltz *verb*
waltzes
waltzing
waltzed
wand *noun*
wands
wander *verb*
wanders
wandering
wandered
wanderer *noun*
wanderers
wane *verb*
wanes
waning
waned
wangle *verb*
wangles
wangling
wangled

want *verb*
wants
wanting
wanted
want *noun*
wants
war *noun*
wars
warble *verb*
warbles
warbling
warbled
warble *noun*
warbles
warbler *noun*
warblers
ward *noun*
wards
ward *verb*
wards
warding
warded
warden *noun*
wardens
warder *noun*
warders
wardrobe *noun*
wardrobes
★ **ware** *noun*
wares
warehouse *noun*
warehouses
warfare
warhead *noun*
warheads
wariness
warlike
warm *adjective*
warmer
warmest
warmly

warm *verb*
warms
warming
warmed
warmth
warn *verb*
warns
warning
warned
warning *noun*
warnings
warp *verb*
warps
warping
warped
warp *noun*
warps
warrant *noun*
warrants
warrant *verb*
warrants
warranting
warranted
warren *noun*
warrens
warrior *noun*
warriors
warship *noun*
warships
wart *noun*
warts
wary *adjective*
warier
wariest
warily
was
wash *verb*
washes
washing
washed
wash *noun*
washes

. . . .

★ Wares are manufactured goods. ! wear, where.

washable
washbasin noun
  washbasins
washer noun
  washers
washing
washing-up
wash-out noun
  wash-outs
wasn't verb
wasp noun
  wasps
wastage
★ **waste** verb
  wastes
  wasting
  wasted
waste adjective and noun
  wastes
wasteful adjective
  wastefully
watch verb
  watches
  watching
  watched
watch noun
  watches
watchdog noun
  watchdogs
watcher noun
  watchers
watchful adjective
  watchfully
watchfulness
watchman noun
  watchmen
water noun
  waters

water verb
  waters
  watering
  watered
watercolour noun
  watercolours
watercress
waterfall noun
  waterfalls
waterlogged
watermark noun
  watermarks
waterproof
water-skiing
watertight
waterway noun
  waterways
waterworks noun
  waterworks
watery
☆ **watt** noun
  watts
✿ **wave** verb
  waves
  waving
  waved
wave noun
  waves
waveband noun
  wavebands
wavelength noun
  wavelengths
waver verb
  wavers
  wavering
  wavered
wavy adjective
  wavier
  waviest
  wavily

wax noun
  waxes
wax verb
  waxes
  waxing
  waxed
waxwork noun
  waxworks
waxy adjective
  waxier
  waxiest
* **way** noun
  ways
✱ **weak** adjective
  weaker
  weakest
  weakly
weakness
weaken verb
  weakens
  weakening
  weakened
weakling noun
  weaklings
wealth
wealthy adjective
  wealthier
  wealthiest
  wealthily
weapon noun
  weapons
* **wear** verb
  wears
  wearing
  wore
  worn
wear noun
wearer noun
  wearers
weariness

- -

★ To **waste** something is to use more of it than is needed. ! **waist**.
☆ A **watt** is a unit of electricity. ! **what**.
✿ To **wave** is to move your arm in greeting. ! **waive**.
* You use **way** in e.g. *can you tell me the way?* ! **weigh, whey**.
✱ **Weak** means 'not strong'. ! **week**.
* To **wear** clothes is to be dressed in them. ! **ware, where**.

weary adjective
wearier
weariest
wearily
weasel noun
weasels
weather noun
weather verb
weathers
weathering
weathered
weathercock noun
weathercocks
★ **weave** verb
weaves
weaving
weaved or wove
woven
weaver noun
weavers
web noun
webs
webbed
website noun
websites
wed verb
weds
wedding
wedded or wed
we'd verb
wedding noun
weddings
wedge noun
wedges
wedge verb
wedges
wedging
wedged
Wednesday noun
Wednesdays
weed noun

weeds
weed verb
weeds
weeding
weeded
weedy adjective
weedier
weediest
weedily
☆ **week** noun
weeks
weekday noun
weekdays
weekend noun
weekends
weekly adjective and
adverb
weep verb
weeps
weeping
wept
weft
✪ **weigh** verb
weighs
weighing
weighed
✱ **weight** noun
weights
weightless
weightlifting
weighty adjective
weightier
weightiest
weightily
weir noun
weirs
weird adjective
weirder
weirdest
weirdly
weirdness

welcome noun
welcomes
welcome verb
welcomes
welcoming
welcomed
weld verb
welds
welding
welded
welder noun
welders
welfare
well noun
wells
well adjective and
adverb
better
best
we'll verb
well-being
wellington boots
plural noun
well-known
went see go
wept see weep
were see are
we're verb
werewolf noun
werewolves
west adjective and
adverb
✳ **west** noun
westerly adjective
and noun
westerlies
western adjective
western noun
westerns

- -

★ The past tense is **weaved** in e.g. *she weaved her way through the crowd* and **wove** in e.g. *she wove a shawl.*
☆ A **week** is a period of seven days. ! weak
✪ You use **weigh** in e.g. *how much do you weigh?* ! way, whey.
✱ **Weight** is how heavy something is. ! wait
✳ You use a capital W in **the West**, when you mean a particular region.

westward *adjective*
and *adverb*
westwards *adverb*
wet *adjective*
  wetter
  wettest
wet *verb*
  wets
  wetting
  wetted
wetness
we've *abbreviation*
whack *verb*
  whacks
  whacking
  whacked
whack *noun*
  whacks
★ whale *noun*
  whales
whaler *noun*
  whalers
whaling
wharf *noun*
  wharves *or* wharfs
☆ what
whatever
wheat
wheel *noun*
  wheels
wheel *verb*
  wheels
  wheeling
  wheeled
wheelbarrow *noun*
  wheelbarrows
wheelchair *noun*
  wheelchairs
wheeze *verb*
  wheezes

wheezing
wheezed
whelk *noun*
  whelks
when
whenever *conjunction*
◎ where
whereabouts
whereas
whereupon
wherever
whether *conjunction*
✳ whey
✱ which
whichever
whiff *noun*
  whiffs
while *adjective* and *noun*
while *verb*
  whiles
  whiling
  whiled
whilst *conjunction*
whimper *verb*
  whimpers
  whimpering
  whimpered
whimper *noun*
  whimpers
whine *verb*
  whines
  whining
  whined
✱ whine *noun*
  whines
whinny *verb*
  whinnies
  whinnying
  whinnied

whip *noun*
  whips
whip *verb*
  whips
  whipping
  whipped
whirl *verb*
  whirls
  whirling
  whirled
whirl *noun*
  whirls
whirlpool *noun*
  whirlpools
whirlwind *noun*
  whirlwinds
whirr *verb*
  whirrs
  whirring
  whirred
whirr *noun*
  whirrs
whisk *verb*
  whisks
  whisking
  whisked
whisk *noun*
  whisks
whisker *noun*
  whiskers
whisky *noun*
  whiskies
whisper *verb*
  whispers
  whispering
  whispered
whisper *noun*
  whispers
whist

- -

★ A whale is a large sea mammal. ! wail.
☆ You use what in e.g. *what are they doing?* or *I don't know what you mean.* ! watt.
◎ You use where in e.g. *where are you?* ! ware, wear.
✳ Whey is a watery liquid from milk. ! way, weigh.
✱ You use which in e.g. *which one is that?* ! witch.
✱ A whine is a high piercing sound. ! wine.

whistle *verb*
  whistles
  whistling
  whistled
whistle *noun*
  whistles
whistler *noun*
  whistlers
white *adjective*
  whiter
  whitest
whiteness
whitish
white *noun*
  whites
whiten *verb*
  whitens
  whitening
  whitened
whitewash *noun*
whitewash *verb*
  whitewashes
  whitewashing
  whitewashed
Whitsun
Whit Sunday
whiz *verb*
  whizzes
  whizzing
  whizzed
who
whoever
★ whole *adjective*
  wholly
whole *noun*
  wholes
wholefood *noun*
  wholefoods
wholemeal
wholesale *adjective*

wholesome
wholly
whom
whoop *noun*
  whoops
whoopee *interjection*
whooping cough
☆ who's *verb*
❍ whose *adjective*
why
wick *noun*
  wicks
wicked *adjective*
  wickeder
  wickedest
  wickedly
wickedness
wicker
wickerwork
wicket *noun*
  wickets
wicketkeeper *noun*
  wicketkeepers
wide *adjective* and
  adverb
  wider
  widest
  widely
widen *verb*
  widens
  widening
  widened
widespread
widow *noun*
  widows
widower *noun*
  widowers
width *noun*
  widths

wield *verb*
  wields
  wielding
  wielded
wife *noun*
  wives
wig *noun*
  wigs
wiggle *verb*
  wiggles
  wiggling
  wiggled
wiggle *noun*
  wiggles
wigwam *noun*
  wigwams
wild *adjective*
  wilder
  wildest
  wildly
wilderness *noun*
  wildernesses
wildness
wildlife
wilful *adjective*
  wilfully
wilfulness
wiliness
will *verb*
  would
will *noun*
  wills
willing *adjective*
  willingly
willingness
willow *noun*
  willows
wilt *verb*
  wilts
  wilting
  wilted

· ·

★ You use whole in e.g. *I saw the whole film.* ! hole.
☆ You use who's in *who's* (= who is) *that?* and *I don't know who's* (= who has) *done it.* ! whose.
❍ You use whose in *whose is this?* and *I don't know whose it is.* ! who's.

wily *adjective*
wilier
wiliest
wimp *noun*
wimps
win *verb*
wins
winning
won
win *noun*
wins
wince *verb*
winces
wincing
winced
winch *noun*
winches
winch *verb*
winches
winching
winched
wind *noun*
winds
wind *verb*
winds
winding
wound
windfall *noun*
windfalls
windmill *noun*
windmills
window *noun*
windows
windpipe *noun*
windpipes
windscreen *noun*
windscreens
windsurfer
windsurfing
windward

windy *adjective*
windier
windiest
windily
★ **wine** *noun*
wines
wing *noun*
wings
wing *verb*
wings
winging
winged
winged
wingless
wingspan *noun*
wingspans
wink *verb*
winks
winking
winked
wink *noun*
winks
winkle *noun*
winkles
winkle *verb*
winkles
winkling
winkled
winner *noun*
winners
winnings *plural noun*
winter *noun*
winters
wintertime
wintry *adjective*
wintrier
wintriest
wipe *verb*
wipes
wiping
wiped

wipe *noun*
wipes
wiper *noun*
wipers
wire *noun*
wires
wire *verb*
wires
wiring
wired
wireless *noun*
wirelesses
wiring
wiry *adjective*
wirier
wiriest
wirily
wisdom
wise *adjective*
wiser
wisest
wisely
wish *verb*
wishes
wishing
wished
wish *noun*
wishes
wishbone *noun*
wishbones
wisp *noun*
wisps
wispy *adjective*
wispier
wispiest
wispily
wistful *adjective*
wistfully
wistfulness
wit *noun*
wits

- -

★ **Wine** is a drink. ! ~~whine~~.

★ **witch** noun
  witches
witchcraft
with
withdraw verb
  withdraws
  withdrawing
  withdrew
  withdrawn
withdrawal noun
  withdrawals
wither verb
  withers
  withering
  withered
withhold verb
  withholds
  withholding
  withheld
within
without
withstand verb
  withstands
  withstanding
  withstood
witness noun
  witnesses
wittiness
witty adjective
  wittier
  wittiest
  wittily
wizard noun
  wizards
wizardry
wobble verb
  wobbles
  wobbling
  wobbled
wobble noun
  wobbles

wobbly adjective
  wobblier
  wobbliest
woe noun
  woes
woeful
  adjective
  woefully
wok noun
  woks
woke see wake
woken see wake
wolf noun
  wolves
woman noun
  women
womb noun
  wombs
☆ **won** see win
wonder noun
  wonders
wonder verb
  wonders
  wondering
  wondered
wonderful adjective
  wonderfully
won't verb
✪ **wood** noun
  woods
wooded
wooden
woodland noun
  woodlands
woodlouse noun
  woodlice
woodpecker noun
  woodpeckers
woodwind
woodwork

woodworm noun
  woodworm or
  woodworms
woody adjective
  woodier
  woodiest
wool
woollen
woollens plural noun
woolliness
woolly adjective
  woollier
  woolliest
word noun
  words
word verb
  words
  wording
  worded
wording
wordy adjective
  wordier
  wordiest
wore see wear
work noun
  works
work verb
  works
  working
  worked
workable
worker noun
  workers
workforce noun
  workforces
workman noun
  workmen
workmanship
workout noun
  workouts

. . . .

★ A **witch** is someone who uses witchcraft. ! which.
☆ You use **won** in e.g. I won a prize. ! one.
✪ **Wood** is material from trees or a lot of trees growing together. ! would.

works *plural noun*
worksheet *noun*
  worksheets
workshop *noun*
  workshops
world *noun*
  worlds
worldliness
worldly *adjective*
  worldlier
  worldliest
worldwide *adjective*
worm *noun*
  worms
worm *verb*
  worms
  worming
  wormed
worn see wear
worry *verb*
  worries
  worrying
  worried
worrier *noun*
  worriers
worry *noun*
  worries
worse *adjective* and
  adverb
worsen *verb*
  worsens
  worsening
  worsened
worship *verb*
  worships
  worshipping
  worshipped
worship *noun*
worshipper *noun*
  worshippers

worst *adjective* and
  adverb
worth
worthiness
worthless *adjective*
  worthlessly
worthwhile
worthy *adjective*
  worthier
  worthiest
  worthily
★ **would** see will
wouldn't *verb*
wound *noun*
  wounds
wound *verb*
  wounds
  wounding
  wounded
wound see wind
wove see weave
woven see weave
☆ **wrap** *verb*
  wraps
  wrapping
  wrapped
wrap *noun*
  wraps
wrapper *noun*
  wrappers
wrapping *noun*
  wrappings
wrath
wrathful *adjective*
  wrathfully
wreath *noun*
  wreaths
wreathe *verb*
  wreathes
  wreathing
  wreathed

wreck *verb*
  wrecks
  wrecking
  wrecked
wreck *noun*
  wrecks
wreckage *noun*
  wreckages
wrecker *noun*
  wreckers
wren *noun*
  wrens
wrench *verb*
  wrenches
  wrenching
  wrenched
wrench *noun*
  wrenches
wrestle *verb*
  wrestles
  wrestling
  wrestled
wrestler *noun*
  wrestlers
wretch *noun*
  wretches
wretched *adjective*
  wretchedly
wriggle *verb*
  wriggles
  wriggling
  wriggled
wriggle *noun*
  wriggles
wriggly *adjective*
  wrigglier
  wriggliest
✪ **wring** *verb*
  wrings
  wringing
  wrung

- -

★ You use **would** in e.g. *would you like to come to tea?* ! wood.
☆ To **wrap** something is to cover it in paper etc. ! rap.
✪ To **wring** something is to squeeze it hard. ! ring.

wrinkle *noun*
wrinkles
wrinkle *verb*
wrinkles
wrinkling
wrinkled
wrist *noun*
wrists
wristwatch *noun*
wristwatches
★ write *verb*
writes
writing
wrote
written
writer *noun*
writers
writhe *verb*
writhes
writhing
writhed
writing *noun*
writings
written see write
wrong *adjective* and
adverb
wrongly
wrong *noun*
wrongs
wrong *verb*
wrongs
wronging
wronged
wrote see write
wrung see wring
☆ wry *adjective*
wryer
wryest

xenophobia
Xmas *noun*
Xmases
X-ray *noun*
X-rays
X-ray *verb*
X-rays
X-raying
X-rayed
xylophone *noun*
xylophones

Yy

-y and -ey
Nouns ending in -y
following a
consonant, e.g. **story**,
make plurals ending
in -ies, e.g. **stories**,
and verbs, e.g. **try**,
make forms in -ies
and -ied, e.g. **tries**,
tried. Nouns ending
in -ey, e.g. **journey**,
make plurals ending
in -eys, e.g. **journeys**.

yacht *noun*
yachts
yachtsman *noun*
yachtsmen
yachtswoman *noun*
yachtswomen
yam *noun*
yams

yank *verb*
yanks
yanking
yanked
yap *verb*
yaps
yapping
yapped
yap *noun*
yaps
yard *noun*
yards
yard *noun*
yards
yarn *noun*
yarns
yawn *verb*
yawns
yawning
yawned
yawn *noun*
yawns
year *noun*
years
yearly *adjective* and
adverb
yearn *verb*
yearns
yearning
yearned
yeast
yell *noun*
yells
yell *verb*
yells
yelling
yelled
yellow *adjective* and
noun
yellower
yellowest

. . . .

★ You use **write** in e.g. *to write a letter*. ! right, rite.
☆ You use **wry** in e.g. *a wry smile*. ! rye.

yelp verb
yelps
yelping
yelped
yelp noun
yelps
★ **yen** noun
yens or yen
yeoman noun
yeomen
yesterday adjective
and noun
yesterdays
yet
yeti noun
yetis
☆ **yew** noun
yews
yield verb
yields
yielding
yielded
yield noun
yields
yippee
yodel verb
yodels
yodelling
yodelled
yodeller noun
yodellers
yoga
yoghurt noun
yoghurts
✿ **yoke** noun
yokes
yoke verb
yokes
yoking
yoked

✱ **yolk** noun
yolks
Yom Kippur
yonder
✴ **you**
you'd verb
you'll verb
young adjective
younger
youngest
young plural noun
youngster noun
youngsters
your
you're abbreviation
yours
yourself pronoun
yourselves
youth noun
youths
youthful adjective
youthfully
you've abbreviation
yo-yo noun
yo-yos
yuppie noun
yuppies

Zz

zany adjective
zanier
zaniest
zanily
zap verb
zaps
zapping
zapped

zeal
zealous adjective
zealously
zebra noun
zebras
zenith noun
zeniths
zero noun
zeros
zest
zigzag noun
zigzags
zigzag verb
zigzags
zigzagging
zigzagged
zinc
zip noun
zips
zip verb
zips
zipping
zipped
zodiac
zombie noun
zombies
zone noun
zones
zoo noun
zoos
zoological adjective
zoologically
zoologist noun
zoologists
zoology
zoom verb
zooms
zooming
zoomed

★ The plural is **yens** when you mean 'a longing' and **yen** for Japanese money.
☆ A **yew** is a tree. ! ewe, you
✿ A **yoke** is a piece of wood put across animals pulling a cart. ! yolk
✱ A **yolk** is the yellow part of an egg. ! yoke.
✴ You use **you** in e.g. I love you. ! ewe, yew.